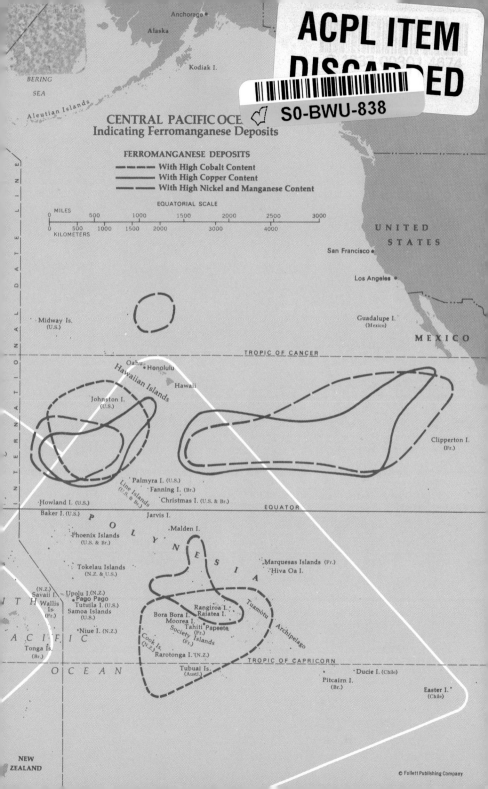

CENTRAL PACIFIC OCEAN
Indicating Ferromanganese Deposits

FERROMANGANESE DEPOSITS
- – – – With High Cobalt Content
- ――― With High Copper Content
- – – – With High Nickel and Manganese Content

EQUATORIAL SCALE

MILES
0   500   1000   1500   2000   2500   3000

KILOMETERS
0   500   1000   1500   2000   3000   4000

BERING
SEA

Anchorage

Alaska

Kodiak I.

Aleutian Islands

UNITED
STATES

San Francisco

Los Angeles

Midway Is.
(U.S.)

Guadalupe I.
(Mexico)

MEXICO

TROPIC OF CANCER

Oahu • Honolulu

Hawaiian Islands

Hawaii

Johnston I.
(U.S.)

Clipperton I.
(Fr.)

Palmyra I. (U.S.)
Line Islands   Fanning I. (Br.)
(U.S. & Br.)   Christmas I. (U.S. & Br.)

Howland I. (U.S.)

EQUATOR

Baker I. (U.S.)

P   Jarvis I.

O

L   Malden I.

Phoenix Islands
(U.S. & Br.)

Y

N

E   Marquesas Islands (Fr.)
S   Hiva Oa I.

Tokelau Islands
(N.Z. & U.S.)

I

A

(N.Z.)
Savaii I.   Upolu I. (N.Z.)
Wallis   • Pago Pago
Is.   Tutuila I. (U.S.)
(Fr.)   Samoa Islands
(U.S.)

Rangiroa I.
Raiatea I.   Tuamotu
Bora Bora I.
Moorea I.   Tahiti Papeete
Society (Fr.)   Archipelago
•Niue I. (N.Z.)   Islands
Cook Is.   (Fr.)
(N.Z.)

ITH   Tonga Is.   Rarotonga I. (N.Z.)
(Br.)

ACIFIC

OCEAN   Tubuai Is.
(Austl.)   TROPIC OF CAPRICORN

• Ducie I. (Chile)
Pitcairn I.
(Br.)

Easter I.
(Chile)

NEW
ZEALAND

INTERNATIONAL DATE LINE

4-14-75

The dream of a Pacific paradise with swaying palm trees, turquoise waters and generous, self-sufficient, beautiful natives has for centuries excited the imagination of so-called civilized man. Sadly, even these professed dreams are no longer possible to entertain, since this once beautiful part of the world is now nearly destroyed, in ecological as well as economic terms. In his new book, Pacific expert Robert Wenkam exposes the corporate and colonial greed which has ravaged the Pacific islands, exploiting the resources there, sullying fishing waters, gouging minerals from the earth and the oil soaked seas of these idyllic Eastern islands. When the white man first came to these islands he brought disease and Western religion—both destructive to the life style of previous generations. But the destruction did not end with the first wave, as Wenkam shows, but continues unabated, as if compulsively bent on destroying the dreams forever.

The Great Pacific Rip-Off

The Great Pacific

Rip-Off

Corporate Rape in the Far East

by Robert Wenkam

FOLLETT PUBLISHING COMPANY
Chicago

Library of Congress Catalog Card Number: 74–80336

ISBN: 0–695–80488–X

First Printing

Liberty cannot be
preserved without a
general knowledge
among the people.
Let us dare to
read, think, speak,
and write.

John Adams

Contents

1 The Pacific Tourist Blight   6

2 The Birth and Death of Hawaii   16

3 "The Life of the Land is Preserved
in Righteousness"   30

4 The Beginning of the End   43

5 The American Lake   53

6 The Ocean of Many Islands   65

7 The Americanization of Paradise   75

8 The American Administration of Illegality   88

9 Home Is the Sea   101

10 The Rape of Mindanao   122

11 Land Beyond the Wind   139

12 Taking Up the Corporate Burden   151

13 A Most Unsordid Act   170

14 Dividing the China Seas   194

15 That's All There Is   213

List of Maps

Major ferromanganese deposits in the Pacific
Ocean   end papers

Island of Nauru   44

United States Trust Territory of the Pacific Islands   54

Concession areas in southeast Asian Pacific
region   102–103

Concession areas in the northern Pacific   195

Territorial seas claimed by the People's Republic
of China   199

NOTE: Concession areas outlined on pages 102, 103, and 195 indicate areas where concessions occur and where certain companies and nations are involved in extraction. Specific sites of operations are not indicated, nor are onshore concessions.

Other Books by Robert Wenkam

New England
Text and photographs by R. Wenkam

Micronesia: Island Wilderness
Photographs by R. Wenkam. Text by K. Brower

How To Photograph Hawaii
Text and photographs by R. Wenkam

Hawaii
Text and photographs by R. Wenkam

Micronesia: The Breadfruit Revolution
Photographs by R. Wenkam. Text by B. Baker

Maui: The Last Hawaiian Place
Text and photographs by R. Wenkam

Kauai and the Park Country of Hawaii
Text and photographs by R. Wenkam

Hawaii Nei
Text by Ruth Tabrah, photographs by R. Wenkam

Acknowledgments

My first extensive introduction to the Pacific occurred shortly after World War II when I traveled the Pacific Ocean from Christmas Island to Iwo Jima as a member of a joint army-navy survey team. The team was set up to produce an inventory of what had been left of the islands after the war.

In later years the governments of the Territory of Guam and independent Western Samoa hired me to create a photographic file of their islands for tourist promotion. *Life* magazine sent me to the Philippines to photograph volcanoes, and for six years I photographed Hawaii for national tourist advertising. It was a great way to learn the Pacific and meet the people who lived there.

The East-West Center Institute for Technical Interchange gave me a grant to do a book on Micronesia. Dave Brower, president of Friends of the Earth, sent me to Borneo with Ken Brower to prepare preliminary work for an exhibit format book on the world's third largest island. At other times I have just sailed around the islands.

It is through these experiences and a home in Hawaii, that I have learned to think like an islander—because I am an islander and the Pacific is my home.

To keep myself up-to-date on this complex island world, I have acquired a small library, subscribed to several publications, and listened to many people everywhere.

First and foremost among publications is the informative *Pacific Basin Reports,* a monthly report service published in San Francisco for financial institutions and Pacific businessmen. *The Pacific Islands Monthly,* from Australia, is a down-under view. The weekly *Micronesian Independent,* which is printed and written on Majuro Island in Micronesia, offers an excellent once-over lightly for the U.S. Trust Territory Islands.

There are individuals: G. N. Appell, a Maine resident and anthropologist of Brandeis University to whom I am considerably indebted for his extensive knowledge and understanding of the people of Borneo that gave the last chapter its inspired thrust and direction; Dan Luten of the University of California Geography Department who put the Pacific island ecology into perspective for me; Hawaii Congressional Representative Patsy Mink who has always helped me through the political maze of Washington, D.C.; Brock Evans, Washington representative for the Sierra Club and the Federation of Western Outdoor Clubs and its wonderful staff; and Herb Luthin, editor and friendly consultant, who first suggested that my knowledge of the Pacific Islands and Southeast Asia should be bound between the covers of a book.

I would like also to thank personally the many individuals who live in the Pacific Islands and in Southeast Asia who are struggling to preserve their homeland and their life-style. They must remain unnamed. It is they who pointed out to me that there must be a peaceful revolution in the economy of the world; otherwise, there will be a violent revolution.

R. Wenkam
Honolulu
(June 25, 1974)

The Great Pacific Rip-Off

Introduction

4,500 YEARS AGO, at the time when Chinese civilization was developing in northern Asia and the Egyptians were building pyramids, early explorers from Indochina established thriving communities in the central Pacific Ocean. They constructed stone temples and fortresses on Ponape Island before utilizing sophisticated navigating skills to sail southeast and beyond to the Samoan islands. Their restless children later moved to the Marquesas Islands where they paused and prospered before succeeding generations sailed on in their efficient double-hulled canoes to establish native empires throughout the Pacific. On Easter Island, Tahiti, and Hawaii, they created new languages, cultures, and traditions by the time of the downfall of the Roman Empire.

Magellan sailed across the Pacific about 1,500 years later, missing almost everything in what amounted to a mad dash around the world when measured by leisurely Polynesian travel schedules. In the process he accomplished little more than to antagonize people already living on the islands by claiming every bay and beach for the Spanish Crown. The natives presumed that at the very least he could share a small boat, but Magellan felt differently. He killed them, then had the audacity to name Guam, Isla de Ladrones—the Isle of Thieves.

Toward the end of the eighteenth century, while Americans were cleaning up after their revolution, Hawaii was discovered for the second time in nine hundred years. The first discovery, by Polynesians, had changed the islands little, but the second discovery was by a different sort of man. Captain Cook started out quite innocently. In fact, he expressed some concern after leaving Tahiti, for his fatal impact upon the islands, but he ended up with the same kind of boat trouble as Magellan. When he went ashore to help retrieve a longboat that had been liberated in Kealakekua Bay, his men shot into the crowd of Hawaiians who promptly retaliated, killed Cook, and children playing in the area ate his heart.

The story of man's inhumanity to man is the history of the Pacific still being told in the continuing struggle of brown people against white interlopers, who, whenever they found some place new, claimed it as their own and planted a cross upon the land as moral justification for their deeds.

This book is a story of the Pacific, told in terms of its land and traditions. It is the story of many islands and many people who have never stopped fighting to survive, whose land has been repeatedly occupied by strangers and a people who have often been cheated by their own.

The story is a cry of pain, for the people have been hurt. The land has been harshly trampled upon by the Spanish, Dutch, Japanese, French, Portuguese, British, and Americans who, at one time or another, claimed every island except one as their own. The fragile balance between man and his environment has been seriously disturbed, and the violent struggles between man and man have never ceased.

This is the story of a million islands and the sea and how alien man has encroached upon them irresistibly and persistently. Today, the islanders have learned that their Pacific Ocean domain encompasses the richest fisheries resources of any ocean, millions of acres of virgin timber, the world's most extensive deposits of copper, cobalt, manganese, and tin, and perhaps the largest reserve of crude oil anywhere on earth.

This is also the story of the world's developed nations, the so-called civilized powers, and their scramble for the last remaining raw materials to fuel their wasteful, materialistic life-styles. These powers have shamelessly divided the Pacific's last remaining resources—people and minerals—among themselves. They seem oblivious to the revolutionary insurgents—both peaceful and violent—who plead not only for simple justice and a fair share of the profits, but demand a new world where finite resources will fully benefit those who sail the oceans, hunt in the forest jungle and live a subsistence life in village clusters on tropical islands and Asiatic lands.

As for those who do not want paved roads and tin roofs, they will sit back and watch from their grass thatched huts in rare good humor, possibly wiser and healthier than all the others, eating yams from their own gardens, and enjoying the sun with no clothes on at all. For after the timber, minerals, and oil are all gone, the Pacific islanders who have refused to dig and drill and saw, respecting the land and living on it, not by it, will still enjoy a way of life inherited from their ancestors who started it all so many thousands of years ago.

This is the last story for the others.

1

The Pacific Tourist Blight

HAWAII is a life-style housed on a string of semitropical islands floating in just the right place. Away from the South Pacific where it is too humid, not so far into the North Pacific as to be too cold, but safe from the regions where stormy seas and typhoons rage, Hawaii boasts no seasons. The climate is so good that native Hawaiians had no word for weather. The living is so good they had no swear words.

Missionaries came to Hawaii over 150 years ago, but many resigned from the church, became prosperous in business, and introduced the concept of private property without explaining the consequences. As traders, businessmen, and tourists poured in, the Hawaiians lost everything —including their kingdom.

The blight of tourism began when Yankee sailing ships were Hawaii's transportation link with California. Honolulu harbor was a major crossroads port of the Pacific. During the bubonic plague scare at the turn of the century, territorial health authorities identified waterfront rats as the culprits. To clean out the rats, the Honolulu Chamber of Commerce sponsored a voluntary one-cent-a-ton tax on all cargo shipped over Honolulu docks. The cleanup campaign was successful, but the tax was not repealed, and soon there was the problem of what to do with the money.

In 1920 the Chamber of Commerce agreed to use the surplus rat funds to establish a bureau to bring in tourists.

Matson Lines, a local steamship company, quickly expanded its passenger operations and created Waikiki as a resort destination, building new Moana and Royal Hawaiian hotels for its ships to fill. Skillful advertising and promotion made Hawaii a "South Pacific paradise," and exotic images of grass skirts and hula girls spread across the mainland.

The first small black and white national advertisements appeared in *Sunset* magazine. Opulent color spreads appeared later, created by the best photographers in the country. Anton Bruhl did most of his photography in New York. Everything Hawaiian was shipped to him—hula skirts, coral, coconuts, fish nets, and all the visual ingredients of a Hawaiian landscape, including the little grass shack. When Pan American Airlines began operating flying boats across the Pacific, plumeria and ginger flowers were shipped daily by air to Bruhl's East Coast studio. I don't think he ever saw Hawaii.

Famed photographer Edward Steichen, founder of the photography department of the New York Museum of Modern Art produced his color advertisements in Hawaii. The subject was to become a popular classic over the years —Waikiki Beach, with an outrigger canoe and Diamond Head. Mainland editors loved it. A Steichen photo of model Jinx Falkenburg at Waikiki became a *Saturday Evening Post* cover. Hawaii became the dream vacation land.

But the promoters had their problems. For one thing the old tourist bureau forbade photographers to show a dark-skinned Hawaiian beachboy on the same surfboard with a white girl. Local beachboys were always kept at arm's length from visitors. In later years when I was photographing magazine advertisements, the advertising agency asked me not to show Diamond Head with rows of high-rise buildings obstructing the famed profile. Hotels were getting in the way of the scenery tourists had come to see, particularly the hotels that look so much like World War II fortifications. The claim is made that the best view of Waikiki is from the roof of the Sheraton-Waikiki Hotel, because there you cannot see the hotel.

Other problems have appeared over the years. Tourists contribute substantially to the fifty-two million gallons of untreated raw sewage pumped daily into the ocean five miles from Waikiki beach. On days when the south wind is persistent, stringy solids drift perilously close to Waikiki's popular surfing grounds. Tourism has become an industry symbolic of scenic trespass, overuse, and environmental exploitation. Claiming to be a clean industry when compared with conventional industrial activity, its traffic noise, jet exhaust fumes, highway construction, and reckless destruction of visual beauty are seldom mentioned when adding up the financial gains.

Major airlines are committed to filling the seats of expensive Boeing 747 jets regardless of the adverse consequences to Hawaii's fragile and priceless scenic beauty. Absentee hotel operators maximize profits at the expense of Hawaii's easygoing island way of life, trampling the aloha spirit that once made every visitor a friend rather than the source of a large tip. The tourist industry and its tax-financed marketing agent, the Hawaii Visitors Bureau, advertise the golden people of Hawaii not unlike a supermarket bargain. Hotel developers carelessly mine the best beaches and scenic areas as an inexhaustible natural resource instead of a fragile and limited asset.

The Hawaii Visitors Bureau estimates that over two million tourists visited Hawaii in 1973, leaving behind some $890 million in cash. The tourist returned home with happy memories worth a lifetime of saving. But a little less of Hawaii remained unspoiled.

Continued growth of Hawaii's tourist industry may be good dreaming for the land developer, but to the environmentalist it is a nightmare. A computer projection based on the last ten years' tourist growth rate reveals that business will be very good 100 years from today, when 60 trillion, 450 billion tourists will visit Hawaii. Nine million visitors will deplane at Honolulu International Airport every hour! The computer at the State Department of Planning and Economic Development was unable to determine what this will do to Hawaii's environment, for it cannot produce a printout of the quality of life. The programmers are unable to punch love, beauty, and the aloha spirit into a computer tape.

The same computer warns Oahu residents who continue buying cars at the 1970 rate that they face a bleak future in thirty years. If by the year 2001 the State Department of Transportation has succeeded in constructing highways capable of accommodating every car then on the island, all of Oahu, except for the mountaintops, will be paved over!

Perhaps such projections are absurd. But even so, it is the reckless economic philosophy of growth ad infinitum which must be seriously questioned—not the environmentalists' cries of alarm. If being paved over is not a desirable objective, when does the paving stop? When will the warning signs be erected to slow the tourist boom and to stabilize the population to prove the computer wrong? It may already be too late for Waikiki. In fledgling resort areas around the Pacific in Samoa, Fiji, and Micronesia, Waikiki is already a well-worn adjective describing how *not* to do it.

Financier Chinn Ho, president of Hawaii's Capital Investment Company, said, "Let's accommodate the tourists!" He organized the Diamond Head Improvement Association to obtain city resort zoning at the foot of Diamond Head to build high-rise hotels. Improvement—that's what the National Natural Landmark needed! By the early 1970's, the citizens said "no," in a stormy series of public hearings that culminated in the election of Mayor Frank Fasi, who sided with the campaign to save Diamond Head. For the first time in the history of such controversies, the Hawaii Visitors Bureau testified against the building of more hotels. So did the Chamber of Commerce and the building trade unions. The Save Diamond Head Association, composed of forty community groups, had acquired some unusual support in quashing the old economic philosophy that growth and more hotels were good—no matter where.

Local militant conservationists decided the tax-supported Hawaii Visitors Bureau was promoting tourism and neglecting the interests of island residents. So they organized the underground Hawaii Residents' Bureau and distributed thousands of handbills on the mainland urging potential visitors to "Please don't visit Hawaii until we are able to save what's left! . . . . You can't buy ALOHA!" The leaflet showed a drawing of canned, "instant, imitation Aloha in heavy syrup distributed by the friendly skies of Air Pollution Corporation." There is no evidence that anyone's vacation plans were changed, but the annual economic report of a Honolulu bank did remark that 1971's lower tourist growth was partly due to derogatory comments by conservationists.

The international environmental organization, Friends of the Earth, inspired legislation to collect a tourist head tax of five dollars a day, earmarked to purchase parklands and open space for public use. At the first legislative hearings in Hawaii's handsome new capitol building, I was the only person to give public testimony in support of the bill. No one else. The next year I was joined by Art Rutledge, porky leader of the AFL-CIO Hotel and Restaurant Workers Union. He also supported the idea. The third year around, advocates of the tax were heartened by the attendance of Honolulu's newly elected mayor, speaking for a tax of $2.50 a day and urging that tourism pay its own way. The tourist industry screamed, forecasting economic disaster and erosion of the "aloha spirit." The politicians obediently pigeonholed the bill again, noting that it did not appear to be a solution to the problem.

Veteran Hawaii politician Tom Gill has long supported a hotel-room tax similar to surcharges in many mainland cities across the country, saying its revenues could help both Waikiki and the fiscally troubled state government. Gill also claims the tourist industry needs to encourage more $100-a-day hotels like Laurence Rockefeller's successful Mauna Kea Beach Hotel, and less "cut-rate package tours" by visitors who "split a hamburger" for lunch and are strangling the "golden goose" of tourism. According to Gill, "A lot of those who come on package tours probably would not recognize good service if they saw it."

Of course, the problem is one of too many tourists who provide jobs for too many residents on a group of islands too small to lodge everyone. "The loveliest fleet of islands that lies anchored in any ocean"—as Mark Twain exclaimed—is in trouble.

At the eight or so native Hawaiian feasts (luaus) held weekly in Honolulu, any attempt at serving authentic food, offering island hospitality, or playing traditional Hawaiian music has been abandoned. The hapless tourists, after paying a stiff bill averaging $15 per person, are herded into hotel dining rooms like cattle, fed several meager samples of Hawaiian food and some American fillers to keep them satisfied—all on paper plates—drink some watered-down rum out of plastic cups, then are sung to and laughed at by talent-deficient entertainers who try to be like Tongan fire-walkers and Tahitian hip-shakers while piously claiming to "preserve Hawaiian culture." In an interview with Associated Press writer Robert Murphy, the Hawaii Visitor Bureau's director of special events, Kalani Cockett, Jr., said commercial luaus "have caused more complaints than any other attraction in the state." But he added that the tourists "are just going to have to put up with these commercial jobs" until the HVB can arrange for more traditional feasts sponsored by local civic groups and churches. It is symptomatic of the Hawaiian tourist industry that it cannot even put on a proper Hawaiian show.

But mainlanders, sick of crime, prejudice, and pollution in their own hometowns, clamor for escape to Hawaii. The South Pacific paradise created by publicity stunts is still the end of the rainbow. Never mind that Hawaii's

Aloha Week is celebrated with plastic leis from Hong Kong and the "fresh" mahimahi fish on restaurant menus is often shipped frozen from Taiwan. So what if the "Hawaiian" pageantry is fake, embellished with imitation warrior helmets of dyed chicken feathers. The rainbows and flowers and surf are real. So are the scenery and the gentle people who seem not to mind this intrusion on their island home. The soft landscape seems forever green; the rivers and streams bright and clear; every day is a sleepy Sunday and the winter week a shirt-sleeved summer.

Hawaii is paradise for the lazy where the poor still live in shacks, sponge off the rich, swim in nothing, and revel with a conscience comparable to a mynah bird's. Instead of concrete, there are coral and sand to walk upon. Romantic fragrances of ginger, pikake, and plumeria mingle with fresh trade winds blowing over snowy summits and through rustling woodlands spared from volcanic wrath. Who can resist paradise?

Mark Twain said of the visitor to Hawaii: "When you are in that blessed retreat, you are safe from the turmoil of life; you drowse your days away in a long deep dream of peace; the past is a forgotten thing, the present is heaven, the future you can leave to take care of itself. You are in the center of the Pacific Ocean; you are miles from the world; as far as you can see, on any hand, the crested billows wall the horizon, and beyond this barrier the wide universe is but a foreign land to you, and barren of interest."

Although Captain Cook discovered Hawaii for the Western world, the Polynesians discovered it for themselves much earlier and ended their Pacific migration. There was no better place to go. Now an overpopulated America has rediscovered Hawaii's delicious life-style and wants to share the dessert.

The renting of islands to visiting tourists on a short-term basis is only one of many recent human activities that have significantly altered these fragile ecosystems and rendered them vulnerable to decay and deterioration. The inherent contradictions involved in tourism make it mandatory that careful consideration be given to all aspects of the island's environment if only for one important reason —the more unspoiled it is the greater its tourist potential. The epitome of civilized man's dream is to get away from it all, probably to a carefree existence on an untouched tropical isle with abundant sunshine, papayas and mangos, orchids, and virgin brown maidens. It is the theme of tourist advertising, yet each visitor to this paradise destroys a little of the fragile image and ecological balance, not only for himself, but also for every visitor to follow. Depredation and corrosion increase with every tourist who walks down the airliner ramp. To accommodate the visitor is to destroy a little of the treasure he came to enjoy. The development side of tourism is almost antithetical to conservation, since development is synonymous with modernization and resource exploitation. With every development there is destruction of natural values.

Spokesmen for the tourist industry recite at length the positive environmental roles the industry plays in protecting scenic beauty and cultural assets they sell. *Sunset* magazine publisher Bill Lane, speaking at the Pacific Area Travel Association 1973 environment workshop in Kyoto, Japan, said, ". . . some of us have been trying for a long time to tie tourism and environment together; it has been encouraging to find that in recent years, this critical relationship has been more and more recognized—namely, that travel and the environment generally work in harmony, one complementing the other. . . . But important to the purpose of this workshop, we would have a bad case of 'environmental myopia' if we were to ignore the increasing examples around the world where this industry does *not* enhance the environment and, indeed, is a contributor to various forms of serious pollution—whether it be a deterioration in the natural or social environment. A high rate of muggings, pickpockets, and prostitution can, for instance, be an equally serious *social* environmental problem as dirty water and air are in our *natural* environment."

Protestations by hotel owners, airlines and tour agents who claim to be socially responsible fade into silence, however, in the face of any truly controversial issue that demands a decision pro or con. The history of tourism in Hawaii and the Pacific is a constant reminder to conservationists and historical buffs that the tourist industry can be counted on for little help in preserving parklands, open spaces, and historical sites, stopping beach and ocean pollution, reducing noise and traffic, eliminating obnoxious signs and roadside selling, enacting progressive zoning ordinances and promoting long-range planning to preserve the island environment. In fifteen years of effort as an active citizen conservationist, I pleaded again and again with the Hawaii Visitors Bureau, a predominantly business-oriented arm of the tourist industry, to take an active role in community environmental efforts. Only once did they agree—to oppose high-rise hotels at the foot of Diamond Head to save the most famous landmark Hawaii tourism possesses.

A definitive inventory of environmental tragedies across the Pacific would be a requiem to governmental stupidity and must serve as an example of apathy within the tourist industry. It is often bewildering to learn that the citizen conservationist who frequently opposes tourism is working so adamantly to save the tourist industry from itself. The industry may claim no responsibility—but then neither does the tourist who demands airports, highways, harbors, and water and sewers immediately upon his arrival.

Conceding as we do that we are the world's most intelligent creatures, we should also consider the fact that —along with the lemming—we are the only animal capable of destroying ourselves. It may be opportune to tarry for a short while in our mad rush, and give reverence to life and nature. Dave Brower, president of Friends of the Earth, says, "Perhaps it is about time for man to try to come back to his senses, all of them. Better that he does, before becoming too enamoured of his overriding technology and overbearing intellect.

"What we need is not an expanding economy, but an expanding individual," cautions Brower. "The individual can expand and have no trouble understanding other living things, if he can manage to renounce some of his dependence on man-made ephemera and to spend more time with things as they were, are, and may still be."

It is not too late to leave the Pacific alone. Not too late to refuse domination by an insane economy of growth and technological madness which discards every quality that is wholesome, beautiful, and good, in the name of profit and progress. There must not be a hotel on every beach—a road on every mountain—a tower on every skyline. To allow every visitor equal access to every island worthy of a visit is to destroy the people of the Pacific, their culture and their islands. To allow entrance to every visitor able to afford a ticket will destroy the Pacific treasure. At some moment, at some place—perhaps soon—the people of Hawaii must say, "There is no more room at the inn."

2

The Birth and Death of Hawaii

THE constellation that the Greeks called Orion was known to the early Hawaiians as Na Kao. The Hawaiians who watched Na Kao march across the zenith every winter night saw him as a giant warrior. They saw darts on his belt, darts that split the clouds over the island peaks and brought down the sacred rains. Along with Naholoholo, the western evening star, Na Kao held a favored place in the Hawaiian heaven.

Na Kao was still below the horizon an hour before midnight in July 1962, as a small group of warmly clothed men, 10,000 feet high on Maui's Mount Haleakala, watched Naholoholo assume his place in the sky and blend with the wide sweep of the Milky Way. Occasionally a shooting star darted toward the distant horizon. The night was clear and cloudless. A chilling breeze rustled the plants that grew between the jumbled basalt blocks scattered across the summit.

The men who stood on the summit, and their colleagues, had built what seemed like a moon station on the volcanic mountain. The cold black lava of the southwest rift zone now supported Air Force trailers bristling with electronic gear and radar screens. Occasionally, from the direction of the trailers, a shaft of light pierced the darkness and momentarily revealed a silhouetted figure darting into the doorway of the instrument-laden Atomic Energy Commission laboratory. The men were waiting on the chilly mountain to observe and record an atomic explosion in the ionosphere. I was on assignment for *Life*.

A short-wave radio, lying between the legs of my camera tripod, fed back static gathered from the air between Maui and Johnson Island, 800 miles distant in the South Pacific. The noise was interrupted at intervals by an unemotional voice giving the countdown to zero. It was a monotonous countdown, begun abortively five times during the week. Tonight it would be completed. The Thor rocket was off its pad on Johnson Island and rising rapidly into the night.

The usually familiar stars of the Milky Way seemed unreal as scientists, armed guards, and photographers peered intently toward the southwest. The countdown continued for several minutes. The sky seemed to move and then wait, as the unknown voice rose higher in pitch and began to speak in seconds. I reached toward my group of cameras, opened the shutters and waited for zero.

There was no sound. In the briefest of instants, the world was gone. There was no color and no shape, all was empty and white. There was nothing to see or feel. The sky, sea, and earth were wiped out in a white glare.

Just as suddenly, there was darkness again. But now the stars were gone. Night closed in quickly and pushed against the startled human beings huddled on the mountain. A bright green star appeared where none had existed before and, with horrible swiftness, grew monstrously into an exploding ball of fire—800 miles away and 240 miles above the earth's surface, yet at arm's length. No one dared reach out. The silent flame changed in seconds from green to bloody red, then irresistibly spread its bright stain across space, polluting the heavens in the afterbirth of a hydrogen bomb.

The stars came out again. The Milky Way glowed anew against the sky. Doors opened and stayed ajar, the familiar yellow tungsten light casting reassuring shadows across the lunar landscape as high-energy electrons in the ionosphere continued to glow in long arcs across the sky, dramatically revealing the earth's magnetic field between the North and South poles. Rainbow curtains of an artificially induced aurora borealis shimmered in the north in the eternity before the heavens stopped bleeding.

Then Na Kao, the warrior constellation, rose and joined Naholoholo in the sky. The technicians and photographers packed up their equipment and departed, leaving the mountain top alone.

The heavens seemed almost the same again, but the people who had been on the mountain top that awesome night were not. They felt uneasy about the new world that had been thrust upon them so suddenly and wondered if the new world could still find a place for the old.

The high summit crater of Haleakala was still venting molten lava when the forebears of the first Hawaiians began moving eastward in their long migration across the Pacific. The ancestors settled in the Samoan Islands about 1500 B.C., then sailed farther eastward to the Marquesas, where they paused and prospered. Sometime between 200 B.C. and 400 B.C., they moved again, this time dispersing to Easter Island, Tahiti, and Hawaii.

The voyagers had no written language, and traditions were passed on orally, through chants. In this old but sure way, stories of the homeland were carried across the seas and generations to children born in lands unknown to their grandparents. And so it was that as the first Hawaiians stepped ashore after the long, arduous voyage from the Marquesas, the new land did not seem alien. The volcanic islands they saw looked exactly as their ancestral Samoan home, Savaii, had been described to them. They named the biggest island Savaii or Hawaii. Then they crossed the channel from Hawaii and landed on the island to the north, pulling their waterlogged canoes ashore at a spot they named Samoa, or Hamoa. This second island, with its new Samoa, was named Maui after the Polynesian demigod who had safely escorted the travelers across the pathless seas.

Stories of the demigod Maui are recounted in exotic languages by inhabitants of primitive villages scattered across some thirteen million square miles of sea and land, from the atolls of Micronesia to the lonely islands of Hawaii, many weeks' sail north from Tahiti and the Marquesas. "Ko Maui tinihanga koe" (You Maui of a thousand tricks, you) is the Maori version of a maternal reprimand common to a thousand Pacific islands. Royalty of almost every Pacific land claims Maui as an ancestor. In the Hawaiian Islands, King Kalakaua and Queen Liliuokalani noted him in their genealogies.

According to the chanted legend, Maui was neither man nor god. He deserted the gods of the underworld to join man on top of the earth. Many islanders claim that it was Maui who lifted the heavy skies high enough that man could walk upright instead of crawling on all fours. And he created the lands of the seas as well. He starved his blind grandmother to get her jawbone as a magical weapon. Then he cut off his own ear for bait, and using the jawbone as a fishhook, he pulled up many sizes and varieties of fish from the ocean. His catch became the Pacific islands.

According to the Kumulipo, a Hawaiian creation chant that ties Maui's adventures together in an epic series, Maui also used his mother's pet mud hen as bait. The pet's wing was broken off in Maui's struggle to wrest the bird from his mother, and when he fished with the imperfect bait, he caught a broken-up land—the Hawaiian Islands.

Two millennia after Maui's broken lands were discovered and settled by the Polynesians, British Captain James Cook approached Kauai Island. In February 1778, he wrote "many of the inhabitants put off from the shore in their canoes, and very readily came alongside the ships." Landing at Waimea, he named this strange land in honor of his sponsor, the Earl of Sandwich.

It was an auspicious meeting. The people of Hawaii, for whom the demigod Maui was a proudly-claimed ancestor, met Captain Cook, harbinger of a civilization that worshipped a different god and which brought as its gifts commerce, exploitation, and conquest. Cook himself did not survive the meeting. But once the Hawaiians and their islands were written on Western maps, it was they who suffered in the long run.

Cook compared Hawaii unfavorably with Tahiti, but found on Kauai "a greater quantity of gently rising land, [which] renders it, in some measure superior to the above favourite islands, as being more capable of development."

The white man's discovery of the islands opened up new opportunities for the businessmen who sailed from Europe and America. Fortune hunters joined conservative financiers in acquiring land on all the islands, legally or otherwise. The Hawaiian civilization was corrupted by American business. King Kalakaua, in an all night poker game, demonstrated the mood of the times. The King, playing with San Francisco sugar baron Claus Spreckels, contemptuously slammed his cards on the green felt table, proclaiming, "I have five kings," pointing to himself as the fifth.

The monarchy's objective throughout a century of expanding commercial activities was, simply, to increase royal revenues. Inspired by missionary advisers in the government, the monarchy lent full support to a single-use land policy and a plantation system of land utilization. Little attempt was made to encourage homesteading or to establish family farms. Most of the valuable lands suitable for large-scale agriculture, much of the beach land, and desirable future urban areas were quickly dispersed through widespread grants to large plantations and private estates.

The native Hawaiian population was dropping alarmingly by the time Mark Twain first visited Hawaii to write home about the tropical paradise. In 1873 he wrote: "The natives of the islands number only about 50,000 and the whites about 3,000, chiefly Americans. According to Capt. Cook, the natives numbered 400,000 less than a hundred years ago. But the traders brought labor and fancy diseases —in other words, long, deliberate, infallible destruction; and the missionaries brought the means of grace and got them ready. So the two forces are working along harmoniously, and anybody who knows anything about figures can tell you exactly when the last Kanaka will be in Abraham's bosom and his islands in the hands of the whites. It is the same as calculating an eclipse—if you get started right, you cannot miss it. For nearly a century the natives have been keeping up a ratio of about three births to five deaths, and you can see what that must result in. No doubt in fifty years a Kanaka will be a curiosity in his own land, and as an investment, will be superior to a circus."

The few remaining forests diminished as great sugar plantations spread across the land. As the forests receded before the commercial leviathans, barren fields of dry, red earth fed giant dust clouds. Red dust, carried by trade winds, blew miles out to sea at Waimea and Kehaha on Kauai Island. For days at a time during trade-wind weather, ships could not see the harbor and were forced to wait offshore.

The land was changing, but industry prospered. In a few decades Hawaii was to boast the largest sugar plantation, the largest fruit farm (pineapples), and the second largest family-owned cattle ranch in the United States.

The corporate formula for use of public lands in Hawaii is revealed dramatically in the history of lands occupied by Kauai's Kekaha Sugar Company. The story of how a government-sponsored land monopoly determined not only the economy of an island community, but also the very mood and appearance of the land.

Outright purchase of large land grants by the plantations had been stopped long before the Kekaha Sugar Company was founded. The Kingdom's policy of leasing lands instead of selling them had been initiated in order to halt the rapidly dwindling public domain. Later, the United States Congress, in writing the organic act establishing the territory of Hawaii, included provisions that protected Hawaiians from being stripped of their land heritage, and the leasing policy was continued for that purpose.

Kekaha began its corporate history in the early 1900s as the only Hawaiian plantation completely on government-leased land. Businessmen of the time must have raised their eyebrows as Kekaha cleared land, planted cane, and constructed a grinding mill at great cost, all with only a fifteen-year lease. But the venture proved quite profitable.

As Kekaha's first lease renewal time approached, plantation manager Hans P. Faye became concerned when the new Territory of Hawaii asserted that, upon termination of the lease, expensive mill machinery would revert to the government, in addition to buildings, irrigation ditches, and other improvements. Faye disagreed with the territorial government and in a letter to C. T. Bailey, commissioner of Public Lands, he offered to buy the land on which the innovations had been made, pleading that he could not make needed mill improvements without full ownership. Without objection, Commissioner Bailey deleted the forty-acre mill site from Kekaha's 28,000-acre master lease, and following the provisions of the organic act, placed the land on the auction block for competitive bidding.

Only two Honolulu men registered to bid on March 13, 1922: W. T. Bottomley, acting as agent for Kekaha, and his close friend, E. White Sutton of Bishop Trust Company. The auction took only a few minutes. The short-term leases on pastures and rice fields went to Kekaha at the opening, or upset, price of $3,000 annual rental. The fifteen-year sugar-land lease also went for the upset bid of $103,000 plus 7½ percent of gross sugar receipts. Kekaha had no other bidder for its mill, so the Territory, having agreed that Faye's offer for the forty-acre mill site, camp lands, and improvements was fair and equitable, sold the mill outright to Kekaha in fee simple for $150,000 cash.

Competitive bidding on ranch lands took only slightly longer. Sutton raised the $3,600 upset price by five dollars. Bottomley smiled and raised it another five. "Sold," said the territorial land agent, and Kekaha acquired the ranch land lease for $3,610.

With factory improvements completed and secured by

fee simple ownership of the mill site, manager Faye examined his company's leased acreage closely for new cane lands so he could feed greater tonnage into his modernized mill. Additional raw sugar could be produced profitably with little increase in overhead, and Kekaha could also safely increase planting without fear of losing leasehold lands. Without the mill, Faye correctly reasoned, no one would ever be able to outbid Kekaha, which would obtain every future lease at the upset price.

Faye wrote Commissioner Bailey, asking if Kekaha Sugar Company might be able to lease the Mana game reserves. The Territorial Division of Fish and Game said they "were not interested in creation of a reservation" at Mana, although at the time of the 1922 public auction the lands were specifically excluded from the sugar lease and designated as a game reserve. The plantation-oriented Territorial Land Department promptly answered Faye, requesting that he submit an offer for the 583 acres. Of course Faye did, and the only remaining migratory bird ponds on Kauai were leased at public auction to Kekaha Sugar Company for an annual rental of $900, the upset price.

Kekaha dispossessed the Hawaiian stilts, migratory birds, and ducks from their native habitat. The ponds were filled and planted in cane. In 1936 Governor Lucius G. Pinkham's Executive order setting aside Mana land for a territorial airport was also canceled. The airport lands were leased to Kekaha, which promptly planted them in cane. The territory's unwritten policy of promoting a single industry and a single land use was revealing itself as Kekaha expanded rapidly on all available land, eliminating the small farmer and showing little sympathy for conservation concepts encouraging protection of unique flora and fauna.

As the second round of fifteen-year lease negotiations opened in 1936, Kekaha was enjoying great prosperity.

Capital stock had been doubled by the issuance of stock dividends directly or indirectly earned from government-leased land. During the thirteen years of this second lease, average yearly cash dividends were 27.1 percent on capital stock. The company had clearly profited beyond all reasonable expectations.

Since water rights and irrigation ditches were publicly owned and since there would be no sugar or profits without tremendous quantities of water, it was reasonable to assume that there be a fair division of profits between the company and the territory. Instead, Kekaha proposed a new lease agreement even more favorable to itself than the old one.

Hearing of the proposal, Kauai's maverick Senator Charles A. Rice launched what was perhaps the first direct challenge of Kekaha's land monopoly and long land tenure. He wrote the Territorial Land Commission objecting to the proposal as "unfair to the government." And he wrote to the assistant U.S. Secretary of the Interior to complain about the low rentals paid by the sugar plantations. He suggested that homesteaders would be willing to pay more. "While I understand that not all of the government land leased to plantations can or should be cut up because of the irrigation and harvesting elements, I believe that at least 100 more of these homesteads could be disposed of on Kauai with a general good effect on the population." He gave as an example lands on eastern Kauai. Here the government lease on sugar land had not been renewed, and instead had been divided into sixty-one three-acre plots for homesteading and sale at auction. "As a result of this opportunity, citizens of the territory now own their own lands and homes, with surrounding gardens. There was spirited bidding at the auction. More than forty of the lots brought more than the upset price."

Leasing of large blocks of government land at low cost to the sugar and ranching industries had long blocked the creation in Hawaii of an independent, farm-owning population, and was described by the 1937 Congressional Statehood Committee as "one of the outstanding evils of Hawaii's present economic setup." Senator Rice agreed.

Governor Joseph Poindexter received a concerned note from the U.S. Department of the Interior that stated,

"The decreased income to the territory is undoubtedly causing an increase in the taxes paid by the people of Hawaii." The governor asked for an investigation. It had become obvious, even in Washington, that government land leases were being manipulated to keep the land available to only a favored few.

This high-level correspondence did not ruffle the land commissioner. His office was dedicated to furthering the best interests of Hawaii's fastest growing and most profitable industry. After receiving a letter from the Kekaha Sugar Company stating they wanted payment made as originally requested—on a sliding-scale percentage of gross —and would have nothing to do with a division of net proceeds, he asked the land board to approve Kekaha's application for a new lease. The board complied. It ignored Senator Rice's objections, unanimously approved the application, and moved for the auction to be held. As an added measure to make it more difficult for outside bids in the future, board member Charles Hite, then also secretary of Hawaii, moved that the power plant and campsite lands of the plantation be sold outright, although they were completely surrounded by territorial lands. The legal requirements were met and the cards stacked against any outside bidders for the Kekaha lease.

The outside bidders who did appear were dealt with in summary fashion. In the fall of 1937 a San Francisco businessman, George Rodiek, made a lease proposal "which, at all times, would give the landowner (i.e., the territory) fifty percent of the profits made by the operating company." He further proposed "that the cost of purchasing the present mill or the erection of a new plant, should be deducted from the lease rental . . . by doing this, the territory of Hawaii would own the entire project with all operating factors at expiration of the lease." Land Commissioner Whitehouse could, with ease, have expressed interest in this proposal of obvious benefit to the territory. His reply was simply, "law does not permit this."

Whitehouse dealt similarly with native Hawaiians

who sought homesteads on Kekaha lands. One day he
opened a registered airmail letter from Kauai carried by the
new interisland airways. It was from Henry K. Aki in
Lihue, writing for a "blank application for homestead in
the island of Kauai." Whitehouse was pleased to answer
what he thought to be a routine request and directed Aki
to D. F. Hurley, land agent in Lihue. Hurley informed
Honolulu that Aki wanted several dozen copies and would
Whitehouse "please send us a supply."

Whitehouse wrote Hurley anxiously by return mail,
asking what was going on over on Kauai and "what land,
or lands, Henry Aki plans on having petitions filed?" The
new airmail service brought a prompt reply: "Please be
informed that he refers to the lease to the Kekaha Sugar
Company . . . he said that he 'will see that the Hawaiians
get a chance to own their own homes.' "

Now even the Hawaiians were after the Kekaha lands.
Four hundred residents of Kauai were said to be ready to
file, and twenty-five actually petitioned the governor requesting homesteading lots on Kekaha lands. Mostly farmers already skilled in sugar growing, they wanted their
own farms on the Hawaiian Home Lands in the Mana
and Kekaha uplands. They wished to move homes and
families onto the land. The farmers declared that this
would not stop sugar production at Kekaha, but it would
result in independent farmers growing cane which would
be sold to the Kekaha Sugar Mill for processing. The great
water resources high in the Kokee Mountains, owned entirely by the government, would make it an easy matter
not only to grow sugarcane, but to permit the development of private, diversified farming and dairy industry as
well. Kekaha Sugar Company had already proved the
feasibility of the homesteaders' arguments by operating
its own truck farm on the very same Hawaiian Homes
Land.

The planters pointed to a provision they had written into the homesteading law during previous legislative
sessions, a provision that excluded the territory-owned

lands available for homesteading. In the end, the threat from persons seeking homes was met easily by industry. Governor Poindexter stopped the homesteaders' plea for land simply by rejecting their petition.

On June 8, 1938, the Kekaha lands were leased at public auction for the upset price of $130,000 to Kekaha Sugar Company. There were no other bidders.

World War II put a temporary end to the land debate. Kekaha was in full production, supplying sugar for the war effort. By 1942 the upland plantation farms were producing more than 600,000 pounds of vegetables a year. Clearly the land was suitable for truck farming, and Hawaiian farmers would have done well there. After supplying local markets, Kekaha sold surplus fresh produce to Kauai wholesalers in Lihue. Large quantities were also consumed by the army and some even found their way to Honolulu. By 1943, 800,000 pounds of produce were being harvested, principally beans, corn, summer squash, cabbage, potatoes, tomatoes, carrots, rutabaga, lettuce, peas— almost anything that the company could find seeds to plant. Everything seemed to grow well.

At the end of World War II, Hal Hanna, territorial representative from Maui, reopened the land debate. Speaking before the legislature, he stated, "Former Territorial Land Commissions literally gave thousands of acres of Hawaii's land leases to the big interests of the territory for a mere song." He claimed that the territory realized, for pasture lands and sugar and pineapple lands, only seven or eight dollars a year per acre. Considering the large amount of government land under lease, Hanna concluded, "in a community as wealthy as Hawaii, somebody is getting away with something. The territory receives too little."

The legislative flurry died quickly. While Democratic Governor Ingram Stainback echoed Hanna's charges, Republicans representing sugar interests still controlled the majority vote and quietly pigeonholed the bills introduced by Hanna. Not until statehood, fifteen years later, was any serious attempt made to revise Hawaii's public-land laws.

Meanwhile, Kekaha expanded its land-reclamation program. An extensive drainage canal and pumping system was installed for irrigation and for pumping swamp seepage into the sea. Sandy flatlands and drained lowlands were filled with bagasse—sugarmill trash—and mud from cane washing equipment, then flooded with waste water to speed up decomposition in an organic land recovering program. The new land was planted with sugarcane or used for irrigated pasturelands and alfalfa fields. Intensive land use continued to be a major program at Kekaha in its efforts to increase land production to its maximum. In the winter of 1953 Kekaha Sugar signed a new lease. As usual there were no other bidders for the lease.

Fortune magazine once described the system that kept Hawaiian agriculture from collapsing in a competitive world as *paternalistic semi-feudalism*. This system depended on a single industry for control over private and public lands. Upon admission into statehood, the system and the paternalistic laws that perpetuated it became obsolete, and by common agreement among legislators, their regular 1961 session was to be a land legislature.

It *was* to be, but it failed to pass a new land law. The Senate-House Conference Committee, which was attempting to hammer out compromise legislation, failed to reach agreement. Liberal and conservative principles resisted compromise, and discussions bogged down completely on the question of the sale of public lands for commercial use. The basic stand of the new postwar Democrats was that the state should not sell its lands. Their Republican counterparts took the position that the state should do its utmost to promote economic development and that public lands should be made available, even for outright sale.

Democratic Representative David McClung proposed that land leases be limited in size so that small-scale agricultural enterprises would have opportunity to develop. The sugar industry quickly took issue, saying that a 500-

acre lease limitation would threaten the operation of Kekaha Sugar Company. They asked if the representative meant to force the plantation management to negotiate sixty separate leases from the land board and compete at public auction with countless other parties for the use of land on which its continued operation depended.

The next legislature, a year later, successfully compromised by agreeing that the final determination of land exchanges and sale of public lands for public use would be by legislative act. But the main body of Hawaii's land laws went unchanged and the political struggle over land reform continued to be a major issue in subsequent elections.

Political scientists Robert Horwitz and Norman Meller, in a review of Hawaii's land and politics, said: "The protagonists in this struggle had truly been 'playing politics,' but in a more basic sense than that term generally implies. The resolution of the land issue would, as they saw it, vitally affect the very character of Hawaii's regime, for the ownership, control, and utilization of her lands affect the quality of life of virtually every inhabitant of the Islands. The principles underlying the land issue were fundamental, for the protagonists rightly understood that while land laws of one sort are compatible with a plantation economy, extreme differences in wealth and status, and concentrated political power; land laws of another kind will promote the development of varied economic enterprises, more egalitarian division of wealth, and broader participation in government. The land issue in Hawaii has been—and will continue to be—linked inexorably with the extent to which the Island's regime is more or less oligarchic, or more or less democratic."

So long as fundamental differences of opinion about the nature of the good life and the just society divide Hawaii's citizenry, the issue of land and politics will continue to be stoutly contested in Hawaii's state capital.

3

"The Life of the Land Is Preserved in Righteousness" (Motto of the Kingdom of Hawaii)

HAWAIIANS considered the use of land a communal right, not something to buy and sell. Natives did not understand the concept of private property introduced by Boston missionaries and later exploited by American sugar pioneers. And no one explained the actual consequences of land ownership. It was only necessary to register the plot with appropriate descriptions at the office of the land agent. Many Hawaiians neglected to take even this simple step. They wondered why, after having lived on the land for as long as they could remember, it was suddenly necessary to describe how far it was from the large corner stone to the grass hut and the nearest mango tree.

Hawaiians, who spent most of their lives fishing and farming, soon learned that their land could pay for fish hooks and taro. The fact that land could be used only once for this purpose was never fully understood. Land agents for sugar plantations on Maui would seek out land-owning Hawaiians who worked on other islands, offering to buy the land they no longer used in Maui. Poorly paid Hawaiians generally agreed.

In one transaction I discovered while browsing through various plantation land-office files, Kamakea, a native Hawaiian, borrowed $250 from a land agent. The agent accepted as collateral the mortgage on Kamakea's undivided interest in twenty-two acres. A week later, the agent signed over the mortgage to a small sugar plantation which, in turn, leased the land from Kamakea for fifteen years, paying him $750 after subtracting the loan. Fifteen years later, a larger plantation, having acquired the assets of the original sugar company, transferred the leased land to its ownership records and continued harvesting sugarcane. Kamakea and his children were never notified that the lease had expired. Nor were they told that the plantation claimed Kamakea's land as its own under adverse possession laws formulated by Honolulu representatives of the sugar industry who advised the Hawaiian Kingdom.

This entirely legal if somewhat confusing procedure was repeated again and again in Hamoa, Hana, and Kaeleku, on Maui Island. The plantation did nothing to compensate the holders of undivided interests unless they complained. The few landowners who realized what was happening were paid their asking price without question.

An elderly Hamoa resident, Nalae, attempted to keep the family land untouched and undivided by creating a primitive trust. In his will, dated 1866, he wrote:

"In the name of the living God, I hereby give and devise my property unto my heirs, and to be divided as follows:

"Unto my wife, two aho (fish lines), one net, one ax, one file, one house, three hooks.

"Unto my grandchild, one aho, two nets, one large ax, one file, one package of hooks.

"Unto my son, Kamiki, I give and devise my real property, being our hui land at Mokae. This devise is for his lifetime, and upon his death he is to devise the same unto Kamila in the same manner. . . ."

Nalae's son did as the will requested, but on the son's death Kamila, who was Nalae's youngest daughter, sold one-third of the land she inherited to an enterprising agent for $150. She withheld her house lot, but only until the next day, when she was persuaded to sell that too—for one dollar. The agent then sold the original acreage to Kaeleku

Sugar and kept the lot on which the house stood for himself.

Increasing numbers of children and grandchildren continued to reduce their undivided interests in the land until the fractional ownerships almost defied computation. The Kaeleku Sugar Company records show a $75 land purchase of, "not less than an undivided 315/672nd interest in and to an undivided interest in the whole land of 315/2016nd in the land . . . situated at Mokaenue . . . containing an area of 2.45 acres. The area conveyed being not less than 0.382 of an acre." The Hawaiian land ownership system devised by Polynesian chiefs had been saner than this, and Hawaiians had trouble understanding.

Older Hawaiians returning to retire on their land often found their parcels lost in a sea of tasseled sugarcane. Entire village sites were plowed under. Stone walls, trees, and boundary markers had been obliterated. The land was no longer theirs. By adverse possession, it belonged to the sugar plantation.

Annie Pak Chong, a thin, weathered Hawaiian-Chinese woman, still lives on the Hamoa lands her ancestors passed down through several generations. She is one of the few who over the years have successfully resisted encroachment by ranchers and sugarcane planters.

When the latest of several landowners allowed his cattle to graze freely across Annie's land (property that he claims to have purchased from the sugar plantation) Annie posted "Keep out" signs and strung barbed wire to keep invading ranch cattle away. Her land, a remnant of a land grant from King Kamehameha IV, is now much reduced in size, having been subdivided and resubdivided until, for the most part, only fractional interests remain. But it is the last of a great heritage, and Annie intends to keep her land. She claims clear title and has resisted every effort to take the land away. I talked with her in a tiny kitchen, my tape recorder on the table before us.

"When I was eight years the house was there," she told me, pointing across the field to the remains of a rocky foundation. "I remember the house was there, and my father used to raise chicken. We has a little chicken house below this on the opposite side. But I was only eight years. I'm fifty-nine, fifty-eight this year. So that's about fifty years ago."

The facts of land ownership were difficult to ascertain, but the new rancher, a wealthy mainland industrialist, was impatient. "Why can't these people understand that I own the ranch now," he said. He personally directed loading the ranch bulldozer onto a flatbed trailer, and the trailer departed for Annie's land, a mile down the Hana road from Hana Ranch headquarters.

"They use to rent the lands from the Hawaiians," Annie continues. "Since the plantation time, we kept on using our land because part of this was rented to the plantation, and part of it—we living there. And the plantation was leasing until Mr. Fagans came here. Then he started to raise cattle and then he didn't pay us no rent for the land, no nothing. So we fenced the undivided interest and we used our interest."

In the early morning, a Hawaiian cowboy drove the ranch truck to Hamoa, towing the bright yellow D-8 bulldozer. The wide load forced oncoming cars off the narrow paved road to allow the rumbling truck to pass without delay. The ranch manager, his red hair blowing in the open cab window, sat quietly beside the Hawaiian driver who had some misgivings about his morning work.

"He told us that we didn't own here," Annie says, "and I told him: I said no. I said my mother has the interest here and we own here. She lived here all her lifetime and we lived here all our lifetime after my mother. And her grandmother lived here all her lifetime. We put the fence there after the cane was over, see. So we put cattle in. He told we didn't own the place."

The D-8 was unloaded at the top of the hill. The shiny blade bit into the wet earth covered with a stubble of grass, and the machine moved forward, drowning out the sound of rocks thrown at the steel behemoth by Annie's brother.

The rocks bounced off as the bulldozer easily snapped the ohia fence posts, jerking twisted barbed wire into the air. "He came here, he bulldozed the boundary fence. Twice he did that on the fence we put on the boundary. We put the fence back twice. After he bulldozed it we put the fence back twice. Then afterwards, he threw me in land court, threw the whole thing in land court. It's my great grandfather's tomb that's on that round hill. It's a round tomb, on top of that hill. Yes, my mother's grandfather. And our great-grandmother is over there in those trees. And my grandmother and my grandfather is buried below the beach, between the two fishpond."

White-face Herefords slowly followed each other into Annie's green kuleana, now stripped of its boundary fence and open to grazing among the gravestones. Through years of litigation the problem of ownership of the land Annie lived on went unresolved. It still goes unresolved today, but twenty years after the bulldozer felled her fence, new owners of Hana Ranch presented Annie an exchange deed for her land. She promptly erected a new fence.

In a time when ethnic minorities everywhere are fighting in defense of racial integrity and self-determination, the question is often asked why native Hawaiians failed to seriously challenge the take-over of their island and their land by American sugar planters and traders.

Feeble resistance by supporters of the last Hawaiian Queen, Liliuokalani, composer of *Aloha 'Oe*, only emphasized the general apathy of Hawaiians as a racial group. They seemed willing to accept virtual extermination of their cultural traditions by missionaries, and suffered widespread decimation of their race by Western disease (bubonic plague, smallpox, measles and syphilis) and loss of their land to Western concepts of economic democracy and private property.

Following annexation of the islands as a territory of the United States in 1898, white planters and traders supported the Hawaiian delegate to the U.S. Congress, Prince Jonah Kuhio, in his plea for Hawaiian homesteading land.

This gesture was apparently a reaction to adverse criticism of their ruthless take-over of the sovereign Hawaiian kingdom. Congress authorized the establishment of an Indian-style reservation system, ostensibly offering the Hawaiians an opportunity to return to the land. The only requirement was that they farm it and live on it.

Unfortunately, after American businessmen and the military took the choicest parcels, most of the land remaining for the Hawaiians was marginal at best, little suited for small-farm agriculture, and without water or access. After numerous farms had failed, it also became clear that few Hawaiians really enjoyed the hard work of farming. They found easy loopholes in the agreements, and many subleased the land to pineapple growers and ranchers who paid them a nominal rental.

In time many homestead areas, particularly in Honolulu, deteriorated into rural slums as traditional Hawaiian family relationships broke down in the clash with the competitive urban demands generated by a money economy. Traditional family relationships were disrupted by a cost of living so high that both mother and father were forced to work. In some cases the artificial security of a free homestead seemed to smother the Hawaiian spirit. Adults were too often on welfare and their children delinquent.

Opportunities for Hawaiians in skilled employment were scarce, and what success they did achieve appeared to them to be racial tokenism rather than opportunity for a proud contribution to society. Too often the hotel-room maid, the bellboy, and the janitor were Hawaiians. There were more dropouts than graduates from high school, and the police lineup seemed increasingly to repeat Hawaiian surnames.

It was only a matter of time before young part-Hawaiians became radicalized. They pointed to the increasing urbanization of Hawaii and the accompanying depreciation of rural life-styles as the social culprits. Disrespect for the land allowed speculators to run bulldozers across agricultural fields with little opposition until the rising

prices of land and housing crowded all but the most affluent off the land. Honolulu was identified by federal agencies as the second most expensive city in the world, in terms
of daily living cost, and it became evident that perhaps a
closer concern for land use was needed: perhaps unre-
stricted growth and subdivision of the land of Hawaii were
mistakes.

When Hawaii is thought of as a closed island ecosystem, the folly of continued urbanization becomes self-evi-
dent. Not only is the future economic solvency of sugar and
pineapple jeopardized, but so are the scenic assets of a
valuable tourist industry. Even more, the island rapidly
becomes too expensive for the people who work in Hawaii
to live in Hawaii.

The state itself took the first step to help preserve
agricultural lands by withdrawing primary zoning rights
from county governments and initiating land-use zoning
by the state for all lands, public and private. This helped
reduce destructive chamber of commerce competition between the individual islands and made difficult the acquisi-
tion of favorable zoning decisions by private developers—
the state being more difficult to corrupt than the counties.

Gradually an aroused community began to resist the
encroachment of sprawling subdivisions upon agricultural
land and the expansion of hotel facilities into scenic and
historical areas. Battles were won and lost in the state and
county political arenas, but even the losses were gains in
some ways. Every loss saw a newly irate community or
social group decrying the irresponsible, partisan legislators,
builders, and developers. The matter of saving the land became a political issue.

The basic issue of stockholders' interests versus people
became relevant when in 1972 the Kohala Sugar Company
on Hawaii Island announced it would shut down because
the company was no longer earning sufficient profits. Suddenly everything became clearer—the use of the land was
better understood. The sugar workers' union and the
county governments demanded that Kohala continue in

operation. The county recommended buying the company and having the people of Hawaii grow the sugarcane.

That kind of radical proposal was promptly turned down, but Herbert Segawa, former president of the Hawaii Island Chamber of Commerce, says, "personally, I am concerned for Kohala sugar. Government cannot turn its back on the people. It must step in and assist or look to other avenues, for it must save the community."

As the 1970s began, seemingly unrelated events created headlines. They have emerged as a pattern of positive action:

• When the state of Hawaii completed the purchase of Kahana Valley on Oahu's windward shore to create a new state park, authorities immediately issued eviction notices requiring the Hawaiian residents to move from the valley. The residents refused, and the resulting outcry forced the Division of State Parks to reevaluate its construction plans. Perhaps it would be appropriate after all, they said, for Hawaiians to live in a park on their land.

Kahana residents wanted to take part in the concept of a living park and were supported by the governor's task force for Kahana Valley. A bill was introduced in the legislature, determining that "if the Land Department finds . . . that the original residents of the park area enhance the land or have a culturally or historically valuable life-style, these residents shall be allowed to remain on the state park lands." It would have been a great cultural step forward for Hawaii to officially recognize the Hawaiians' plea but the bill failed to pass. At the same time, no further move was made by the state to evict the 140 residents of Kahana Valley.

Speaking for the valley Hawaiians, Lydia Dela Cerra, whose mixed racial parentage is revealed in her name, said: "This valley has housed our ancestors for many, many years. Isn't it a privilege that we, the offspring of Hawaiian ancestry, should be given rights to remain in the valley which once held the Hawaiiana [traditions] of the natives here, which is slowly dispersing into thin air?"

A new pattern was appearing in the valley dwellers'
plea, one that echoed a different cry from that of conventional environmentalist objections to expanding highways
and sprawling subdivisions. The Hawaiians were presenting a petition to the private estates and public land administrators stating that the land they lived on was theirs by
right of birth, that no one owns the land, that "the land is
ours to hold in trust for our children and generations to
come." Suddenly the controversy developed into a political
challenge of the basic concepts of private property and laws
perpetuating corporate landowners and estates.

• On Oahu, pig farmers in Kalama Valley and young
counter-culture people united in an effort to preserve the
small farms and house lots at Henry Kaiser's Hawaii Kai
Project, which were to be replaced by expensive residential
subdivisions. The farmers lost, but only after staging a sit-in
in front of the bulldozer. Police dragged them away as they
pleaded for the right to live on the land that Hawaiian Prin-
cess Bernice Pauahi Bishop inherited from their ancestors
and the Bishop Estate's trustees had leased to Kaiser.

The struggle may have begun in the mid-1960s, when
newly-elected Governor John Burns appointed me to the
State Land Use Commission, to help implement the only
statewide zoning law in the nation. I worked closely with
the State Director of Planning and Economic Development
to oppose urban zoning of Oahu's south shore beyond
Sandy Beach. When the Kaiser Hawaii Kai development
people learned of this opposition to their plans, Henry
Kaiser himself drove downtown to the Land Use Commission office and, with his associates waiting hesitantly in the
hallways, loudly expressed his extreme displeasure at a
public zoning body that would deny him the right to do
anything he wanted with his land. Kaiser said he would sue
and threatened to abandon the entire multimillion-dollar
Hawaii Kai project unless he immediately received permission to build hotels on Sandy Beach in Kalama Valley and
on every ridge. The progress and growth-oriented commission quickly retreated, and I was unable to muster suffi-

cient votes to prevent Kaiser from receiving almost everything he demanded.

The small farmers and Hawaiian families living deep inside Kalama Valley were never consulted. No public hearing notices were posted along the dirt roads leading inland among the dry, windblown kiawe trees bordering Sandy Beach. The zoning change was decided by Kaiser.

The hopes of Kalama Valley farmers and squatters, enjoying a semisubsistence life-style, were briefly revived when a bill was introduced in the 1971 legislature suggesting that the rural life in southern Oahu should not completely disappear. Senator Nadao Yoshinaga charged that "the proposed urban development of Kalama Valley is an example of mismanagement and misuse by the land owner, a charitable trust, and is a threat to the welfare of the State."

Senator Yoshinaga's bill called for a study of population stabilization in a racially and economically mixed community, which would include former residents of the valley who were forced out to make room for the Kaiser subdivision. He also asked for a planned land development program that would include open spaces, recreational, agricultural, and conservation areas. He further asked for individually-styled communities appropriate to counterculture life-styles of people who want to live on the land in their own way in hand-built structures exempt from conventional building codes. Education for children and adults would be integrated into community life and include participation in civic, artistic, and cultural affairs.

The bill was defeated by a legislative majority that would have none of this rural life-style nonsense.

Yet the right to build their own "country-style" home without the restrictions of expensive zoning and building codes is, in part, what many citizens are asking for. The need for concrete sidewalks is hardly necessary if you prefer bare feet. But in requiring the removal of a simple beach shack built by young people in Waianae, Honolulu Building Department staffer Herbert Muraoka said the owners must have a building permit and at least build a safe structure. He said, "They have to follow the same kind of construction as conventional building construction. By that I mean they have to use nails. They can't hold it together with ropes." Old Hawaiian technics used in grass shacks are no longer acceptable at city hall.

In the spring of 1972, a disenchanted group of young people met again at Henry Kaiser's development near Sandy Beach to offer a requiem for the last open shoreline of the Bishop Estate on southern Oahu Island—a shoreline being bulldozed for development into a modern resort-hotel complex. The evicted farmers were there along with young part-Hawaiians and friends of every racial mix, dancing to a rock beat and asking in plaintive song why only the rich could live in Hawaii.

• On the big island, ten organizations joined together to oppose the construction of public golf courses and a realigned highway near Kealakekua Bay where Captain Cook first landed. They called for a public hearing and complained that the Bishop Estate had "never discussed any of these plans with us. They should find out what the Hawaiian people want."

Concern was expressed for the Hawaiians who lived on small land parcels along the isolated Napoopoo shore. They claimed that the Bishop Estates planned a community of 8,800 persons with eighty-eight acres of hotels and that the crowds of people would "force us off our land, deny us our beaches, and pollute our fishing waters." Their spokesman said zoning would not protect the Hawaiians, because "the tax collector will take away everything when the rich mainlanders move in."

• Hawaiians living in the Kahaluu Valley along Oahu's upper Kaneohe Bay joined the cultural rebellion, forming their own community association to oppose irresponsible government-sponsored development and to protect traditional rural life-styles against the onslaught of urban subdividers steadily advancing north from Honolulu.

"We love our land," said Lucy Naluai, the quiet chairman of Hui Malama 'Aina Ko'olau, a community organization whose goals include the "protection and loving care of our kuleana," the personal property handed down through generations after the great division of land among the commoners and the chiefs by King Kamehameha IV.

"We also love our ancestors," cried Naluai, "and we cannot and will not see them ripped out of the land by bulldozers. They kill a little bit of us every time they take our land."

Some of the people evicted from Kaiser's development moved to Kahaluu, where according to Hui Malama spokesmen, they are "broken people, many of them forced to live on welfare because their sources of income were destroyed and their rents went up. . . . Now, there are no more Kahaluus that they can go to."

The demands of Hui Malama were simple—stop all capital improvement projects financed by public funds that would accelerate population growth and increase land costs and taxes. They criticized highways crossing the island, which "will allow many people . . . from Honolulu to move to Kahaluu and make Kahaluu into a rich suburb. There will be a lot of expensive housing development which we cannot afford."

The proposed Kahaluu flood-control project "will make commercial, resort, and industrial development possible . . . [and] further drive up the cost of the land," according to Hui Malama. "If the land is not cleared and bulldozed there will be no floods to bother us, and a new sewage treatment plant will not be needed if no more people move out here, and if the highway isn't built the people won't come. . . ."

Another Hawaiian association has given its support to a congressional reparations claim for native Hawaiians, asking for "compensation for losses resulting from the overthrow of the Hawaiian Kingdom through the use of the armed forces of the United States, acting illegally and without proper authorization." They want $1 billion in ten an-

nual payments plus title to all federal lands in Hawaii
which become surplus to government needs. Their attorney
says the claim is just as valid as the settlement Alaskan
Indians and Eskimos received in Congress.

Leader of the group, former city councilman Kekoa
Kaapu, said his organization "is now seeking justice for
events which occurred eighty years ago, which deprived
the Hawaiian natives of their land, civil rights, country and
dignity."

The Hawaiians, born of the islands and the custodians
of the rich culture and traditions of a Polynesian civilization, see their language and unique life-style disappearing.
With perhaps less than 8,000 pureblooded Hawaiians remaining, they see the entire race nearing extinction. They
do not pretend they can stop development, but they do ask
to participate in the decisions that shape their future and
their land.

"We demand that it be development that builds on the
life of the people," says Hui Mālama, "that preserves our
values and that nourishes the children and grandchildren
of all the native people of Hawaii. We cannot any more
allow development that destroys the things that make
Hawaii what it is."

4

The Beginning of the End

ASTRIDE the equator in the southwest Pacific
Ocean far to the west and south of Hawaii is the smallest,
loneliest nation on earth. Though it lacks nearly every at-
tribute one might expect of a viable modern state, the tiny
island Republic of Nauru has survived as an independent
nation since January 31, 1968. Nauru must import its water,
for uncertain rainfall makes water catchments useless. Poor
soil permits little agriculture, and jagged reefs surrounding
the island have no harbor breaks to provide protection from
tropical storms. There is no commercial fishing, few natural resources, and no scenery or pleasant beaches to invite
tourists to play on. All Nauru has is itself—probably the
largest deposit of phosphate anywhere. The entire island is
phosphate—ancient deposits of marine organisms built up
on coral reefs—a valuable component of fertilizer that is
also Nauru's only source of income.

Shaped like a skimpy sugar doughnut with a rapidly
growing hole, Nauru covers 8.2 square miles. A tour around
the island takes only fifteen minutes of dodging potholes in
the road and an ugly breed of Nauruan pigs. The hole of
the doughnut is a phosphate mine exposing the bare heart
of Nauru. This is all that remains after a hundred years of
continuous mining by German and British colonists, Japanese invaders, and now independent Nauruans exploiting

43

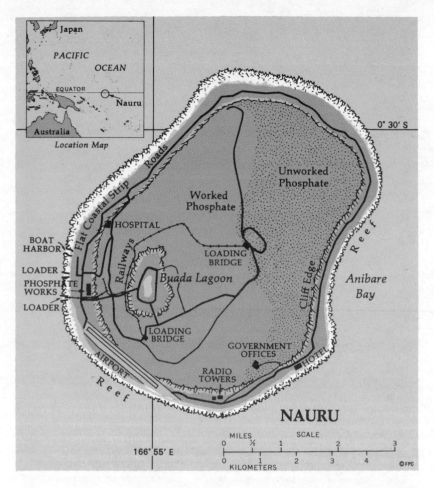

NAURU

their own valuable resources. When the noisy clam-shell excavating shovels and smoking loading trucks move on, fifty-foot-high pinnacles of bleached white coral remain as evidence of the marine origin of Nauru phosphates, built up over millions of years during higher stands of the sea. The pinnacles clutter the open strip mine like a dead forest, testimony to the decay and death of an island nation first settled about 2000 B.C. It is in some respects a disorderly microcosm of the Pacific Islands. But unlike other parts of the earth, in sad disarray, the Nauruan people have made plans to escape their colossal island wreck.

The ancestors of the present Nauruan people arrived on Nauru perhaps 4,000 years ago when the brown people of Southeast Asia launched their outrigger canoes and sophisticated sailing rafts to venture into the unknown Pacific and settle on new lands across the horizon. Their accomplishments in navigation and logistics at such an early date eclipse the endeavors of Cook and Magellan —sailing in vessels that were larger and less responsive to the unpredictable winds and currents of the open sea. While the first European explorers were satisfied to visit and return home with sketches of "savage natives" and collected flower samples, the first oceanic voyages by Asian peoples included complete family groups which carried not only the seeds of edible fruits and medicinal plants—coconuts, breadfruits, taro—but also cultural grafts for new civilizations on thousands of Pacific Islands.

Before the Vikings reached Greenland and North America, traveling on what were basically large rowboats, Melanesians were sailing with the aid of fore-and-aft rigged sails and center-boards on swift, double-hulled canoes easy to maneuver and maintain on course. Even their rafts could be sailed upwind more efficiently than the later square-rigged ships that dared venture into the open ocean.

Sailing canoes are still widespread in the Pacific. And the navigational skills required to sail by canoe across the ocean with speed, comfort, and accuracy is a common trait among islanders who have no knowledge of contemporary navigation technology or use of a compass. Their ability to navigate far beyond the sight of land through intimate knowledge of the stars, winds, and currents, enabling them to return again and again to tiny, remote islands scattered across the Pacific basin, is testament to an enlightened civilization that thrived for thousands of years without written languages.

Their sailing canoes are marvels of innovative design and construction passed down through generations of craftsmen who drew no plans and wrote no books of instruction. In a single island group all the canoes possess identical design details. They look as though they were prefabricated instead of being laboriously constructed by hand—from memory.

Unusually seaworthy "flying proas" fitted with removable lateen sails and masts sail smoothly and swiftly across long Pacific swells imparting a sense of security that a passenger finds absent in conventional motor boats. I sat astride the hull of a small three-man canoe in the Namonuito Islands, watching in amazement while a naked crewman walked the sail fore and aft, tacking before the wind, the open hull never taking water over the bow or stern. Made with gently convex hulls and free-jointed outriggers counterpoised by loaded platforms, the canoes sailed trimly and with incredible stability, sliding smoothly through cross-running seas, bending gently before gusty winds, slipping little water over gunwales that were only inches above the water. The canoe moved with a characteristic gentle zigzag so useful in navigating by the stars, and I could appreciate claims of stability made for these small craft that allows them to ride out fierce seasonal storms that move northwestward on yearly tracks through the central Pacific islands.

The Melanesian peoples were hardly primitives; they were architects, politicians, and navigators. Two thousand years before Columbus challenged the concept of a flat world and braved grotesque monsters at the edge of the earth, the Pacific peoples developed an extraordinary knowledge of the sea and sky, and they evolved complex astronomical systems. They were able to identify and locate every star seen from the Southern Hemisphere. According to Herman Friis in his history of the Pacific basin, "European impact interrupted a spreading process whereby sidereal and lunar months were being coordinated, and westerners were astonished at the facile accuracy with which Caroline navigators sketched maps to oblige. Star bearings, voyaging times, and alternative landfalls were precisely indicated."

Anthropologists may never learn the routes of early voyages of exploration spread over many millions of miles and several thousand years. The first Melanesian pioneers to discover Nauru probably were exploring northward out of New Guinea and the Solomon Islands at the same time their racial compatriots were exploring northeast Asia by land and sea to found Chinese civilization.

The first European to see Nauru arrived almost four thousand years later. Captain John Fearn, searching for whales in the southwest Pacific, landed on Nauru for provisions, and described the island as "extremely populous," with "houses in great number." Later white visitors were mostly sailors and escapees. A trading ship captain recorded in 1843 that, "this island, and many others in the Pacific, is infested by Europeans who are either runaway convicts, expirees, or deserters from whalers and for the most part men of the very worst description." In this same decade the Nauruans, apparently encouraged by the white expatriates, massacred the entire crew of the American whaling brig *Inda* out of Boston, after a dispute over coconuts. For many years after, traders and whalers treated the islanders with considerable respect.

The most unusual arrival on Nauru was a thirteen-year-old boy, Ernest Milner Hindmarsh Stephen, who was dumped on Nauru in 1880. The boy's father had allowed his son to make a trip on the trading ship *Venus*. When the captain decided not to return to the boy's home port with his full cargo, he left Ernest with a trader on Nauru. Not until eight years later did the boy's father finally trace his son to Nauru. When Ernest was found at the age of twenty-one, he had a native wife, three children, and his own trading store.

Intertribal scuffles between competing tribes of Nauruans was common, but not until white traders introduced guns was the balance of power severely upset. Beginning in 1888 the fighting was extremely bloody and only eventual German occupation prevented Nauruans from exterminating themselves. The island was like a battlefield. In ten years over 1,000 combatants were killed in continuous wars.

Imperial Germany gained control of Nauru as part of the late nineteenth century agreements in which major European powers divided the Pacific into spheres of influence. Germany occupied the island in October 1888, when the gunboat *Eber* arrived with the military governor. The island was a shambles.

The Germans banned alcohol, including fermented coconut juice introduced by Gilbert Islanders, demanded surrender of all firearms, and arrested the twelve warring chiefs, confining them in a copra shed under guard. Once the total of 765 rifles, guns, and pistols had been turned in —almost one for every man, woman, and child on the island—the chiefs were released, and the war was over.

It wasn't long before the Germans discovered that their newly acquired island was almost all phosphate, perhaps the purest phosphate found anywhere in the world. Phosphate promptly became a profitable export and extensive mining has been under way ever since, with few interruptions even for world wars. The British kicked out the Germans during World War I, then they ran both the phosphate works and the islands under a League of Nations mandate in collaboration with Australians until early 1942, when Japanese Imperial forces took over.

Japanese military commanders, concerned about divided loyalties and limited food and water, exiled 1,200 Nauruans to Truk Island in Micronesia for the duration of World War II and continued production with indentured labor. The island was subject to frequent air raids and bombing runs, but the complex phosphate loading facilities were never touched by American bombers. One day after the announcement of peace between Japan and the United States, the local garrison surrendered to Allied naval units and island mining supervisors began oiling up loading machinery that had been idled during the shipping blockade. Only 737 Nauruans returned home from exile. The others,

463 men and women, died of starvation, disease, and Japanese brutality on islands in the Truk lagoon.

Under a United Nations trusteeship agreement, the Australian government took over control of Nauru, rehabilitated phosphate processing machinery and began shipping the much fought over phosphate directly to Australia. In 1968, Nauru won its independence and in 1970 the Nauru Phosphate Corporation became the property of Nauru—but with quarry operations still run by Australians.

Members of the Nauruan Parliament and Head Chief of the traditional local government council, President Hammer DeRoburt is a survivor of the Truk exile and leader of the long struggle against foreign domination. He describes the day independence was achieved as a "Day of Deliverance" when Nauru became not only politically independent but free of foreign phosphate diggers. Income from the phosphate mines, now owned by the people, would be used exclusively by Nauruans themselves, and DeRoburt proceeded to convert Nauru into an unusual island corporate state with free hospital, medical, and dental care, free education, modern housing, and a comprehensive pension plan for every island citizen. Two modern, well-equipped hospitals, a dental clinic, and nine schools providing education from infant level through secondary grades were financed totally from income generated by phosphate sales.

The 4,000 people of Nauru earn over $4,000 per capita in royalties from the 1.6 million tons of phosphate that is shipped away from the island each year in bulk ships that the islanders also own. This income enables native Nauruans to live an almost entirely imported existence on their phosphate republic in the middle of the Pacific.

Nauru may be the only nation to boast of a constantly increasing foreign exchange balance in its favor. With only one export, the people of Nauru have earned millions of dollars using conventional capitalist gambits—exploiting raw materials and getting someone else to do the hard work at low wages. Chinese and Gilbertese contract laborers are imported as phosphate miners. They live in bleak slums of dreary tenement housing that contrasts adversely with the more substantial Nauruan dwellings along the shore road.

Under DeRoburt's aggressive leadership, the increasing phosphate profits have been invested in numerous overseas ventures. In the land of their most recent colonial rulers, Australia, Nauru has under construction the tallest office building on the choicest real estate in downtown Melbourne.

"Australia is still very important to us," says DeRoburt. "We send our pupils to school there, sick people who cannot be hospitalized here are sent to Australian hospitals, and a large part—nearly all of our phosphate, as a matter of fact—goes to Australia and New Zealand, and on this we depend very much."

Originally, the Australian Nauru Centre Tower was to have been forty-seven stories—just a fraction shorter than an older white-owned office building nearby—but four more floors were added before construction began. DeRoburt insists the increase in height was motivated purely by economics and not by one-upmanship. It was necessary to purchase more land next door and level an old building on the lot to obtain new zoning approval. Total cost of the land and building may exceed $45,000,000, the largest single investment so far by DeRoburt and possibly the forerunner of similar expensive building projects in other overseas countries.

Millions of dollars have been invested in Australian trust funds, bonds, and blue-ribbon stocks. There's even a steamship company, the Nauru Pacific Shipping Line—a wholly Nauru-owned Pacific line carrying cargo and passengers between south sea ports and, in shippers' vernacular, "other ports with sufficient inducement." Nauru Pacific's *Kolle D,* the 33,000-ton heavyweight of the line, made her maiden voyage from Nauru carrying phosphate to Australia. The modern bulk carrier then toted a full load of wheat to Vladivostok in Siberia before beginning work on an all-year chore hauling wood chips from Tasmania to Japan. The ship *Rosie D* is on tourist cruises to South Pacific ports from Australia. The *Enna G* was to run a scheduled service to Samoa via Fiji and Tonga until she became a casualty of striking crewmen in New Zealand before her first voyage began. Twenty-three Fijian seamen walked off the ship, complaining that their $123.50 a month pay was woefully inadequate. When government officials flew in twelve Nauruan strike breakers, the ship was blacklisted by the New Zealand Seaman's Union, and DeRoburt learned quickly that making money with money was far more difficult than simply digging it out of the ground.

Air Nauru was his next venture. Beginning with a small, leased American jet, the fledgling international airline soon was flying Dutch-manufactured F-28 twin-jet aircraft from Australia to Nauru and on to Majuro with stops in between. Negotiations are underway to expand operations to Japan via Ponape and Guam, but DeRoburt must first overcome strong objections of Continental Airlines-owned Air Micronesia and of Pan American, both of which would like to fly the same trail-blazing north-south Pacific route. Air Nauru is keeping alive the slogan, "getting there is half the fun." In an age when air travel can often be frustrating, this all-first-class airline pampers its passengers continuously from the moment they step aboard. There are Australian beer, multicourse meals, tropical fruits, bonbons, and a choice of beverages in a veritable orgy of service by gracious Gilbertese and Nauruan hostesses.

Among the swarm of new post-war nations, Nauru may be the most financially successful, even if its future is limited. The Nauruan investment program of phosphate income is in a race against time to return foreign-earned profits (of an expected one billion dollars) before the phosphate is gone. The mine is expected to last only another twenty-five or thirty years. Then the doughnut hole will be empty; it will flood with brackish water, and the island will provide neither income nor home. Their investments, Nauruans say, should be sufficient at this time to sustain a comfortable way of life for many generations after Nauru is no longer habitable.

The Australian government has offered to resettle the Nauruans in Australia when the phosphate mines are exhausted, but DeRoburt says his people prefer a self-governing island environment somewhere so they can maintain their own community and customs. For this reason, many island businessmen in nearby Micronesia have become wary of Nauru cash, fearing that Nauru is only interested in land, and her investments are only made with an eye toward eventually controlling land. Nauru is still searching for an unused country.

Huge diesel dump trucks shuttle back and forth between active digs and the clattering machines that separate and crush the rock before loading it into railroad cars for transfer to nearby cleaning plants. Spindly cantilever trestles carry the processed phosphate by conveyor belt off shore to bulk carriers waiting at anchor in deep waters beyond the reef.

Nauru digs deeper within itself, excavating its bowels for sale to the highest bidder to stay alive for a while longer. The weird, bleak landscape of jagged pinnacles and scrub brush is an ecological disaster, yet the destructive excavation continues with little thought of land reclamation, for Nauru intends to destroy itself to buy enough money to sail away to another island to live at another time.

5

The American Lake

WESTWARD from Hawaii, south of circumnavigator Magellan's first trek across the Pacific, in the five million square miles of Pacific Ocean north of the equator between Hawaii and the Philippines, are scattered 2,200 islands comprising a unique island community, yet a significant part of the earth's environment. It's a substantial part of the earth's surface—above and beneath the sea— little known, relatively unexplored, and inhabited by over 110,000 Micronesian and Chamorro people occupying a combined land area smaller than the smallest American state, Rhode Island.

Europeans named the land Micronesia—tiny islands— and called the people Micronesian. If American administrators had only asked, they would have learned the true name of these islanders who speak fourteen different languages and comprise six different ethnic groups, for without pretense they naturally call themselves "the people."

Since 1521 when Ferdinand Magellan raised the Spanish flag on Guam, the tiny islands north of the equator have been told what to do by international traveling salesmen and clerics from Germany, Japan, and the United States. They've been "saved" by Spanish Catholics, German Lutherans, Japanese Buddhists, and American Seventh Day Adventists—in that order—and have been told what *not* to

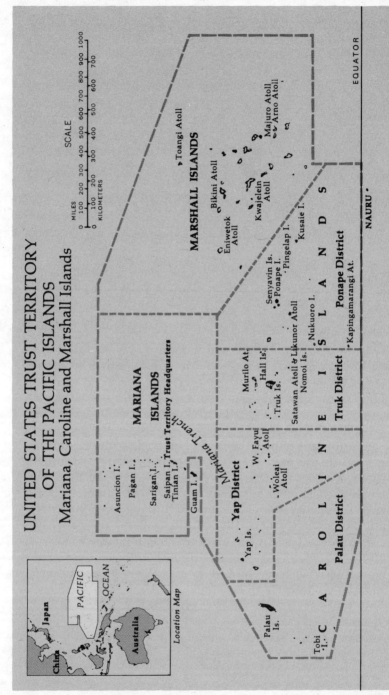

UNITED STATES TRUST TERRITORY
OF THE PACIFIC ISLANDS
Mariana, Caroline and Marshall Islands

Location Map

China
Japan
PACIFIC
OCEAN
Australia

SCALE

MILES 0 100 200 300 400 500 600 700 800 900 1000
KILOMETERS 0 100 200 300 400 500 600 700

MARIANA
ISLANDS

Asuncion I.
Pagan I.
Sarigan I.
Saipan I. Trust Territory Headquarters
Tinian I.
Guam I.

Marianas Trench

Yap District

W. Fayu Atoll
Woleai Atoll
Yap Is.

Palau
Is.

Tobi I.

Palau District

C A R O L I N E   I S L A N D S

Murilo At.
Hall Is.
Truk Is.
Satawan Atoll & Lukunor Atoll
Nomoi Is.

Truk District

Senyavin Is.
Ponape I.
Pingelap I.
Nukuoro I.
Kapingamarangi At.
Kusaie I.

Ponape District

MARSHALL ISLANDS

Toangi Atoll

Bikini Atoll
Eniwetok Atoll
Kwajelein Atoll
Majuro Atoll
Arno Atoll

NAURU

EQUATOR

©FPG

do by a varied claque of militarists who in the final analysis told everyone what to do.

Yet, the natural beauty of the land and the traditional culture of an island civilization have in large part been untouched by intruding colonizers, traders, and politicians from Asia, Europe, and America. Of the 2,200 islands, only a scattered fifty are inhabited. Across the three million square miles called Micronesia—the Trust Territory of the Pacific Islands—many are occupied only by a dozen Micronesians or a seasonal copra harvesting party.

Geologically, the islands range from the volcanically active Marianas Islands, the extinct volcanic high islands of Palau, Yap, Truk, and Ponape to the low island atolls in Yap, Truk, and the Marshalls. Between Guam and Truk is the Marianas Trench, the deepest waters of any ocean on earth.

The exploration of America into the western Pacific islands began a hundred years ago when Boston-trained Hawaiian missionaries arrived in the Marshall Islands. Whalers and traders from every land followed in motley array. The foreign cultural and technological invasion was interrupted only by two world wars that did little more than blend political allegiances among native people who never achieved a nation or even a common language. Yet, in time, it may be the Americans who give them the common purpose and language that build a nation, as they resist the territorial imparity of an island floating in the middle of the American lake.

Before Walter J. Hickel was fired as secretary of the interior, he pleaded with President Nixon's then National Security Advisor, Henry Kissinger, to recognize the people of Micronesia and their need to own their own land. Kissinger replied, "There are only 90,000 people out there. Who gives a damn?"

The Micronesian people have no vote and no elected representatives to carry their plea to Washington. Today's United States High Commissioner, appointed by the president without review or consent by the Senate, has veto powers over any action of the U.S.-sponsored Congress of Micronesia. At the same time, as a concomitant to the strategic trusteeship agreement, the commissioner suffers veto by the Pentagon over his one-man rule. There has been little modification in the procedures of colonialism. Only the names have changed.

United States Navy administrators converted Micronesia and Guam into a huge military reserve at the end of World War II and built nuclear testing facilities on Kwajalein, Eniwetok, and Bikini. The Central Intelligence Agency (CIA) constructed elaborate training facilities for Chinese counter-revolutionary insurgents on Saipan, teaching Taiwan Nationalists tricks of spying and sabotage preparatory to dropping them by parachute into the People's Republic of China. The ill-conceived project was abandoned after the U.S. Department of the Interior assumed administrative control of Micronesia. When the Marianas were formally incorporated into the Trust Territory, the CIA's costly staff housing complex became headquarters for U.S. civil administrators. The few remaining facilities from Japanese days were left to rust and decay with few accomplishments of any consequence credited to the string of incompetent political appointees who offered no real plans for the future except to keep everyone else out.

I went fishing in 1968 with Rear Admiral Carlton Jones who was in charge of the U.S. Navy's Marianas District at the time. His responsibilities also included the Pacific Islands. After we cleared the mouth of Guam's Apra harbor navy base in the "Admirals barge," I asked him about the future of Micronesia. "Why not invite the Japanese businessmen back to rebuild the economy destroyed by war? Can't we allow the Japanese tourists into Micronesia?" My questions were rhetorical but I hoped for an answer and I got one. "The Japanese will never return to Micronesia," he said, with the firmness of a jingoistic military officer still fighting the last war. He was also very wrong.

There is no lack of examples to show how little control the Micronesians have over their lives or their land. When the Atomic Energy Commission (AEC) sought to bury radioactive waste underground in old salt mines at Lyons, Kansas, the people rose in wrathful opposition to the proposal. The AEC hastily backed off and began looking for another disposal site.

They thought of loading it aboard a rocket and shooting the deadly stuff into space, toward some unknown galaxy. There would have been no chance of its ever returning to earth, they said. But someone reminded the scientists that rockets have failed on lift-off, and that plan had to be dropped.

Why not bury the waste in the Pacific in the bottom of the Marianas Trench in Micronesia, near the place where the United States tested early atomic bombs?

The problem is that, although America's burgeoning nuclear power plants are described as "pollution free" by electric utility companies anxious to build the efficient power generators in large numbers to solve their energy problems, nuclear power plants are definitely not free of pollution. Disposal of dangerous radioactive waste produced by conventional nuclear reactors is a major unsolved problem demanding solution within the next few years.

Exhausted nuclear fuel rods removed from reactors aboard nuclear submarines, aircraft carriers, and power plants may possibly be the most dangerous material produced by man—with the possible exception of the hydrogen bomb itself. Of the spent fuel, ninety-eight percent are radionuclides that effectively decompose in 150 days. But the remaining two percent, recovered during waste processing, is composed of the most deadly matter known to man, Plutonium 239. It is a cancer inducer far worse than comparable nonradioactive pollutants such as lead, arsenic, and cadmium, which retain their detrimental properties forever.

Plutonium 239, with a half-life of 24,400 years, is capable, in extremely minute quantities, of giving off

highly lethal alpha particles capable of completely destroying living tissue when injected internally and producing
terminal cancer. A quantity about the size of a baseball is
enough to combine with other nuclear ingredients to make
a single hydrogen bomb capable of destroying Chicago.
The United States' weapons arsenal apparently contains
sufficient atomic bombs at present, so we have surplus of
waste Plutonium 239—an ugly by-product of the atomic
age that will not go away. With a decay half-life of many
thousands of years, it requires permanent storage without
any possibility of human contamination "for hundreds of
thousands to millions of years," according to Cyril Slansky,
nuclear chemist for Allied Chemicals radioactive waste
processing plant in Idaho. But Slansky has found an alleg-
edly safe repository—in the bottom of the 36,000-foot
depths of the Marianas Trench, southeast of Guam in
Micronesia.

Recent geological discoveries affirm a slow plastic flow
of the earth's mantle as the continents drift apart and the
ocean floor puckers in long undersea trenches and sub-
merged mountain ridges. Hopefully the radioactive waste
can be sealed in corrosive-proof containers and dropped
into the deep ocean trenches. Ultimately it is expected to
be sucked deeper into the earth's hot interior as the ocean
floor drifts together—hopefully before the waste container
leaks. Slansky says extensive oceanographic research has
found that the Pacific Ocean deeps have "slow moving currents whose return of a dissolved substance from the
bottom to the surface (where most living matter resides)
would take approximately 1,000 years. By burying the waste
in the ooze in the deeps, one might double or triple the
return time." By this casual adjudication, should the
United States decide to use its Pacific lake for a nuclear
garbage dump, Guam may have only 3,000 years to live—
if the American nuclear waste floats to the surface.

Twenty-five years of American colonial blundering
have created neither a viable economy nor a democratic
community. By even minimum American standards, Mi-

cronesia is a poverty ridden land. Losses of cultural traditions, natural resources, and wildlife have been enormous. Giant breadfruit trees on Ponape split apart the
untended ancient ruins of Micronesian history two thousand years old. Inept bureaucrats strip sand from one-of-a-
kind beaches for construction of unneeded jet runways.
They dredge live coral reefs for deep water harbors in
fundamental ignorance of adverse ecological consequences.
Proposals have been made to flatten islands and to cover
barrier reefs for international airports. Investors invite
foreign surveys to prepare feasibility studies to harvest the
wealth of the sea. They strip mine for phosphates and destroy deep coral reefs to obtain pink coral for tourist beads.
Research and development studies to dispose of radioactive
nuclear waste seem almost anticlimactic in the apparent
urge to lay waste to Micronesia in the name of economic
development.

The approaching critical level of environmental disaster is clearly revealed in the district centers where dangerous concentrations of people, flinging aside traditional
cultural restraints in a headlong rush to acquire the economic benefits of a money economy, are polluting their
land, the oceans, and lagoons with accompanying destruction of a valuable island life-style. The adverse ecological
changes are hidden in the wilderness of a thousand scattered islands like a time bomb with a sputtering fuse.

High altitude jet trails smear the sky over remote
islands where airliners had never before been seen. Plane-
loads of tourists are beginning to tread fragile tropical islets,
raid untouched beaches for shells, dive into hidden lagoons,
and photograph the bare breasts of native girls. Ecological
and cultural disruption continues in the name of economic
development. Native traditions and language are polluted
by shallow tides of western civilization engulfing proud
peoples whose island landscape and biological uniqueness
are trampled and purchased by rampaging businessmen,
opportunistic politicians, and swarming tourists, who ignore their traditional values and communal ideals.

The flimsy French swimsuit received a Micronesian name when Operation Crossroads exploded atomic test bombs under and over the remote Micronesian Bikini atoll. The name became instantly famous in scientific laboratories and beach resorts around the world, but few are aware that thirty years after the mushroom cloud rose over Bikini, the lagoon fish are still too poisonous to eat and land crabs crawling up the gently sloping white beaches are still "hot" radioactively. Navy Seabees cleared the small island of dangerously radioactive buildings and blockhouses by bulldozing them into the lagoon and dumping them at sea. Their solution to atomic contamination is to keep it out of sight.

Redstone Arsenal headquartered in Huntsville, Alabama, took over Kwajalein atoll ten years after United States troops captured the low islands from Japanese occupation forces and immediately began transforming the island group into a Pacific missile range test facility. Micronesians were evacuated from the scattered lagoon islands and confined in American-style ghettos adjacent to the main Kwajalein Island and the northern test site at Roi-Namur.

A new kind of light illuminates the night sky for the Marshallese natives renowned for their ability to navigate trackless Pacific water in outrigger canoes by reference only to the stars. The glare of chemical rockets launched from Kwajalein pads brightens the night and warns observers to seek shelter as deadly experimental missiles streak skyward to intercept intercontinental ballistic missiles (ICBM) fired from Vandenberg Air Force Base in southern California. An on-target hit showers the Marshall Islands with metal fragments, littering the calm lagoon with antiballistic missile (ABM) parts.

The naval air station on the bulldozed flatlands above Agana, Guam, offers a mid-ocean sanctuary for swarms of scheduled transpacific airlines sporting the familiar names of Pan American, Continental, and Trans World Airlines (TWA). Their jet fumes mix with the exhaust of private cars crowding the single highway encircling tropical Guam, producing a thin haze that has begun to persist on still mornings. Continental Airlines' route from Minneapolis to Saipan island hops through Micronesia with stops in each district center, landing on coral runways dredged from island lagoons and cleared from coconut groves planted by German rulers a half century ago.

The impact of jets and dollars on a subsistence economy and tropical environment severely disrupts the surface serenity associated with the traditionally languid tropics. The waving palms, turquoise lagoons, and half-moon beaches are still there to photograph, but behind the palms and below the calm waters looms a cultural and ecological chain reaction nearing critical level.

On the back streets of Koror, teen-age boys stone the unlucky white visitor caught on the streets alone at night. Truk authorities are forced to close the bars to restive youths reacting violently to a future without jobs or security, in a money economy estranged from traditional village life of shared responsibilities. The conventional concept of private property and democracy taught by Peace Corps volunteers proves revolutionary on islands where village chiefs control land use and political power in the old communal style.

Extensive loss of breadfruit trees, source of a Micronesian staple food, is threatened by a disease infestation spreading unchecked among the islands. Banana crops have been lost to diseases. In the Palaus, entire copra plantations have been totally decimated by rampaging coconut beetles, wiping out the food and the income of dependent islanders. Thousands of Trukese natives are faced with serious food problems through loss of the breadfruit tree, their most important staple food, while Marshallese natives harvest copra for sale at world market prices that fluctuate beyond their control.

Beneath the sea the disruption of the underwater ecological balance by radioactive waste, shell collectors, reef dredging, and power plant thermal effluent has reduced the triton mollusk and the associated sea life to a degree that the crown of thorns starfish (*acanthaster planci*) has reached a critical population level. Normally a casual occupant of the reef, sharing space and food with myriad crustaceans and tropical fish, the giant starfish suddenly began swallowing the live coral in an ecological horror story. It digests the coral organism and leaves behind a dead skeleton—host for algae growth resulting in sharply increased toxicity for reef-feeding fish. The Bikini lagoon, where before the A-bomb only a few varieties of toxic fish thrived, has steadily increased in toxicity, and according to Bikini chiefs who visited their former home, fish that were never before poisonous are now deadly.

Leeward of the oil-fueled U.S. Navy power plant beyond Guam's Apra Harbor where thousands of gallons a day of hot circulating water is discharged over the reef, an increase in the toxicity of inshore fish has been observed. The same phenomenon has also occurred near the raw sewage outfall from the capital city of Agana where the dead coral reef was first noticed by University of Guam scientists. Bulldozing for new subdivisions in the hills above Agana washes increasing quantities of red earth into the nearby ocean after every tropical squall, mixing alien material into the sea water, destroying the natural habitat for sea life. Shellfish were the first to disappear. Then the reef.

The extent of damage to Guam's reef system was not known until after the 160-mile-per-hour winds of Typhoon Karen in 1962 tore up tons of dead coral reef, tossing it inland. Accompanying high seas immediately began eroding the exposed shore, and curious skin divers discovered that most of the reef was dead. Thousands of tiny fish normally clustering around the live coral were gone. The reef was reduced to a pile of crumbling chalk.

Forty percent of the reef surrounding Guam was dead; twenty-four miles of living reef had been destroyed. The remaining live coral was swarming with a giant sixteen-pointed starfish, two feet across, consuming the live coral reef barrier at the rate of half a mile a month like a raging forest fire. Lying like an aquatic plant in the midst of a coral garden, the reddish-brown crown of thorns starfish devoured the living rocklike coral by direct ingestion through the walls of the stomach. Where it had grazed, the coral surface was bleached, glaring white. The dead coral skeleton was soon covered with a dull ooze where bright coral colors once blossomed in profusion.

In Palau, school children were put to work picking starfish off the reef and bringing them ashore to die on the beach. Teams of starfish hunters were organized in every district to inject the predator with an ammonia solution, whereupon the starfish obligingly disintegrates. Even after many years, the acanthaster continued to multiply faster than man could stop the spreading menace, for the acanthaster's natural enemy, the triton mollusk, that kept the starfish in check over the centuries, was in many areas no longer a reef dweller. Like an unknown amoeba from outer space the acanthaster multiplied alarmingly. When cut in half, each piece grew a new set of tentacles covered with spines poisonous enough to cripple a man. The monster shellfish consumed in days coral reefs that had required two hundred years to grow, while the natives faced disaster as their food resources from the reef and sea disappeared. In time the islands themselves might have been washed away, destroying the people, the land, and an embryonic nation in a major ecological disaster unparalled in the history of mankind. It was a classical example of a disruption of the ecological chain. No one is certain that the threat has been stopped. And it could happen again.

For a millennium, the islands of the western Pacific have been aging in the sun. For four hundred years they have been occupied by alien powers, swept by wars not of their making, populated by a peaceful, seldom angry people bending before alien governors like coconut palms before typhoon winds. Change was imperceptible in a people and a land where remote village life echoed social traditions of many thousand years past—until the paradise of the Pacific became a missile testing ground and tourist resort.

When Air Micronesia's mini-skirted blonde stewardesses first stepped from their airliners on Yap Island to pose for snapshots with the grass-skirted local girls, a cry of shame rose from the proud Yapese women. The short skirts were disgraceful, they complained. They sat bare-breasted in a thatch-roofed terminal building but their legs and ankles were modestly covered by long grass skirts decreed since ancient times.

Exploding ABM and MIRV missiles sprinkle the Kwajalein lagoon with metal fragments that future archeologists may find difficult to explain. Spraying tropical insects with chemical pesticides to change native subsistence living to midwest farming; exploiting ocean waters for commercial fisheries to feed continental populations thousands of miles away; clearing the jungle for resort hotels that cater to the affluent traveler; mining the seabed and exploiting natural resources; dumping waste and fighting destructive wars—all these are the astringent benefits from America and Japan. They are thrust upon the Micronesian people without opportunity for choice or refusal and without regard to the ecological or cultural consequences, however good or bad that might be.

6

The Ocean of Many Islands

I WAS lying on the soft, warm sand looking over the quiet waters of Truk lagoon. Suddenly the distant horizon was severed by a geyser of water erupting into the clear sky. A dull boom followed across the lagoon within a few seconds as oceanographers on the white-hulled schooner anchored off Udot Island measured the seismic echos bounced from the deep lagoon floor. The scientists were looking for oil in a very improbable geologic location, but the intensive search for raw materials in the Pacific basin has resulted in even the Truk lagoon being scraped, dredged, dug in, drilled, and punched with dynamite charges. Little has been found, but the search continues, amply financed by United States and Japanese corporations, sometimes working together on cooperative expeditions.

Today's activities are a far cry from the situation forty years ago when, in the decade of American isolationism prior to World War II, Truk was the subject of considerable imaginative speculation by radio commentators and feature writers. Truk was spoken of in mysterious terms as an impregnable Imperial Japanese naval base, constructed in secret by Emperor Hirohito's militarists as part of a campaign to conquer the world. The United States military was convinced that Truk was an impregnable bastion. After

Pearl Harbor, American admirals assumed the worst and offered Truk as evidence of Japanese aggression. The stage was set again for the ravaging of a peaceful island landscape by foreign nations acting without respect for an innocent people.

American admirals were quite mistaken in their belief that Truk was an impregnable super-fortress. The Japanese never intended it to be anything other than a fleet anchorage and advanced staging area. Shallow coral reef shelves surrounding lagoon islands made construction of major naval base facilities prohibitively costly. Not until 1941 were even small cranes and floating drydocks moved in. Water and foodstuffs had to be shuttled in tiny sampans to warships anchored in deep water between island roadsteads. Even when garrison troops finally arrived in January 1944 with anti-aircraft guns, they posed no threat, for effective United States submarine attacks on Truk's lifeline with the homeland sank freighters carrying their food and accessory radar equipment. And the troops spent their time constructing pillboxes and growing vegetables on a slowly starving island.

After the Americans captured Majuro and Kwajalein in the Marshalls they began to look to Truk. On February 16, 1944, five American carriers positioned ninety miles from Truk launched the first flight of seventy fighter-bombers one hour and twenty minutes before sunrise. Arriving over Truk at dawn, they were surprised when they met no opposition. They were six days late—the Japanese fleet had escaped. But the Americans bombed the place anyway.

The Micronesians thought the war was over. The Japanese fleet was gone and the Americans did not send their own fleet in to take over. Only a small destroyer showed up one day at the South pass in the outer Barrier reef to accept the Japanese surrender.

Truk was in chaos. No food had arrived for over a year, and Trukese natives, Japanese troops, and exiled Nauruans were barely existing at a subsistence level. Trukese caught gathering their own coconuts had been shot climbing the palms. Hundreds died of malnutrition. There were simply too many people on the small islands to survive without imported food. Islanders and Japanese troops, pummeled by incessant bombing raids, starved or turned to cannibalism.

All Micronesia was the same. The battlefield of the great foreign powers became a cemetery for thirty years of Japanese economic development—harbors, roads, and airports were destroyed. The economy of the innocent Micronesians was set back a quarter of a century.

The American military government that succeeded Japanese administrators did little except keep everyone else out until the United Nations, at their first meeting in San Francisco, transformed Japan's oceanic empire into an American lake and approved documents that created for the United States a trust territory of the Pacific Islands. This certification of colonial power specifically granted the United States military forces the right to fortify the islands although they had no particular plans in mind at the time. The military did, however, feel the islands would make excellent targets for testing nuclear bombs and proceeded accordingly without informing the Micronesians of the consequences and expressing little relevant concern for their welfare. Ten years after the Marshall Island atoll of Kwajalein was captured by Admiral Spruance, it was transformed into a test facility for atomic bombs.

It had all happened before. The Micronesian historical experience of four centuries under foreign rule helped explain their "shrug of the shoulder" attitude as the United States took over. American military governors said the natives were lazy; in fact, they simply didn't give a damn any more. Native leaders wondered what name their country would have next year? Under the Japanese it had been Nanyo. What language would their children be required to learn? What religion would be best? Should they bow? Or shake hands?

Magellan almost missed Micronesia on his voyage

around the world in 1521. He did find Guam. Unfortunately for the Chamorro people of Guam there was abundant water and tropical fruits lacking on other islands in the central Pacific. Guam in later years became a Pacific port of call for Spanish galleons hauling gold from the Philippines to Acapulco.

Spanish priests and civil governors accompanied by armed soldiers were sent to the Mariana Islands to convert "primitive" natives and force alien Spanish rule upon the naked Chamorros. The natives disagreed violently with the invaders over the way of life to be practiced, and when Father Diego Luis de Sanvitores baptized a Chamorro child on Guam against the wishes of his parents, the priest was killed by the enraged villagers. The Spaniards retaliated and began killing the relatively defenseless Chamorros. Cruel fighting raged on and off for a quarter of a century. Between deadly diseases and the brutality of Spanish troops, an estimated 100,000 native people died, virtually decimating the Chamorro population. At the end they practiced infanticide to avoid raising their children to live under Spanish rule. In a few years all were gone—an island society vanished forever.

The Chamorro people were among the first native people of Oceania to defend their island life-style and traditions against the cruel onslaught of European civilization. In these islands the drama of destruction was first performed—a pattern of cultural annihilation that was later to be repeated again and again throughout the Pacific with rifles, bayonets, venereal gonococci, and atomic bombs.

The ethnocentric English historian, Kenneth Clark, in his book, *Civilization*, said "the very fragility of those Arcadian Societies—the speed and completeness with which they collapsed on the peaceful appearance of a few British sailors followed by a handful of missionaries—shows that they were not civilizations . . ." Clark dismissed the historical chants of Pacific island peoples as legends, affirming his own racist suppositions that anything not written is not fact, that any non-believer in the Christian God was a savage heathen, and that sex was a sin. Clark justified his argument by observing that the island peoples, ". . . produced no Dante, Michelangelo, Shakespeare, Newton, or Goethe. . . ."

Micronesians did not write down their incredible navigational skills, possessed no blueprints for their carefully designed long-distance canoes, and prepared no anthropological studies of their complex family clans and governmental systems of Nahnmwarkis and High Talking Chiefs. Every island possessed its own distinctive language, but it was never written. Spoken chants were their living history —the facts of an island civilization.

Westerners never understood this native island wisdom. An American anthropologist was prying into the private lives of a Samoan family one day, writing down answers to routine questions that the Samoans felt were hardly important enough to ask and had taken for granted for generations. He did not "want to listen to singing chants," the scholar said. He dismissed them as legends. An elderly Samoan interrupted, saying he knew the names of all the stars and where they were in the sky. The American anthropologist did not think it important enough to write down.

The extensive ruins of Nan Madol on Ponape Island are evidence of an island civilization contemporary with the birth of Christ. This city of fortress temples on canals dredged in the coral reef was constructed perhaps a thousand years before Venice. It was a Venice in the Pacific with oriental temples.

Compare the design of Angkor Thom in distant India, built in 889 A.D., with the impressive Nan Dowan fortress —a temple of Nan Madol erected about 300 years earlier. At first glance the similarity is startling! The differences are abundant, particularly when comparing the rough building block technique of island craftsmen to the fine carvings and fitted stone of the later Indian temple complex. Yet the striking comparison speaks well of a sea-faring civilization which forged complex religious motives into a reef city on Ponape.

They utilized the limited resources of a remote Pacific Island with great skill and inventiveness.

Living was extremely difficult in the temple city of Nan Madol. Stormy seas pushed inshore, and typhoons, shouldered on high tides, must have swept often across the man-made islets. Coconuts, breadfruits, and bananas were plentiful, but providing for the large retinue of Nan Madol Nahnmwarkis would have been impossible in the sandy, salty soil. It was necessary to bring food from nearby Temwen Island and the great fertile valley across Madolenihmw Bay to the west. Water was no problem—it rained almost every day.

Six-sided volcanic basalt rock was used in the construction of Nan Madol. Transported twenty miles from the nearest quarry, huge building blocks, some weighing an estimated five tons, were probably slung beneath oversized log rafts for the journey. Rolled up temporary inclined ramps of broken coral at the building site, the heavy rock logs were laid log-cabin style into structures three stories high with projecting corner caps reminiscent of oriental architectural motifs. The impressive structures on artificial islets represent a stunning achievement for native peoples ordinarily given credit for little more than grass shacks.

A destructive typhoon in the early 1800s forced the last Nahnmwarki resident of Nan Madol, Luhk en Mallada, to permanently vacate his island capital. Venereal disease, smallpox, and tuberculosis further decimated his fellow islanders following visits of New England whalers and traders. The islanders had no natural resistance to the new diseases, and by 1852 two-thirds of the population of Ponape were dead. Maintenance of the unique reef community became impossible. The Venice of the Pacific was abandoned.

Typhoons and tropical storms repeatedly flooded Nan Madol, silting in the man-made canals and breaking down protective stone dikes on the exposed ocean side. Devastating waves swept inland, undermining heavy rock foundations of the vine covered temples. Breadfruit trees and coconut palms split open canal revetments 1,000 years old and encroaching mangrove thickets choked sacred burial grounds and places of worship.

The tropical jungle had almost reclaimed Nan Madol when German administrators replaced the Spanish crown in the late 1800s. Curious about native legends and stories of a phantom city on the reef, the Germans began elaborate archeological excavations in 1907. Ponapeans warned their new rulers not to remove the bones of buried royalty, but German Governor Berg continued personally to dig in the ancient tombs. One night he was kept awake in his camp by harsh sounds from Temwen Island, residence of the last living Nahnmwarki. The next day Berg was found dead.

The Germans came to the little island with an interest in coconut oil. They planted thousands of coconut palms throughout their rapidly expanding Pacific domain, introducing the technique of sun-drying coconut meat to separate it from its shell and then shipping the resulting copra to Europe for processing into coconut oil and cattle feed. Germans developed the classic island occupations of copra production and trading imported goods, in distinct contrast to their Spanish antecedents who took little interest in the Pacific islands beyond a strange urge to baptize everyone.

British concern over German expansion in the Pacific was verified by the appearance of German trading posts on the north coast of New Guinea and the Bismarck Archipelago. Suddenly the simple division of unexplored Pacific areas between Spain and Portugal was no longer valid. Spain's claim on Micronesia, dating from two years after Columbus discovered the West Indies, was no longer enforceable in the face of German and British warships roaming the Pacific. At an 1888 Berlin Conference following the occupation of New Guinea by German bankers establishing Neuguinea Kompagnie (New Guinea Company), Britain signed an agreement giving Germany a free hand

north of New Guinea and west of the Gilbert Islands. This
cut Samoa in half, with America getting the eastern part
and the western islands going to Germany. Tonga and
Niue were declared neutral. Germany had already concluded nineteen separate treaties with Marshallese chief-
tains making moot any argument over the Marshall Islands
north of Samoa.

The Spanish tried to hang onto Yap, but their landing
party arrived a day late—German marines had disem-
barked the day before at the same time German troops
landed at Woleai, Palau, Truk, Ponape, Kusaie, and Pingelap.

Spain was outraged, and appealed to Pope Leo XIII,
who ruled that Micronesia was indeed Spanish property
but granted Germany commercial rights to establish fisheries, plantations, and settlements. Micronesians continued
to resist compulsory conversion to Catholicism and on
some islands—notably in Palau and Ponape—slaughtered
Spanish priests and garrison troops assigned for their protection. Protestant missionaries were generally welcomed,
but blackbirding of unwilling plantation labor from Micronesia for work in Samoa and Hawaii inspired islander dis-
enchantment toward white colonizers. The island peoples
were never able to reconcile the Christian church that, on
the one hand, preached brotherhood and humanity and
at the same time claimed sovereign islands as private property, divided up the oceans, and forcibly kidnapped island
men.

The United States joined the rank of colonial scaven-
gers following the contrived war against Spain in 1898. At
the end of the war the United States dismembered Spain's
overseas empire and expressed its own imperialistic aims
in new island acquisitions spanning the Pacific. Americans
assuaged their conscience with a payment of $20 million
for the Philippine Islands and independence for Cuba.

America's knowledge of Pacific geography was limited.
When Admiral Dewey's representative sailed into Apra
harbor on Guam to accept the Spanish surrender, the gov-

ernor did not mention the outer Mariana Islands or Micronesia. The governor did not even know there was a war on. The American navy captain in charge seemed perfectly satisfied with receiving Guam and during subsequent peace negotiations Spain never mentioned her Micronesian possessions scattered over three million square miles of ocean. One month later Spain sold the rest of Micronesia to Germany for $5 million.

Japan began kicking Germany out of the Pacific before World War I began and completed its takeover of Nanyo after the Treaty of Versailles under terms of a secret agreement with the allies and followed up with a face-saving League of Nations Mandate. Great Britain allowed New Zealand and Australia to assume some of the "white man's burden" in the Pacific and reinforced her economic and political interests in Singapore and Hong Kong.

For over a century, the countries with the most warships have divided the Pacific among themselves. Holland held on to Indonesia. France gradually extended her influence over the Polynesian islands, including Tahiti, the Marquesas, Tuamotu, and Melanesian New Caledonia. Great Britain took over southeast New Guinea and the lesser islands eastward, including the Solomons, Fiji, Gilbert and Ellice Islands. Germany and the United States split Samoa into two parts and Britain and France decided to rule the New Hebrides Islands together, from government houses across the street from each other under terms of a condominium government—locally termed pandemonium. The islands north of Tahiti were claimed by Britain and America. At Christmas Island the United States flag flew over the north shore while a New Zealand commissioner reigned comfortably under his flag near the south shore. In all the Pacific, only the Tongan Islands were overlooked in the imperialistic scramble for wealth and power.

Arbitrarily carving the Pacific into spheres of influence, European statesmen sometimes revealed a profound ignorance of island people. They split traditional language groups apart and ignored nearby atolls important to sea-

faring islanders but unknown to uninterested cartogra-
phers who drew lines based on the number of battleships
rather than ethnic traditions. The southern boundary of
Micronesia was conveniently made to coincide with the
equator. This cartographic nicety rejected the culturally
related Melanesian peoples in Nauru and the Gilbert Islands but included Polynesians living on Kapingamarangi
and Nukuoro atolls who enjoy totally different customs
and languages.

Senator Amata Kubua, Iroji and past-president of the
Congress of Micronesia, commented on one of these lost
islands in a recent Congress session. Opposing premature
return of the eastern portion of Mili Atoll that had been
omitted from Micronesia in the United States Trust Territory Code—"due to some past miscalculation" as he put it
—Kubua asked the Micronesians to consider what the missing Mili Islands can represent if they remain in their present status in the Pacific island wilderness.

"It can represent an island of our country which has
not undergone great changes as a result of the imposition
of the Trusteeship agreement," asserted Kubua. "It can
represent our past history, our cherished customs, our re-
siliency and strength as a people, who struggled and tri-
umphed over the forces of nature and the constraints of
so little land in such a vast sea.

"It can also represent what potentials we have for the
future. It can represent an area which can produce fish and
traditional Micronesian foodstuffs and materials, but can
also be productive in a modern sense as a place for controlled tourism, and a representative of the benefits Micronesia has to offer to international sea transportation and
commerce as a free port.

"In short, Mr. President," concluded Senator Kubua,
"let this part of Mili remain as it is—a representative of
what an independent, free, self-sufficient, and self-reliant
Micronesia was and can become after dissolution of the
Trusteeship."

7

The Americanization
of Paradise

ARNO is to some visitors the most beautiful
atoll in Micronesia—perhaps in the entire Pacific. Little
touched by modern improvements, the village life and
Marshallese thatched homes centered on individual coral
graded plots reflect a traditional life-style of another era.

A classic ocean atoll, Arno combines in its 130-square-
mile lagoon all the attributes of a south sea fiction writer's
dream. Miles of curved white sand beaches fringe an enclosed lagoon muted in color from the glare of cumulus
clouds and the turquoise of shallow waters reflected on
clouds overhead—an ancient ocean beacon for canoe voyagers navigating beyond the sight of land.

Arno's 133 islands are scattered around a deep lagoon.
Tiny islands, totaling only five square miles of sandy earth,
some little more than slight rises of white sand behind a
coral reef, support wind blown shrubs and beach vines
hanging on aged coconut palms. The largest islands are
heavily forested with coconut plantations (planted by the
German commercial companies), wild bananas, pandanus,
papayas, and limes, arrowroots and huge breadfruit trees
mixed with isolated plantings of cultivated sweet potatoes.
Only a dozen of the islands arranged in a great oval around
the lagoon are permanently occupied. Most are visited only
briefly by itinerant copra harvesters and local fishermen

waiting out sudden tropical squalls. The population is probably about 800, a figure some consider the maximum allowable for Arno if present desirable environmental and cultural amenities are to be maintained.

Pacific travelers have always talked knowingly of Arno's famous love school on Lunger Island, where Marshallese mothers sent their daughters at puberty to learn the arts of love. Micronesians concluded long ago that a good sex life made for a good home life and girls who graduated from the unique school staffed with all-women tutors are still referred to proudly by their husbands as "Arno girls." Nevertheless, many Marshallese deny it all as a fanciful story concocted by lonely whalers wanting to tell exotic south sea tales back home.

I was stranded on Arno last year. As a trip leader for Wilderness Expeditions, I had planned to take several guests in a chartered boat to Ene Island on Arno Atoll when we encountered rough weather in the channel and ran low on fuel. The seas were relatively smooth close in to Majuro where the high massed coconut palms softened the wind and the wide reef bent aside ocean swells. But as we proceeded further into the open ocean separating Majuro from Arno, a frightening change occurred as we encountered severe northerly winds. Our small boat was suddenly tossed upward into the sky and then immediately thrust downward between towering walls of blue water as we rode giant swells sweeping across our path from the northeast. From crest to trough they measured perhaps fifteen feet, and the top was a continually breaking wave looking like an angry horse tossing its flowing white mane to the winds. We approached the waves diagonally and as our boat sliced through the thin topknot of froth we were drenched by driving wet spray that enveloped our boat and its uncomfortable passengers. Our captain opened his throttle wide on the downhill backside of the giant wave and surfed to the bottom before an oncoming swell caught us and pushed us into the wave ahead. Constantly shoved, rolled, and drenched, my squinted eyes smarted from salt water and my hands were sore and red from trying to stay seated in the bouncing boat. It was eleven miles between islands and the rough seas were extending the trip to about two hours, forcing an alarming increase in fuel consumption.

Soon I could glimpse waving coconut fronds blowing in the gusty wind as the boat momentarily crested on the highest waves before sweeping downward again. We were nearing shore and the captain turned to ride the sweeping backsides of swirling breakers curling shoreward, looking for a way down the other side, then hurriedly slipping back under full power before the huge following wave broke into a curl. He searched carefully, watched the ocean all around him, then suddenly gave the engines full throttle and headed for the beach on a wave that steadily grew in size, but did not break as it pushed us closer toward shore.

The captain said he could not take us further. He did not have enough gas to go on. I objected, explaining that I had made arrangements with the Ene Island magistrate to stay overnight on Ene and share meals with his family. We had no food with us—only our tents and the clothes on our backs, but our captain was quite firm in his demand that we must jump off, now! The waves were running high and with the wind blowing us closer into shore, I dropped overboard along with everyone else into the churning surf and waded ashore. I hoped we would be able to travel overland to our planned destination—island by island around the lagoon—to Ene, about ten miles away. It might be possible.

I called everybody together and we carried our bags to a school house nearby. We could spend the night there. I had asked that everyone bring air mattresses and overnight sleeping sheets, so using liberal coatings of mosquito repellant we prepared for the night. Arno villagers came over at dusk with a large aluminum tea kettle full of hot coffee, a jar of sugar, and two large loaves of bread so fresh and tasty, they needed no butter. It was good to eat the thick, firm slices obviously made without preservatives—only flour, yeast, and water. We satisfied our hunger and went to sleep.

I had been told there was one car on Ene Island, a Datsun pickup truck owned by the Ene magistrate. By use of a walkie-talkie radio operated by Nikja Namdrik, the local Arno policeman (who had no jail, no courtroom, no uniform, and—until we arrived—no problems), I learned that at low tide, when the road was passable between islets, the Ene magistrate would drive over to get us. We could expect him about ten o'clock that night. A later radio call informed us that the magistrate was ill, but his brother would drive over.

No Datsun came that night, or in the morning at low tide. Nikja radioed again, and he told us that since the brother had never driven the truck at night he decided not to take chances on the dark road, and when the morning low tide occurred, he forgot. So we had no boat and no truck. Majuro was too far away to call directly, but with the help of Nikja we called another nearby island which relayed our call to a third island with a larger radio. They in turn called Majuro and informed authorities that we were stranded on Arno and needed a boat.

No boat arrived. I was quite concerned, since we had no food of our own. I found Nikja and reminded him of our problems and he got on the radio again. Nikja spoke very little English and I was never quite sure that the urgency of our situation was fully realized by him, but he carried on an animated conversation in Marshallese, and finally turned to me saying that Majuro understood our needs and would arrange for a boat. This was considerably different from what I wanted—confirmation that a boat was on the way, but it was not possible to make any demands. Obviously the boat captain decided to pick us up later. The fact that we would miss our flight to Ponape was no concern to him. After all another plane would arrive later in the week. We would catch that one. Micronesians never could understand why Americans were always in a hurry.

Nikja translated for us the reason why no boat had

come. The day before, it seems, the radio operator on Majuro asked his young son to tell the District Transportation Department that we needed a boat to pick us up in the morning. The boat captain was putting on a movie show for the village at the time and the young boy stopped to watch the movie and forgot to deliver the message! The radioman never followed up; although, he told us later that he did wonder why the boat was still there in the morning.

By this time the native residents of Arno Island were well aware of our plight, and when we strolled down the single island path women and men stepped from their thatched huts to greet us and to offer fresh coconuts to drink. "Yukwe, Yuk," Marshallese for aloha, was rapidly learned and pronounced in several accents.

Arno Island is small—about 1½ miles long and 1,000 feet wide at the widest. The highest pile of sand is ten feet above high water. Coconut, naupaka, breadfruit, and pandanus cover the island with palms leaning out over the white sand beaches. Shells of all kinds litter the beach, and as footsteps approach, crabs scurry away into waves quietly lapping the gently sloping beach. The water is transparent upon the white coral sand, blending into pastel shades of turquoise faithfully reflecting the sky overhead. The village is scattered at random along the length of the island path. Each small house is surrounded by a clearing where broken coral gravel covers bare dirt giving the living clusters a clean, trimmed appearance unique to Marshall Island communities. Each residence is actually several small huts— one for cooking, one for storage, another for sleeping. Sometimes there is one for relatives.

At the far north end of Arno, the people offered us fermented coconut palm juice obtained from the severed palm frond. The sap is drained into hanging bottles in a manner similar to the gathering of maple sap. It was overwhelmingly sweet—too much so for more than a few sips. We grimaced and said we liked it before drinking more fresh coconut water to straighten out our digestive systems.

I left the others on their own at this most pleasant place and hurried to the south end of Arno to confer again with our police friend Nikja. His walkie-talkie was alive with rambling conversations among the islands, including an intriguing exchange between a U.S. Army Civic Action team captain who demanded a boat immediately and several army construction team members whose beer boat didn't show up. I wondered what our priorities were. I heard no comments about any boat coming for us, although Majuro did confirm they knew we were still stranded on Arno. At least we were making ourselves heard. Nikja was disappointed at the lack of definite news, as were we, but he said that Arno was happy to have us visiting their island even if we hadn't intended to, and everyone would like to thank us in the Marshallese tradition. He asked all of us to be back at the school house before noon.

As we slowly straggled in from different parts of the island, two men carried a long unpainted wooden bench from the nearby church to the empty, windowless classroom we had been sleeping in, placing it against the back wall. Directly in front of us four student desks were bunched together forming a large square table. We sat together on the straight backed bench facing an empty room, expectantly waiting while the villagers gathered under a shady pandanus tree outside the school yard. Men, women and children filled woven palm baskets with gifts and armfuls of food. Older women led the procession toward us, singing in the beautiful choral voices heard so often in Micronesian religious services, men harmonizing in low rumbling tones against the almost shrill voices of women, sounding together like a great cathedral organ. The words were Marshallese so we could only hear the emotional sounds that seemed to emphasize their welcome and expressions of hospitality. The entire village was honoring us, as if we were the first white visitors ever to set foot on Arno. It was totally unexpected, a genuine gratefulness for our being their guests.

Each spoke to us personally, "Yukwe Yuk," glad you are here, and shook our hands in the awkward soft grip typical of island people. They were dressed in their finest; the women in colorful cotton prints hemmed modestly below the knee with a little lace on the slip properly exposed—the men in fresh white shirts. They brought with them baskets of coconuts to drink, baked breadfruit, steamed rice with grated coconut, salted fish and fried fish, roast pig and roast chicken. The tables were high with more food than we could possibly eat if we had stayed a month. The two women with us were given beautifully woven handbags. Everyone received long shell leis made of hundreds of tiny seashells. We leaned forward to receive flower leis of fragrant frangipani while maramar flower wreaths were set gently on our heads like royal crowns. We stood quietly, a little uncomfortable, after the emotional splurge of gift giving and salutations, not knowing what would next occur—not knowing how we should respond.

An elderly man stepped forward, the village chief, and carefully spoke to us in Marshallese. The school principal translated. He said the village was very pleased that we visited Arno and was happy to welcome us as honored guests. They were sorry that they could not offer us a proper place to sleep or all the food we needed, but they wanted to do all they could to make our stay enjoyable. He asked us, "to please tell the people of America and Majuro of our island and take with you on your trip all that you cannot eat on Arno."

Each of us thanked the villagers in return, introducing ourselves by name, noting where we lived, and our work. The school principal translated as we spoke with some embarrassment, and the people responded with nervous laughter and obvious appreciation. We glanced around at the gathering of brown and excited faces, thrilled to be on Arno to share this unique outgiving of native hospitality —a traditional Marshallese response to the ocean traveler that must reach back thousands of years into the cultural traditions and history of an island people. We had traveled eleven miles across the open ocean from Majuro and stepped backwards a hundred years. I asked in a dozen different ways how we might return their favors, but they refused to accept payment. It soon became clear they would be insulted if we paid for their hospitality. We had discovered paradise.

Micronesia has sometimes been described as Hawaii two hundred years ago. If so, Arno Atoll is Micronesia a hundred years ago. A short distance across an open ocean channel from Majuro, Arno has escaped most of the anti-culture of its district center and remains an old-fashioned island community with the admired traditions of individual skills, hospitality and pride of personal accomplishment still a way of life. Arno could be described as an island life-style.

Nearby Majuro, the United States administrative center for the Marshall Islands, is made up of three tiny islets: Diarrit, Uliga, and Dalap, all combined by U.S. Navy bulldozers after the war into one long narrow island barely 1,000 feet wide for most of its length. It is perhaps revealing of American acculturation that the once separate islands, joined by coral filled causeways, are now represented by their initials, DUD, on the side doors of small Japanese-made police cars, accurately describing the dreary string of dusty white buildings to English language visitors. The acronym is meaningless to Micronesians.

Majuro's raucous district center life-style has been described as "navy culture," descended as it is from the post-war United States military base housed in the same buildings. It is the antithesis of peaceful Arno, with noisy traffic jams, jet runways, bars, and the associated urban evils including juvenile delinquency, rat infested slums, and pollution—all symptomatic of American administrative failures in the Trust Territory of the Pacific Islands.

The district center slums, repeated identically in every island group, exemplify deteriorating Micronesian culture. The breakdown of traditional family relationships and increasing dependence on scarce jobs doled out in a money economy that is artificially supported by congressional grants exceeding $60 million a year make 110,000 Micronesians, on a per capita basis, the highest dollar recipients of any American foreign aid program. Even Micronesians are having doubts over this spending spree that effectively destroys culture, skills, and knowledge in exchange for political allegiance and economic dependence. Micronesians have begun searching their own history and traditions for elements of an island life-style that can stem the deadly erosion of island society by Americanization.

New Zealand author Ronald Crocombe, professor of Pacific studies at the University of the South Pacific in Fiji, comments on the despair of islanders in his book *The New South Pacific*, writing that, "Dependency erodes respect and generates an ambivalence of gratitude and resentment. Whether economic or cultural, excessive dependency can have serious social and psychological consequences. To see the effects of the total dependency of the Pacific Islands on the United States is to appreciate the impotent bitterness, the slackness, the decadence that can be generated by extreme dependence."

As a Micronesian told me, "So long as you keep your mouth on the U.S. tit you don't even need to suck. It just flows."

Islanders enjoy canned mackerel from Japan. It is easy and convenient, but they are forgetting the skills of spearing fish inside their own reef. Outboard motors need only the turn of a key to start across the lagoon. The fiberglass hull is maintenance free. But the incalculable skills and knowledge required to design and build an outrigger canoe capable of ocean travel are forgotten. It is swift and easy to fly by jet between islands—a trip that takes only hours when perhaps weeks are required by canoe—but the special knowledge of the sun, the sea, and stars passed down from generations of ocean navigators may be lost forever.

Technological achievements of industrial nations have been offered with few strings attached, without the opportunity of refusal, without recognition of the eventual adverse consequences. When Micronesians buy the Sony transistor and Datsun pickup, the price tag is turned over, hiding the eventual true cost. After years of working for the government, the people of Majuro and every other district center have become dependent on a money economy that has ravaged their unique cultural heritage and subverted the ethnic identity of a proud Pacific race. The sons of Marshallese Iroji famed in Pacific lore and history for their ability to sail a thousand ocean miles without compass or map, are today driving taxis in Majuro. Perhaps fifty cars weave continuously back and forth on the two and one-half mile district center road. Everyone seems to be in business for himself, owning a Datsun or Toyota or Mazda import and paying monthly installment payments just slightly more than their gross income after the purchase of gas. Hundreds more work for the Trust Territory government—a favored job. The jobs to avoid are harvesting copra or fishing. How to build a thatched house is already forgotten. Corrugated sheet iron is so much better, even if the next typhoon does blow it away.

Western and European voyagers exploring the Pacific introduced useful woven cotton and iron. They also left behind numerous maladies, all more or less deadly to islanders with little natural resistance to strange diseases. Mosquitos arrived on whaling ships. Missionaries from Hawaii insisted on clothing native women, and respiratory ills became endemic. Even food plants and trees suffered with the arrival of alien insects.

The alienation of paradise continues. United States administrators, inspired by military demands for an American ocean lake with subservient native inhabitants, have erected elaborate bureaucracies to teach indigenous public servants concepts of political freedom and private property, imposing alien political and economic values upon a possibly more appropriate and traditional communal society. Mark Twain suggested, in a satirical plea for Hawaii one hundred years ago, the slogan that apparently still guides American bureaucrats today: "We must annex those people," he said. "We can afflict them with our wise and beneficent governments. We can introduce the novelty of thieves, all the way up from the street-car pickpockets to municipal robbers and government defaulters, and show them how amusing it is to turn them loose—some for 'political influence.' We can make them ashamed of their simple and primitive justice. . . . We can make that little bunch of sleepy islands the hottest corner on earth, and array it in the moral splendor of our high and holy civilization. Annexation is what the poor islanders need. 'Shall we to men benighted, the lamp of life deny?' "

The accumulated adverse consequences of easily available mackerel is difficult to explain to people who are indoctrinated in Peace Corps-taught schools that "growth is good and progress is better." The advantages of manufactured goods versus the hand-made variety is easy to see, so long as easy money is available, but we may be dooming an island way of life before we know its secrets. In arbitrarily teaching the "benefits" of our civilization, we are condemning the Micronesian peoples to a social philosophy of material wealth, growth, and technological progress that has precipitated a frightening erosion of our own once-vaunted standard of living.

The road of "progress" on Pacific islands must not emulate a bankrupt economic philosophy, but should utilize historical perspective in perceiving the unique benefits of an island life-style for islanders. The cherished values of individual achievement and pride of individual accomplishment may already have been lost in the aftermath of the industrial revolution and the Judeo-Christian work ethic. Instead of making art an integral part of our daily lives, we hang a painting on the wall. The New York Museum of Modern Art would place an outrigger canoe on display in its entrance foyer for all to marvel at the grace of its slender, hand-carved hull and functional design. The Micronesians would have sailed it across the ocean.

There is danger of deteriorating health patterns for

native peoples from consumption of manufactured foods
and artificial additives of all kinds. Combined with an increasingly polluted environment, modern food itself has
apparently contributed to the increase in mental breakdowns, high blood pressure, and fatal heart disease in over-
crowded island district centers.

Historians have often related how the impact of western civilization on the inhabitants of the Pacific Islands has
been somewhat less than beneficial. Indeed the arrival of
infectious diseases, alcohol, firearms and alien moral codes
has had an almost fatal impact. The islanders' idyllic way
of life could easily disappear before we fully appreciate its
potential contribution to our own endangered lives.

An extensive medical survey of some 1,200 Ponape
residents has recently been completed by New Zealand
medical research teams. Results are not all in, but preliminary evidence indicates that so-called primitive native
peoples growing their own food and living in old fashioned
ways in remote villages of Ponape are apparently healthier
and may possibly live longer than civilized white administrators working in air-conditioned district center offices.
Incidence of high blood pressure and heart disease revealed
in controlled medical examinations tend to prove that for
a longer, healthier life, subsistence living in a thatched hut
may be best after all.

Director of the Micronesian investigative team, Dr.
Ian Prior, claims that Pacific natives are "now commencing
to suffer for the first time in their history from the same
degenerative diseases that are the primary causes of death
among white men." Evidence is accumulating rapidly that
islanders who once feared only smallpox and flu now face
increasing probability that they will succumb to the white
man's urban plague. Dr. Prior states the facts quite explic-
itly: "Our evidence now shows that the farther the Pacific
natives move from the quiet, carefree life of their ancestors, the closer they come to gout, diabetes, obesity, and
hypertension."

Nutrition Today magazine reports that European and
Maori women between thirty-five and fifty-five living in

New Zealand cities in apparently improved environmental circumstances as measured by European standards, "suffer from hypertension and coronary heart disease four to five times as frequently as do women of the same age and ethnic group who live on atolls in the central Pacific."

It may be a new discovery for us, but three hundred years ago, a Spanish writer on Guam with Father Diego Luis de Salvitores made the same observation. Francisco García reported in 1683 that the ancient Chamorros, "remain in good health to an advanced age and it is very normal to live ninety or one hundred years." The foreign impact was indeed fatal.

There appears to be a correlation between going fast and slow—between longevity and the traveler who uses a jet plane, an automobile, trading boat, or outrigger canoe. The slower you go the longer you live. The material benefits of civilization are apparently more expensive than is revealed by current accounting practices. A cost-benefit analysis of the Gross National Product might well include a column on death.

Several years after the invasion of Micronesia by American forces, United States authorities began negotiations with Yapese chiefs to lease several acres of communally-owned village land for construction of a Coast Guard Loran navigation station. The chiefs were being difficult and, as far as Americans were concerned, unduly obfuscatory in discussing terms of a possible agreement. At one point in their deliberations, after having proceeded for several months without any sign of progress, the exasperated naval commander handling negotiations grew angry and rebuked the Yapese chiefs for taking so long to approve what they knew was going to be done anyway. The high chief, dressed only in a loincloth but speaking four languages—his native Yapese, German, Japanese, and English—slowly leaned forward, speaking carefully to his uniformed adversary. "We have been told what to do," he said, "by Spanish, Germans, Japanese, and now the Americans. We don't know who's next, but I should like you to know we are not in any hurry."

8

The American Administration
of Illegality

THE ex-chairman of the Hawaii Republican
Party and former Honolulu insurance broker Edward E.
Johnston, now the Nixon-appointed High Commissioner of
the U.S. Trust Territory of the Pacific Islands, carefully followed U.S. Interior Department directives forbidding direct
foreign investment in Micronesia under the terms of the
United Trusteeship agreement. The "most favored nation"
clause was seen as limiting investment to the United States
and requiring it to open Micronesia to economic participation by any member of the United Nations if it were
opened to even one other member nation.

This possibility was an anathema to the Pentagon. The
Russians would then be able to send foreign aid money to
Micronesia, and that would be intolerable. A People's Republic of China representative had already personally told
Senator Amata Kabua that China would very much like to
receive a loan application from Micronesia. Chinese Under
Secretary-General T'ang Ming-Chao even added an attractive inducement, saying, "If for some reason payments cannot be met but the people of Micronesia are willing to pay,
the People's Republic of China will cancel the debt." Ming-
Chao explained, "that loans are given with the end result
of obtaining friendship and why should such a goal be
marred at the end when someone honestly cannot pay?"

I flew with T'ang on Air Micronesia's regularly-scheduled flight and took delight in watching the American military suffer from grievous frustration at every stop he made island hopping across the Pacific, landing to refuel at Midway and Guam Naval Air Stations, and pausing to look around carefully during a scheduled stop on Kwajalein Island, the Redstone Arsenal top secret testing base for U.S. ABM intercontinental missile interceptors. It was fascinating to watch the military become so obviously disturbed at an event they had no control over. They consider Kwajalein top secret. It was only twelve months ago that the Kwajalein military police had stopped me from walking beyond the terminal gate.

Japanese merchants are already in Micronesia and have been for years. Easy credit, under-the-counter loans, and bargain-priced Japanese goods combined with an almost total lack of interest by American businessmen has led to domination of Micronesian trade by Japan. Many Micronesians suddenly hit it rich as a result of covert Japanese arrangements in violation of official policy. In Palau a locally-owned general store was saved from imminent bankruptcy by the timely arrival of a Japanese bookkeeper who helped straighten out its financial records. The bookkeeper stayed on and began offering such good advice on whom to order from and how to keep proprietary items in stock that it was difficult to determine after a while who really owned the store. It was obvious who was managing the store. The Palauan owner stayed home and enjoyed his profits while Nanyō Bōeki Kaisha (NBK) proceeded to strengthen their growing monopoly of consumer imports.

Covert fronts to evade direct foreign investment prohibitions have succeeded well in Palau. Van Camp, a subsidiary of Ralston-Purina, has operated a tuna freezing plant in Koror for several years, completely ignored by American administrators. Van Camp came in early, before approval was required under provisions of the Economic Development Act. The U.S. firm receives fish directly from an Okinawan fishing fleet based at Malakal Island, freezes

the tuna whole and ships it to American Samoa where a
Van Camp canning subsidiary processes the fish for American markets. By this procedure Micronesian canned, light
tuna is sold to American buyers exempt from tariff surcharges, since American Samoa is a United States territory. None of the Micronesian tuna is sold in Micronesia.

Japanese fishing fleets also operate illegally out of
Palau, their huge refrigerated mother ship anchored in
Malakal channel to receive swarms of Japanese wood-
hulled boats returning from the rich ocean fishing grounds
of the Philippines Sea. Their mode of operation is quite different. The entire operation is chartered by a Micronesian
business trio whose knowledge of fishing and investment in
the expensive operation totals zero.

Numerous stories are told of Japanese and Micronesians scheming to evade investment regulations. It would
appear that Micronesian businessmen are their own worst
enemy when it comes to enforcing policies designed to
protect the island economy from foreign takeover. Authorities on Ponape watched Japanese carpenters construct
a new hotel that was ostensibly owned by the South Park
Hotel Corporation, a wholly-owned Micronesian company.
They wondered why local men were not on the job. The
Ponape District Economic Development Board instituted
an inquiry after learning that the manager of the hotel
corporation was a Japanese national, Koshizawa Takuro,
and construction costs were being paid from about $150,-
000 presented to the hotel as a gift by Takuro, "with absolutely no special condition or strings attached," according
to the company. The board recommended revocation of
the work permit for the hotel and the entry permit of Takuro, finding that the gift did have strings. Company officials admitted that Takuro was manager but said he had
been given the position in consideration of his goodwill.

The Philippine subsidiary of Mobil Oil enjoys a complete monopoly in Micronesia by way of an exclusive contract signed with the Trust Territory administration.
Continental Airlines operates Air Micronesia and a pair of

multi-million dollar hotels under special permits to serve the United Micronesia Development Association, a locally controlled stock corporation that also handles copra exports and controls a scheduled airline flying $36 million worth of aircraft, two Boeing 727 jets, all with capitalization of less than half a million.

American investors have often circumvented Micronesian policy requiring local ownership through complex lease-back arrangements and sales of debentures not redeemable until some future date when the rules change. The Intercontinental Hotel now under construction on Saipan is owned by the Pacific Micronesian Corporation that actually controls only twenty percent of the stock, although the original lease agreement provided for the required fifty-one percent. Purchase of negotiable debentures has enabled Japan's partly government-owned Japan Travel Bureau, the largest travel agency in Japan, and Keio Plaza Hotel to become working investors in the 200-room project along with Bank of Hawaii's RAMPAC subsidiary in San Francisco. The agreement calls for the Japanese companies to put up $650,000 of the total construction cost which is estimated at $4.7 million. After completion in 1975, the resort hotel will be managed by Keio Plaza with the Japan Travel Bureau in charge of booking Japanese tourists into the hotel. It is expected that eventually the new hotel will be completely controlled and operated by a Japanese hotel chain.

Furukawa International Development Company, the Japanese firm with a name reflecting the new economic nationalism of Japan, has established a joint venture of thirteen companies in the Furukawa industrial group to pay the complete cost of building a $1.3 million seventy-room hotel with ten cottages and flower gardens on a 13,000 square meter site near the new Saipan International Airport which was only recently improved and enlarged to handle the largest jet airliners. The hotel will be built by locally-owned South Seas Incorporated. Its corporate officers represent a typical Micronesian front: David S. Sablan of San

Antonio village, Saipan, secretary; Felipe Mendola of Rota Island, treasurer; Thomas Mendiola of Rota, vice-president; and Clement Jennings of California, president. The Tokyo company will, of course, be in charge of their management.

It is intriguing to read publicity releases of aggressive Japanese firms now returning to their lost territory once a stronghold of the imperial Japanese Navy. In some evocative way, they read like military communiques of another day. Furukawa says, "its advance into Saipan will constitute a stepping stone to its further investments in Rota, Palau, and other Micronesian Islands."

But soon the fun and games of corporate manipulation and evasive fronts will no longer be necessary; the Japanese may redeem their debentures and reclaim the gifts. Secretary of Interior Rogers Morton announced a major revision of United States policy in Micronesia, dropping enforcement of the most-favored-nation trusteeship concept. He said the interpretation that has been followed for so many years no longer applied if respective district Economic Development Boards approved business applications within the guidelines of the Congress of Micronesia's own Foreign Investment Act. Under terms of that Act, U.S. High Commissioner Edward E. Johnston would review any application approved by the Micronesians, but in light of current widespread violation of existing foreign investment restrictions, it is doubtful that many permits would be disapproved as the economic door to Micronesia opens wide.

Military opposition to a wide-open Micronesia was answered by Secretary Morton in accompanying advice on how to veto any objectionable application. Morton instructed the High Commissioner "to base his review (of foreign business applications) on the security of the area and the general welfare and development of the Micronesian people." That would seem to take care of the Russians and Chinese.

The reaction in Micronesia was generally favorable. High Commissioner Johnston obediently said, "I think this is an excellent thing for the Trust Territory." Senator

Amata Kabua, chairman of the Senate Committee on Resources and Development concurred: "We should be thankful to the Interior Secretary for lifting this finally. It's what is needed if we are to become part of the community of the world."

Others were doubtful about being turned loose on the streets of international finance. Said Senator Edward Pangelinan, heading the Marianas future status negotiators: "I think they've opened a Pandora's box and I don't know how we're going to control this monster." His colleague from Yap, Senator John Mangefel, concurred. "I don't agree with it yet," he said. "It shouldn't be lifted at this time."

It was not clear why the United States had lifted restrictions at this time, although the Trust Territory director of Resources and Development, expatriate Wyman Zachary thought that "lifting of the ban should also bring to the fore some arrangements we suspected in the past that can now be made public." In a later speech to the Micronesian Congress, Senator Pangelinan expressed subtle misgivings over relaxation of investment policy. He surmised the United States is presenting Micronesian politicians with a test: "If we handle this challenge well in a salutory fashion, then I believe we will have demonstrated our responsibility and maturity. . . . If we do not act wisely and in the best interests of our people, then we may find the road to termination of the trusteeship longer than we had thought." Micronesians suspicious of America's long-range goals looked at the apparent relaxation of foreign investment opportunities as a gambit forcing Micronesian leaders to realize that an end to the trusteeship and political freedom could not be achieved before their island economy has been stabilized. To many, Morton's statement was just another delaying tactic to defer early determination of the future political status of Micronesia and to insure continued dependence on the United States.

It is understandable that reaction would differ so. The history of Micronesia reveals desires for ethnic integrity and island culture confusingly mixed with an envy of precooked rice and Datsuns. The contradictions will not be easy to resolve. Micronesians on their way to the bank with tourist profits reflect deep concern for the adverse impact of tourism and foreign development on their cherished life-style. Pedro Dela Cruz, chairman of the Marianas Economic Development Board expressed the prevalent mixed feelings saying that the new policy, "offers us an opportunity to bargain for foreign investments that we desire. But we have to be very careful. We don't want to see this area become another Honolulu. . . ."

Tourism has always been a controversial enterprise in Micronesia. It is Micronesia's only industry of any consequence, and American economic advisors assert that it is the only industry Micronesia can profit from in the long run. Unfortunately, tourism operated the Japanese way leaves very little profit for the Micronesians. As Guam has discovered, when hotels are constructed using alien labor and imported materials from Japan—with food from Japan, served by Japanese waitresses in hotels staffed by Japanese management, escorted on island tours by Japanese tour companies in Japanese-made buses, flying on quasi-governmental Japan Air Lines, using a sheaf of coupons sold by the partly government-owned Japan Travel Bureau—little money is left for circulation in the local economy. Australians refer to the Japanese style of tourism as the "boomerang technique" since almost all of what the tourists spend winds up back in Tokyo. Others have less polite terms for the Micronesian rip-off.

Japanese businessmen are not the only culprits in this shell game of tourist profits. When Continental Airlines was forced to commit themselves to building luxury hotels in every district to obtain exclusive air-carrier rights to Micronesia—and a hoped-for eventual trans-Pacific air route to Japan—they constructed air-conditioned hotels using New Zealand contractors and Chinese carpenters from Hong Kong. They imported every stick and board from overseas despite local attempts to use native materials. The Micronesian, by this procedure, is denied even

the opportunity of apprenticeship to learn the trades necessary to fully share in the benefits of a tourist economy.
When Micronesian employees sued the Continental Airlines hotel on Truk saying they were paid below minimum
wages as agreed to in the master lease for the land, Continental tried to wriggle out, asserting the workers were not
part of the original land lease agreement. Hotel management claimed unskilled local labor was not worth higher
wages. Micronesian Legal Services financed by the U.S.
Office of Economic Opportunity (OEO), took their case
before the Trust Territory court where in mid-trial the U.S.
High Commissioner attempted to get all OEO funds cancelled, claiming the attorneys were not properly representing the people of Micronesia.

Continental Airlines hotels on Truk and Palau import
almost ninety percent of their food and supplies from the
mainland United States, Australia, and Japan, even by-
passing local food wholesalers. Fresh fish and island fruit
are seldom seen on a Continental Hotel menu.

What remains for too many people in Micronesia is
the pittance received from handicrafts, taxi driving, and
bed-making. In the process their dependency on a money
economy becomes complete, and their once hospitable island way of life is drowned in competition for low paying
menial jobs and the shameful scramble for bigger tips.

Even the tourist may be fooled into thinking the trip
is a unique experience. Fiji professor Ronald Crocombe
writes that tourism in the Pacific islands ". . . invests vast
sums on the planned creation of largely spurious images of
primitiveness, condescending notions of simplicity and the
exaggeration of differences. The foreign visitor is seduced
into becoming a participant in the myth so created. . . .
What the travel agent sells the tourist above all else is
status. The artificial myth of exotica which provides a vali-
dation for the purchase of the status receives a fallacious
fulfillment in the presentation of pseudo-traditional per-
formances in the foreign contexts of the hotel lounge. . . ."
Actually it would be quite unusual, under the circum-

stances, for an American or Japanese tourist to visit Micronesia without being convinced he was of a superior race. Perhaps that is in part what the Pacific tourist is purchasing from the travel agent back home.

A Congress of Micronesia Committee Report comments adversely on tourism, saying, "Development of tourism in Micronesia is fraught with hazards. The potential impact on the environment and on other characteristics that now make Micronesia attractive to tourists, is serious. The effect of tourism on Micronesians and their culture is even more serious."

"Tourism is of little value to Micronesia," warned the United Nations Visiting Mission to Micronesia in 1973, "and indeed may have a generally negative effect, unless a substantial proportion of the expenditures generated by the tourists flows into Micronesian hands and the majority of the jobs created are occupied by Micronesians."

It is a warning often expressed by knowledgeable opponents of the growth of tourism in Hawaii, where tourist-related industries pay the lowest wages and demand the most expensive capital improvements from ever obliging politicians. Hawaii's tourist economy requires a disproportionate number of families in which both husbands and wives must work in low paying tourist jobs to support a comfortable standard of living. Yet the taxes they pay do not cover minimum costs of such governmental services as police and fire protection, street maintenance, sewage disposal and education. Mention is seldom made of the adverse social consequences that occur when both parents work and when spreading crime and juvenile delinquency are generated by a resort environment. Despite substantial tax increases, the state of Hawaii sinks deeper into debt with every monthly increase in tourist arrivals. Only military expenditures keep Hawaii's economic head above the polluted waters of Waikiki as swelling rates of immigration and tourist hiring barely compensate for higher percentages of unemployment in a so-called booming economy.

Yapese on Rumung Island were the first to seriously

object to the tourist blight in Micronesia. They had been persuaded by the district administrator to allow small tour groups to visit their remote village. It would not hurt at all, they were told, and villages could charge several dollars for each tourist to spend on community improvements.

Three American tourists duly arrived in Rumung village one sunny morning and immediately proceeded to make themselves obnoxious. One tried to move a huge disc of Yapese stone money away from the house—where it had been placed a generation ago—to a better spot for taking pictures. Another thrust his camera into the grass walls of the nearest house to shoot photos of the family inside, while the third American chased a bare-breasted Yapese girl around the village insisting that she pose for a picture. The people of Rumung were aghast at this flagrant invasion of their privacy and decided that three tourists were already too many. They would tolerate no more, no matter how much the tourists paid. Through their island magistrate they asked the district legislature to pass an ordinance permitting any island to prohibit tourists if they so desired. It did, and Rumung immediately banned tourists forever.

Meanwhile, on the neighboring island of Maap, an occasional Japanese visitor, president of Transpacific Development Company, organized the Yap Nature Life Garden Incorporated. He made a local Maap businessman, Linus Rumamau, president, and convinced seven other villagers that financial opportunities beckoned through development of resort facilities for visitors to their beautiful island. He made them directors.

Tokugo Kuribayashi, also an executive with Nanyō Bōeki Kaisha (NBK), revealed little of his long range plan, deliberately beginning operations on a small scale without constructing permanent buildings. He housed the first paying guests from Japan in tents, building only a temporary kitchen and dining area as the first increment of a resort that would eventually boast forty-seven air-conditioned cottages, a 500-foot-long pier to the barrier reef, and an enclosed deep-water swimming area dredged from the in-

ner shoal waters where coral heads and seaweed would be
removed. Local people were told that there would be a
general improvement of the whole island. The Yap Nature
Life Garden was an apparent euphemism designed to
thwart suspicion of his true intentions.

The first complaint came from adjacent villagers—
Japanese tourists were stealing coconuts. Then the Yapese
women objected to Japanese girls swimming in bikinis.
Proper Yapese may be bare-breasted, but they always wear
long grass skirts modestly covering their feminine ankles.
The bikinis were obviously disgraceful! Tourists were also
wandering uninvited into homes, and fishermen discovered that the lines to their throw-nets that had been hung
in trees to dry had been snapped. The situation rapidly became intolerable. Kuribayashi attempted to explain, but
the people of Maap began demanding that NBK go home.
Within the month, over seventy percent of the adult villagers of Maap Island signed a petition dictated by their
chiefs and translated into English by OEO attorneys in
Colonia, the district center. In their petition the Maap
chiefs reaffirmed that, "we love our land and the ways in
which we live together here in peace, and yet humbly and
still cherish them above all other ways, and are not discon-
tent to be the children of our fathers."

The enraged chiefs said, "it has become apparent to us
that we have been persuaded to subscribe to processes that
will quickly extinguish all that we hold most dear." In
reference to the Japanese tourist development company,
the chiefs claimed the firm had taken advantage of their
goodwill, and by "usurping unnegotiated lands, assuming
nearly dictatorial manners in the area where it operates,
obscuring the nature and the extent of its ambitions and
the inevitable and irreversible injury that these will cause
to our customs and our pride, the company has far exceeded all pretense to legality and welcome to our land. It
plans to make a dead sea of our lagoon, and thus a dead
place of its shores."

Kuribayashi's building blocks and cement were already

warehoused in Colonia and other construction materials were enroute by ship to finish the partially constructed buildings that were said to be forty percent completed. But Kuribayashi was forced to withdraw financial support, and at this the Yap Nature Life Garden corporation collapsed.

The appointed chairman of the Yap Tourist Commission, Jesus Mangarfir, told me the Maap people were not actually opposed to tourists; they simply, "wanted to know what was going on and didn't like strangers poking into their houses." It did seem like a reasonable objection.

The thirty-four Maap chiefs reinforced the arguments in a resolution designed to prevent any recurrence of the NBK invasion. The *pilungs* and *langanpagels,* elders and elected officers, meeting in full assembly, emphatically declared "our love of this˙place and of the ways passed down to us by the generations. We have inherited from our fathers a land that is lovely and provides for us with the fruits of the earth and of the sea. We are few in numbers but we have a brave history and are strong in our resolve to preserve these things that are sweet to us and free to determine the affairs of our island with respect to custom and deference to the law. We meet today," continued the chiefs, "under the shadow of such change and innovation . . . that we are therefore all the more solemnly moved to affirm our united will in the face of the unfamiliar contingencies of this age and the ages to come, so that our home may not be vulnerable to the casual invasions of those who do.

"We constitute ourselves this day and make these bold resolutions in the face of unlawful, discourteous, and avaricious intrusions that imminently endanger our small land and cherished manners, and with faith that we shall prevail to pass on to our children the delight of being of this gentle place."

I later visited Cho'ol Beach with permission of the village magistrate. The brown Yapese children were again playing on their beach, once usurped by alien tourists monopolizing the warm sands. But as I sailed closer across the shallow lagoon waters in a rented outrigger canoe, the children grew silent and apprehensive. I shifted in my seat, preparing to step over the side and they suddenly grabbed for their playthings, running into the jungle to disappear among the palms. When I reached the shore, the beach was deserted, except for one wide-eyed boy cautiously peering at me from behind a coconut palm. He watched me carefully, then dashed out to retrieve a forgotten toy, before he, too, disappeared with all the others.

My Yapese guide said we should leave. I was a tourist. It was easy to see I was not wanted.

9

Home Is the Sea

FOR two thousand years the brown ocean people have explored and lived carefully upon the sea. They found the immense ocean rich in food and an unlimitable passage to everywhere. Its greatness and power justified a special place of importance in religious beliefs. The ocean was a manifestation to fear and worship—the home for a seafaring community which, in its last outreach into the unknown, discovered the Hawaiian Islands.

For aeons, island people caught fish in the ocean and evaporated salt from its brine without expecting any more than was easily replenished by the ocean itself. Not until more rapacious civilizations outgrew their continental borders in a population explosion and demanded greater quantities of raw materials to fuel their industrial demands, did scientific oceanography generate new knowledge of the rich resources of the ocean. Only recently have new technologies developed feasible methods of exploiting the oceans' mineral and chemical wealth within and beneath the sea.

The waters of the Atlantic and Pacific Oceans constitute the world's largest continuous ore body, with dissolved mineral solids of 35,000 parts per million in the 350 million cubic miles of ocean water. Salt is commonly extracted, along with magnesium and bromine in lesser

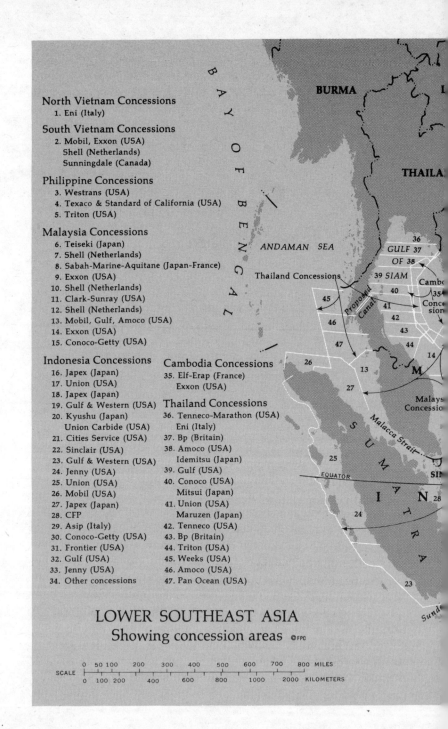

North Vietnam Concessions
1. Eni (Italy)

South Vietnam Concessions
2. Mobil, Exxon (USA)
   Shell (Netherlands)
   Sunningdale (Canada)

Philippine Concessions
3. Westrans (USA)
4. Texaco & Standard of California (USA)
5. Triton (USA)

Malaysia Concessions
6. Teiseki (Japan)
7. Shell (Netherlands)
8. Sabah-Marine-Aquitane (Japan-France)
9. Exxon (USA)
10. Shell (Netherlands)
11. Clark-Sunray (USA)
12. Shell (Netherlands)
13. Mobil, Gulf, Amoco (USA)
14. Exxon (USA)
15. Conoco-Getty (USA)

Indonesia Concessions
16. Japex (Japan)
17. Union (USA)
18. Japex (Japan)
19. Gulf & Western (USA)
20. Kyushu (Japan)
    Union Carbide (USA)
21. Cities Service (USA)
22. Sinclair (USA)
23. Gulf & Western (USA)
24. Jenny (USA)
25. Union (USA)
26. Mobil (USA)
27. Japex (Japan)
28. CFP
29. Asip (Italy)
30. Conoco-Getty (USA)
31. Frontier (USA)
32. Gulf (USA)
33. Jenny (USA)
34. Other concessions

Cambodia Concessions
35. Elf-Erap (France)
    Exxon (USA)

Thailand Concessions
36. Tenneco-Marathon (USA)
    Eni (Italy)
37. Bp (Britain)
38. Amoco (USA)
    Idemitsu (Japan)
39. Gulf (USA)
40. Conoco (USA)
    Mitsui (Japan)
41. Union (USA)
    Maruzen (Japan)
42. Tenneco (USA)
43. Bp (Britain)
44. Triton (USA)
45. Weeks (USA)
46. Amoco (USA)
47. Pan Ocean (USA)

BURMA

THAILA

ANDAMAN SEA

Thailand Concessions

BAY OF BENGAL

GULF
OF
SIAM

36
37
38
39
40
41
42
43
44

Camb
35
Conce
sion

45

46

47

26

13

27

14

M

Malays
Concessio

25

Malacca Strait

EQUATOR

S U M A T R A

SI

28

24

23

Sund

LOWER SOUTHEAST ASIA
Showing concession areas ©FPC

SCALE
0 50 100   200   300   400   500   600   700   800 MILES

0   100 200   400   600   800   1000   2000 KILOMETERS

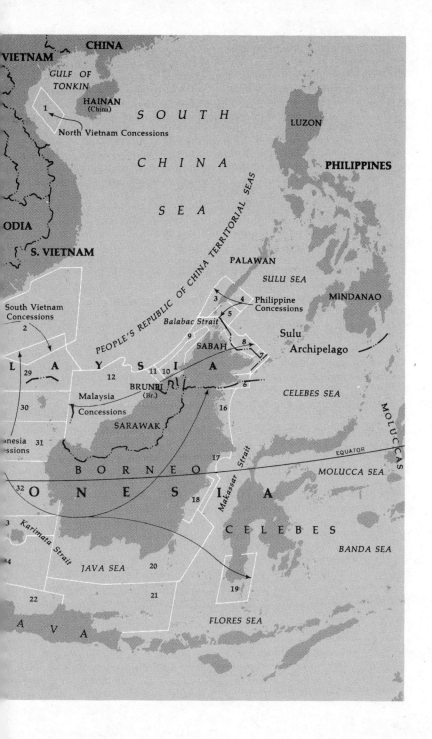

CHINA

VIETNAM

GULF OF
TONKIN

HAINAN
(China)

1

North Vietnam Concessions

ODIA

S. VIETNAM

SOUTH

CHINA

SEA

LUZON

PHILIPPINES

South Vietnam
Concessions

2

PEOPLE'S REPUBLIC OF CHINA TERRITORIAL SEAS

PALAWAN

SULU SEA

MINDANAO

3   4   Philippine
         Concessions

5

Balabac Strait

9   SABAH   8   Sulu
                          Archipelago

L   Y   S   I   A

29

12   11 10

BRUNEI
(Br.)

CELEBES SEA

30

Malaysia
Concessions

6

16

SARAWAK

nesia
ssions   31

17

EQUATOR

MOLUCCAS

MOLUCCA SEA

BORNEO

32   O   N   E   S   I   A

18

Makassar Strait

3   Karimata Strait

CELEBES

4

JAVA SEA   20

BANDA SEA

22   21

19

A   V   A

FLORES SEA

amounts. But the current international scramble for ocean rights was precipitated only recently by development of economical methods for mining surface minerals—minerals found on the ocean floor in manganese nodules that have been formed by oxides as they precipitate out of sea water onto small broken coral pieces, pebbles, and shark teeth. Widely distributed in all the oceans, these potato-sized nodules reach important concentrations (around 15,000 tons per square mile in the central Pacific between Hawaii and Micronesia) at depths greater than three miles. The ore represents great economic potential to the nations —and the miners—who get there first.

A hundred years have elapsed since the discovery of the widespread manganese nodule deposits. Only ten years ago, as George Woolard, Director of the Hawaii Institute of Geophysics, tells it, "manganese nodules were still regarded as a curiosity in the same class as petrified dinosaur eggs and gizzard stones." With the discovery that manganese nodules contain significant proportions of cobalt, nickel, and copper; and with identification of rare earth minerals—titanium, palladium, platinum and gold— as component metals, the common nodules were no longer something of value only to museums or collectors of curiosities. They became valuable ore. The economic feasibility of their extraction from the seabed occurred after professional marine researchers dredged a large haul of nodules from the Tuamotu Escarpment east of Tahiti. The undersea mineral lode proved to be rich in cobalt. Further studies proved the feasibility of commercial mining. The published results sparked investments of almost $100 million by international mining corporations joining in a new-fangled gold rush at the bottom of the sea.

Conservative estimates indicate there are several hundred billion tons of minable nodules in high-grade areas of the Pacific. John Mero of Ocean Resources Incorporated described pictures his firm has taken "of boulders on the ocean floor that must be ten feet in diameter and look like nodules. . . . The largest nodule that I have ever known," reported Mero, "came up in a tangle of telegraph cable and was about four feet in diameter. . . . The biggest dredge bucket I know of that has been put on the ocean floor is a twenty-ton bucket that was used to retrieve nodules as big as a desk. I suppose they get larger, but nothing larger will go into the bucket."

Nodules of industrially useful metals are accumulating in the Pacific at a rate of about ten million tons a year—a rate exceeding present world consumption. Once nodules are being extracted the industry will be faced with an interesting problem of working deposits which re-form faster than they can be mined. Underground ore deposits are generally considered depleting resources, but many ocean deposits are going to be taken out faster than they can be used on land. The existing reserve of metals in the sea may supply the world population for thousands of years even at present per capita consumption levels of highly developed nations.

It is particularly noteworthy, since environmental concerns merit serious consideration, that seabed mining might be accomplished with little measurable environmental damage. Full-scale exploitation of the sea as a source of industrial metal will permit the closing of more objectionable water and air-polluting land mining. No research has been done on the possible injurious impact of mining the ocean floor, but evidence was collected by Hawaii's Dillingham Corporation at their Ocean Bay deep sea suction dredging in the Bahamas where they were strip mining the ocean bottom for barren aragonite. Because of the relative inaccessibility of the ocean floor, few people will ever know the environmental impact of mining the ocean. A Dillingham mining engineer said that continued dredging on the coral bottom releases organic matter. And he speculates that the fish population will be enhanced with the only problem being the interference with mining vessels by fishermen flocking to ocean mining sites.

While environmental pressures and rising demand at

premium prices make the United States a prime market for ocean-produced manganese, copper, nickel, and cobalt, Japan's industrial requirements will also create a demand for seabed mineral development. Most of Japan's copper and all its nickel is imported. Japan purchased about 2.7 million tons of nickel ore from French New Caledonia in 1969. The United States imports almost ninety-nine percent of its manganese for use in steel, ninety-three percent of its cobalt, and eighty-four percent of its nickel. United States controlled mining in international waters could make the country self-sufficient in these minerals and substantially improve our balance of payments.

Future seabed mineral resources offer great opportunities for Japan, and extensive deep-sea nodule deposits east of the Marshall Islands are nearer Japan than New Caledonia. Smaller high cobalt deposits northeast of Ponape and Saipan are even closer. An additional bonus for Japan with its serious air pollution crisis—far worse than in American cities—is manganese nodules' ability to absorb great amounts of noxious sulfur dioxide and nitrous oxide in air pollution reduction devices, thereby offering economic means of reducing pollution in industrial applications and high-sulfur-oil fueled power plants.

Based on oceanographic data developed during the International Decade of Ocean Exploration by the Lamont-Doherty Geological Observatory at Columbia University, Micronesia—and the Marshall Island port of Majuro, in particular—is closer than any other island area to one of the two most widespread and potentially rich deposits of commercial ferromanganese on the floor of the world oceans. The Marshall Islands also lie midway between important ore markets in the Pacific—Japan and the United States—and for this reason Micronesia may share with its companion in good fortune, Hawaii, in international ocean ventures that could well grow into substantial mining operations close to its shores.

Hawaii has no intention of abrogating the commercial advantages of its excellent location immediately northeast of the Marshall Island nodule field and due north of another large field stretching eastward to the Mexican coast. Hawaii already boasts of a foreign trade zone where raw material may be landed and processed, and the refined product transshipped to other countries without payment of American import duties. But Hawaii's excessively high business excise taxes will probably discourage potential investors in deep-sea mining and processing ventures from coming there. Many businesses are likely to search for tax-free home bases in free ports of other nearby island groups where better economic incentives prevail—ports such as those proposed in Micronesia.

Unless developing island nations directly enter into nodule mining and processing operations, the seabed mineral resources may never meet their expectations as a significant source of revenue. Even if present land-derived metal prices hold up for the abundant ocean products, per capita profits would probably not exceed a few cents per person if shared among the less developed nations of the world, as advocated by U.N. resolutions. Accordingly, if Pacific Island peoples are to share in the undersea mineral wealth, they must share equally in control of the Pacific seabed and be actively involved in the ownership and operation of undersea mining ventures.

The example of Nauru, owning exclusive rights to its mineral resources, is illustrative of the financial bonanza to be found in selling to developed countries without middleman concessionaires. Nauru also presents a fearful spectre, for the elaborate deep water port facilities and extensive storage areas of processed and unprocessed nodules would not only be environmentally degrading but the industrial operation would surely destroy the island life-style of the Marshalls. It would propel Majuro and its people overnight into the grubby world of western technocracy and the adverse social and cultural consequences that accompany a commercial seaport and mining enterprises.

The potential conflict over access and ownership of undersea mining operations has already been foreshadowed. Almost half-way around the world, state of Maine lobsters multiplying on the Atlantic continental shelf have been designated as genuine "American" lobsters by federal law. Henceforth, the Lobster *Americanus* can only be trapped by United States fishermen. The states of Maine, New Hampshire, and Massachusetts have petitioned Congress to certify that their official state boundaries extend 200 miles seaward. These states want not only to protect traditional fishing grounds from over-fishing by modern Russian and Japanese fleets, but also to guarantee the integrity of proposed American offshore oil drilling rigs far out at sea on the New England continental shelf.

It is much easier to stake a mineral claim on land than it is to define boundaries 15,000 feet below the sea and a thousand miles from the nearest land. How is it to be regulated? Robert Jenkins, a mining engineer with Hawaii's Dillingham Mining Company, points out that "throughout history, laws have generally followed mining. . . . In fact, mining prospectors and mining companies have in the past often ignored established governments and local laws." Commercial explorations and development of minerals, oil, and timber on Pacific Islands has long been a dominant factor in the enactment of laws to protect the rights of foreign investors clamoring for exclusive privileges to exploit and profit from overseas natural resources.

It is not likely that major international corporations, large enough to entertain visions of expensive seabed mining, will act like old '49ers in the California Gold Rush days. On the other hand, enactment of international laws to regulate open ocean operations outside territorial waters has been consistently avoided by the major ocean-oriented nations, as if the oceans were a no man's sea where sovereign countries venture at their peril. The danger is great that without early cooperation to govern exploitation of the rich seabed resources, peaceful relations between Pacific governments may be disrupted as the respective parties decide for themselves that there are overriding economic advantages in ocean mining.

The role of island communities like Hawaii and Micronesia in determining the future ownership of seabed minerals and the benefits that accrue from their exploitation is clearly revealed in maps delineating the location of these resources. This role may bring about a reexamination by the United States of its rigid adherence to the twelve or three-mile territorial limit designed to protect American rights of innocent passage in narrow geographical straits such as Makassar in Malaysia, and to guarantee the rights of American ships in international waters. The result has been that local airlines operating in the Hawaiian Islands—completely within the state—fly over international waters between the islands where open sea channels average thirty to fifty miles across. The U.S. State Department has insisted on this interpretation, and a task force of the Soviet Pacific Fleet has more than once sailed a zig-zag route between all the Hawaiian Islands to test the principle.

Hawaii's Representative Patsy Mink certainly supports international cooperation in the ocean, but she also affirms that the "ocean for Hawaii, Guam, Samoa, the Virgin Islands and Puerto Rico is our boundary. It is not merely a national resource. A twelve-mile limit to the territorial sea with freedom of transit beyond that means loss to Hawaii of any hope of preserving the territorial integrity of our state where the seven major islands are separated by more than twenty-four miles of ocean."

Contrary to popular belief, neither the boundaries of the state of Hawaii nor of the Trust Territory of the Pacific Islands are legally documented. Legal research indicates that the boundaries of the state of Hawaii are identified as the boundaries of the old territory of Hawaii which in turn, were the boundaries of the short-lived Republic of Hawaii. Closer examination of the Hawaiian Kingdom's claims, however, reveals that King Kalakaua declared his Kingdom consisted of all Oceania including Micronesia. Kalakaua once actually dispatched his only armed warship to Samoa to exercise his claimed suzerainty. A group of Marshallese Iroji later petitioned Kalakaua to include the Marshall and Gilbert Islands in the Hawaiian Kingdom, before Germany and Britain could divide Micronesia between themselves and Spain. Unfortunately the king was too busy at the time with international difficulties brought on by midnight poker and he never acted on the proposal. If he had, the history of Micronesia might be considerably different today.

King Kamehameha III prescribed that, ". . . the marine jurisdiction of the Hawaiian Islands shall also be exclusive in all of the channels passing between the respective islands and dividing them, which jurisdiction shall extend from island to island." The U.S. Ninth Circuit Court of Appeals in ruling against a projected island airline that claimed it should not be required to abide by federal regulations because their operations were wholly within the state, completely ignored the king's declaration. Perhaps after the U.S. Supreme Court rules on Maine's petition to extend its boundaries 200 miles out to sea, the vague boundaries of Hawaii and Micronesia may be more precisely drawn to include natural resources undersea between the islands.

King George Tubou of Tonga, the only Pacific Island group to escape colonial rule, anticipated the problem and in 1887 defined Tonga quite precisely by proclamation: "We do hereby erect as Our Kingdom of Tonga all islands, rocks, reefs, foreshores and waters lying between the fifteenth and twenty-third and a half degrees of south latitude and between the one hundred and seventy-third and the one hundred and seventy-seventh degrees of west longitude from the Meridian of Greenwich."

The present Prime Minister of Tonga followed up his

predecessors' foresight in 1971, inviting the Secretary-General of the United Nations to note the Proclamation, saying it "has been acquiesced in by all countries." He might have included a few contemporary "island squatters" as well, for Tonga took swift action against several expatriates who tried to establish their own Republic of Minerva on two small reefs, barely exposed at high tide south of Tonga. The modern-day colonists planned to dredge a harbor, fill in the reef shoals and build a 2,500 acre city-nation designed by a Glass Age Development Committee. Tonga reacted predictably, and promptly dispatched about a hundred native convicts to the new Republic and built two artificial islands on the reef, annexing them under the names of Teleki Tonga and Teleki Tokelau and proclaiming a twelve-mile territorial sea around them.

In a bold act characteristic of his administration, President Harry Truman on September 28, 1945, precipitated the rush for ocean resources by laying claim in the name of the United States to all resources of the seabed and subsoil of the continental shelf lying outside its historic three-mile limit.

Truman's proclamation of sovereignty over the continental shelf was followed by so many corresponding claims that it quickly became a fait accompli in international law. It was on this basis that North Sea resources were divided between England, Norway, France, the Netherlands, Belgium, Germany, and Denmark. Subsequently the South China Sea was also subdivided and oil concessions granted by various countries around the rim —Malaysia, Cambodia, Vietnam, Thailand, Indonesia, and the Philippines. It may only be a matter of time before the Pacific itself is divided between the oceanic nations.

The United States fears that Indonesia, Fiji, Mauritius, the Philippines, and even Micronesia, may soon boldly and recklessly draw wide baselines far from shore between their outermost islands and reef shoals to enclose most of the ocean. Ambassador Arvid Pardo of Malta warned the U.N. in 1967 that under archipelago proposals "Most of the ocean space and virtually the totality of its living resources and even the greater part of the manganese nodules on the deep ocean floor would come under national control. From a regime of virtually total freedom over oceans we are now passing to a regime of virtual sovereignty over oceans." Should Japan delineate its national boundaries by drawing baselines between its distant islands, it would end up still a small Pacific nation, but should the Pacific be divided in the same manner as Truman mandated division of the North Sea in Europe, Micronesia would become larger than the continental United States, and America would end up controlling a third of the Pacific ocean. The United States and France would divide between them the richest ore deposits in the seabeds of the world.

The implications of deep sea territorial claims in terms of seabed mining could be far reaching, for cobalt-rich deposits of manganese nodules lie on the ocean floor within a few hundred miles of Majuro, Ponape, and Truk. There can hardly be any doubt that the island peoples in Micronesia will be watching with considerable interest when the first deep-sea dredge enters their waters.

The date for enactment of international laws of the sea and an appropriate regime to enforce them is an essential matter. The time is fast approaching when seabed mining on a large scale will commence. Francis Auburn of the University of Auckland law faculty says substantive work on international law by the U.N. Seabed Committee is still to be done. Auburn says, "The Seabed minerals provisions of a convention would then come into force, at the earliest, in 1980. Well before then, on the current views of active ocean miners, exploitation will be in full swing." With regard to manganese nodules, time has almost run out for the U.N. Seabed Committee. It remains to be seen whether only a few developed countries will reap the wealth or whether many countries, rich and poor,

Micronesian outrigger canoe in Namonuito Atoll Lagoon.

Photos by R. Wenkam

Trukese mother on Tol Island in the Truk Lagoon, Micronesia. Upper left: The gradual transition from thatched huts and bread-fruit to a sawn timber table and aluminum pots and pans illustrates the dramatic cultural and economic changes in Micronesia. Below: Handblown glass Japanese fishing floats are gradually replaced by discarded American plastic bottles. A U.S. amphibious tank from World War II is reclaimed by the jungle on Peleliu Island, Palau, Micronesia.

Photos by R. Wenkam

Yapese wearing native "thu" unloads kerosene from the Philippines in Kolonia Harbor, Yap Island, Micronesia. Left: Okinawan fishermen unload tuna at fast freezing plant in Koror, Palau, Micronesia.

Young Micronesians demonstrate in support of United Nations visiting commission on Tol Island in Truk Lagoon. Upper left: Author Wenkam on Namonuito Atoll in Micronesia. U.S. High Commissioner for the Trust Territory of the Pacific Islands, Edward Johnston, at his Saipan, Mariana Islands headquarters. Lower left: Beach on Arno Island on Arno Atoll, Micronesia.

Photo by R. Wenkam

The fortress-temple in Non Madol, the ancient Venice
of the Pacific, on Ponape Island, Micronesia.

Photos by R. Wenkam

PUBLIC NOTICE
POLLUTED WATER
PROHIBITED
FOR USAGE WITHIN 1000 FT.

TIAL DAOB AKIKIONGEL
DIAK A OMENGE MA OMENGEDUB
BA ELSEL A 1000 FEET.

BY ORDER

Photo courtesy Castle & Cooke

Planting pineapple slips (cuttings from mature plants) in the Dole plantation fields on southern Mindanao, Philippines, with Mt. Matutum in the background. The bags of pineapple slips come from the Wahiawa fields in Hawaii. Upper left: Outhouses in Majuro Lagoon, government district center of Marshall Islands, Micronesia. Below: A warning of polluted water in lagoon near Koror, Palau, Micronesia.

Kahana Valley on Oahu Island, Hawaii, has been purchased by the
state of Hawaii for $5 million to be developed as a state park. The
resident Hawaiian people say they will stay. Left: The over-popu-
lated Honolulu crowds up narrow Kalihi Valley on Oahu Island,
Hawaii.

Photos courtesy of Federation of Malaysia

Logging operations such as this Weyerhauser concession on lands in north Borneo (above) and the Jengka Triangle jungle clearing and redevelopment project in Malaysia near the Thailand border (below) threaten to destroy jungle wilderness such as this tropical forest canopy in Kalimentan, Indonesian Borneo (right).

Photo by R. Wenkam

Photo by Ng En Fook, Courtesy Malaysian Information Service

Photo by Dominic Chu, courtesy North Borneo Information Service

Chinese owned hydraulic tin mine, one of over 565 similar mines in Kinta and Selangor states on the Malaya Peninsula, richest tin area in the world. Below: The "Orient Explorer," an American oil-drilling rig operating off the north coast of Sabah in the Sulu Sea.

big and small, will also benefit from the riches of an ocean that the islanders explored a thousand years before the white man dared venture into their sea.

Senator Andon Amaraich of Truk, chairman of the Congress of Micronesia's Joint Committee on Law and the Sea, says the United States cannot adequately represent Micronesian interests concerning rights to seabed resources, because, "our position conflicts directly with theirs." The senator urged that Micronesia have its own representative at any future conferences regarding law and the sea.

The Truk senator said it is the Committee's position that Micronesia "claims general ownership over all waters within the Micronesian island groups, or archipelago, meaning, all waters within straight baselines connecting our outer-most islands" a position the United States has rejected in meetings held so far between the Joint Committee and the Department of State. Micronesia also claims "territorial sea jurisdiction over a twelve-mile-wide zone, measured outward from the archipelago baselines, and a 200-mile seabed and ocean resource zone extending from the twelve-mile zone outward where Micronesia would reserve the rights to all resources" but would not regulate innocent ship passage.

Traditional Micronesian ocean travel using navigational skills a thousand years old were cited in justification of claims to interisland waters. Amaraich quoted from a report prepared by researchers in traditional Micronesian history, asserting that communications between the islands is still maintained by "long and difficult canoe voyages, the latest of which occurred in May 1972 from the island of Puluwat in the Central Carolines to Guam. Micronesians traditionally consider that they own the sea between and around their islands in much the same way they own land."

The report claims that prehistoric island empires, resulting from interchange among large populations on widely scattered islands utilizing highly successful navigation systems, encompassed all of present-day Micronesia. Centuries ago Micronesia was comprised of all the Marianas Islands, the present territory of Guam, all the islands south of Anguar, and the Eastern Caroline and Senyavin Islands, including Yap, Truk, and Ponape. The Marshalls apparently were always considered a distinct political entity, its people traveling eastward 2,000 miles to Hawaii while the separatist Palauans maintained ties with the Philippines only 700 miles away to the west. The ancient political empires encompassed perhaps three million square miles of ocean domain.

In trying to comprehend the significance of these large ocean areas, the report stresses that "the only way one can understand how a Micronesian feels about his sea is to adopt his way of looking at the sea. A Micronesian sees the sea just like land. Asking a Micronesian who owns the sea is like asking him who owns the lagoons or the land . . . or like asking an inhabitant of a continental nation who owns the mountains, forest, deserts, lakes or rivers . . . A nation's territory is its surface habitat, and the sea is at least as important a part of a Micronesian's surface area habitat as is the land. . . . Rights in both categories of surface area exist equally in the minds of men and should therefore be equally respected."

Senator Amaraich spoke further of the islanders' point of reference in an eloquent speech before the 1973 United Nations Trusteeship Council meeting in New York. He asserted most logically that, "Micronesian tradition treats ownership of the reefs, and the seas surrounding the reefs, in the same manner as other societies treat land. An interest in the sea can be passed down, from father to son, in the same way as an interest in land can be passed down in other societies."

An assistant legal advisor to the U.S. State Department, Bernard Oxman, met on Saipan with members of the Committee. He emphasized that the United States was anxious to work out solutions with the Congress so that the United States can fully represent Micronesian interests.

However, Oxman said, "Although the United States has noted unofficial support for the 200-mile jurisdiction proposal as far as seabed resources are concerned, it would be opposed to any plan that would block off huge areas of water to air and sea transport. The United States would also oppose any plan which would disallow for international control of highly migratory species of fish, such as tuna, which travel great distances in the ocean, often through national territorial sea areas."

Concerning fisheries—considered the most complicated aspect of the Law of the Sea, at least from the United States' viewpoint—Oxman said that the large fishing nations such as Japan and the Soviet Union are vigorously opposed to a 200-mile territorial limit, as proposed by Micronesia. He suggested that a compromise might be required in this area. "The United States proposes a 'species approach' that would essentially give coastal nations control over stocks of fish where they exist" (such as reef and shore fish), said Oxman, "including subjecting the entire tuna fish resource to international controls as they are highly migratory."

Although Oxman said the United States is "absolutely committed" to full presentation of Micronesian views at United Nations Law of the Sea Conferences, many members of the Micronesian Congress are not yet satisfied that their views can be reconciled with those of the United States. Marshalls Representative Charles Domnick, for example, says that the United States position on Law of the Sea concerning the tuna issue is a tool "to merely sanction tuna fishing as is." He feels this would result in unfair foreign exploitation of a valuable Micronesian resource.

Many congressmen are also worried about other implications to be considered along with the Law of the Sea issue, most notably those concerning the future political status of Micronesia. Under the proposed draft compact for a Free Association status with the United States, Micronesia would place complete authority over foreign affairs in the hands of the United States. Now, with the United States wishing to represent Micronesia at an international conference on an issue where conflicting views exist, many members of Congress are privately wondering if similar conflicts of interest in other areas will occur under such a compact in the future. Thus, until the Law of the Sea issue is resolved, it may have a major influence on further political negotiations between Micronesia and the United States.

Involved inextricably in Law of the Sea discussions is the ticklish question of rights of innocent passage in international waters. Russia, Japan, and the United States are apparently willing to sacrifice almost anything to guarantee passage for submarines, warships, and oil tankers through narrow navigable straits. If, for example, Malaysia and Indonesia closed three key straits in Southeast Asia (Makassar, Malacca, and Torres), mideast oil for Japan would have to travel all the way around Tasmania below Australia, forcing serious increases in cost.

Eminent authorities have already expressed concern over the possibility of open warfare between the United States and other mineral-starved nations if strict international controls are not adopted soon. Louis Sohn of the Harvard Law School is quoted in a Pacific News Service release: "Assume that an American mining company finds a rich area 500 miles off Hawaii and the Japanese come along and start mining nearby, moving their ships closer and closer. It's an awfully dangerous game."

Lawyer Sohn may be exaggerating a little, since nodule inventories on the books indicate there is more than enough for everybody, although there could be considerable competition for the richest and therefore most economical fields to mine. The controversy most likely to erupt into violence will be over conflicting claims of ownership and control of the seabed adjacent to developing nations which may lay claim to all the profits from seabed mining within their "extended" territorial waters.

The United States wants the oceans "internationalized" beyond the already agreed-upon national rights to continental shelf waters up to 200 meters in depth. An international mining consortium controlled by the mining nations would police the operations and distribute royalties according to some agreed formula, perhaps involving population and length of shoreline of the respective nations. This is the policy being pushed by the U.S. Navy to maintain its alleged right to patrol as close to foreign shores as possible. It is also a policy that would deprive Pacific nations of direct participation in undersea mining and an appropriate share of the rewards. The Navy's arguments differ from those of an industry spokesman quoted in the state of Hawaii-sponsored symposium on seabed mining of manganese nodules, who offered the conclusion that developing nations should be content with the "availability to them of markedly less costly basic materials (for use) by themselves." The United States describes its proposals as "international" when it really means that it would be guaranteed international control of marine resources. This is a proposition few developing Pacific nations would support.

Hughes Tool Company's Summa Corporation, in collaboration with Lockheed Ocean Systems and Global Marine, has already started mining. A huge hanger-like submersible barge is now dredging up manganese nodules on the East Pacific Rise off Nicaragua, a geological formation identified by Russian scientists Dkornyakova and Andryvschchenko in 1970 as part of two major Pacific ferro-manganese ore resource areas. It is a vast field of closely packed mineral-rich nodules extending two thousand miles into the Pacific north of Tahiti.

Accompanied by Hughes's oceanography research vessel, Glomar Explorer, and supporting auxiliary ships, the floating "mine" will selectively sweep the ocean floor in areas of concentrated deposits, using a fifty-foot-wide articulated recovery head to suck up the nodules from three-mile depths and transfer the ore to waiting freighters. Observers estimate the sophisticated equipment should be able to dredge up to 5,000 tons of ore a day for shipment to mainland smelters.

Hughes's competitors are also ready to go. A Tenneco subsidiary, Deepsea Ventures, is using the world's first commercial manganese nodule prospecting ship. But the company is unwilling to invest the additional millions required until Congress passes protective legislation guaranteeing against losses.

A new land rush reminiscent of ruthless pioneer days in Oklahoma is in preparation, and there is little evidence of any more concern for native island people today than there was for the American Indians in less civilized times. The reactionary America Mining Congress is fighting hard for legislation to guarantee that multi-million dollar investments in seabed mining fleets will be safe. Under a proposed law now being considered by Congress, any "qualified" company could buy legal claims to 40,000 kilometer square blocks of ocean floor—about the size of Vermont and New Hampshire combined. It would commit the United States government to underwrite any corporate losses during the next forty years, including "loss caused through any interference by any other person (whether or not violative of international law)." One can only presume the companies are asking in advance for payment of losses that would occur should they by chance start a war. Total cost to the mining companies for this amazing insurance is a bargain $50,000 fee plus small service charges (or $3.33 per square mile). Location of the claims would not be restricted to territorial waters. They could be anywhere on earth—depending on who got there first. The oceans have no landlord and there is no rent to pay. A more blatant law favoring mining interests and selfish nationalism could hardly be imagined.

The Nixon administration has opposed the mining bill, arguing that Law of the Sea negotiations were "moving into a critical stage" and that other nations—upon whom we have been urging restraint in pressing unilateral claims during the negotiating process—might take the Mining Congress legislation as justification for their own preemption of the treaty process.

Senator Lee Metcalf of Montana did not like the idea of waiting. He responded to requests by the influential mining lobby in his own state by introducing the seabed mining bill in the Senate, giving as his reason that we had reached that time "so far as ocean mining legislation is concerned, where we fish, cut bait, or haul for shore."

In an interesting insight into the attitudes of all concerned, the senator said, "Evidently to enhance its bargaining position in the preparatory talks for the 1974 Law of the Sea Conference, the State Department continues to advise the Congress: Now let us just wait and see how well negotiations proceed toward development of an acceptable seabed treaty. We are advised not to pass legislation but not to forget the legislation. This may well be the ideal position for the Congress . . . but I think the time has come to give this bill . . . a fair hearing and then decide whether we want to pass legislation and if so, what that legislation should contain."

Statements in favor of the seabed mining bill, as reported by the citizen's organization, SOS (Save Our Seas), somewhat resemble those put forward in support of the ill-fated supersonic transport (SST), "It is in the American interest to become world leaders in acquiring seabed minerals." *Science* magazine reported further comments: "By diversifying sources and acquiring these metals under the American flag, the nation would become less dependent on the internal affairs of major metals exporters such as Chile, Brazil, and Zaire." Actually if the undersea geologists are correct in their estimates of potential seabed resources, the United States could become self-sufficient in ores we now import, and would bankrupt present exporting countries who might refuse to sell at our asking price.

An exchange between Senator Metcalf of Montana

and T. S. Ary, testifying for the Mining Congress, reveals
the sense of unreality that pervades Law of the Sea discussions:

Ary: "If the United Nations Seabed Committee continues
at its present slow rate, it is unlikely that a treaty will be
ratified in this decade, if ever, and certainly long after the
immediate necessity for a legal regime has passed."

Metcalf: "If you pardon me, I would say you should change
that word decade to centuries."

Ary: "Our committee discussed that, and we thought we
should put decade in rather than until eternity."

Metcalf: "Well, you are more optimistic than I am."

The law of the seabed today is no law at all. It is the invitation for a new land grab of such magnitude and of potential serious consequences that the murderous compaign to
conquer the American Indian nation over a century ago
pales in comparison.

Japan has recently announced that its $8 million man-
ganese prospecting ship will soon be operating in waters
south of Hawaii, gathering information on seabed ore for
Mitsui. The French firm CNEXO, Society Le Nickel, is
conducting exploratory mining cruises north of French
Polynesia. It would appear that both research vessels are
operating in the same waters. Their ore dredges and suction
barges will not be far behind.

The race has begun among the major powers to extract
the wealth of the sea. "It's a tragedy," says Charles Rhyne,
long-time advocate of the rule of law over the ocean's beds.
"We are about to witness the kind of dog-eat-dog competition that characterized colonization of Africa and the New
World. One would think we could learn to place a premium on cooperation rather than greed, quickness, and
force."

By unanimous Resolution, the U.N. General Assem-
bly has set forth principles for a Law of the Sea treaty, stating that seabed resources are to be exploited for the benefit

of mankind with particular consideration to be given developing countries. No nation would exercise rights incompatible with the international regime that would be established under these principles to regulate mining or actually do the mining itself under contract.

With a view toward implementing these principles, President Nixon in 1970 proposed a treaty that would have coastal nations "renounce all national claims over the natural resources of the seabed beyond the point where the high seas reach a depth of 200 meters and would agree to regard these resources as the common heritage of mankind." The treaty would set up an "international regime" to exploit seabed resources beyond that limit. Should Nixon's proposal be implemented the Pacific islanders would have no claim to their abundant seabed resources, the richest anywhere on earth, since the Pacific Islands do not possess a continental shelf over which they can claim resource rights. It would appear to be quite unjust that after 400 years of enforced colonial exploitation by developed nations, that when the oceans are about to yield some of the last remaining natural resources, a sophisticated international regime would deprive the island people of their last worldly goods, and divide it among everybody else. It is an act that would forever deny the Pacific islanders the opportunity for self-sufficiency and economic independence.

It does seem strangely contradictory at the very time we should be striving for one world, that nationalistic determination has become the goal of developing nations striving for economic independence, while the developed countries utilize international legal concepts to claim the earth's last natural resources to feed their rapacious, materialistic societies.

It may be too late to internationalize the world's last remaining resources. Now that we have almost exhausted our own finite supply and denied the Third World countries a fair share for so long, we may be forced to pay for our needs in a buyer's market. And that could be expensive.

10

The Rape of Mindanao

IT WAS after midnight when our rusty tramp freighter moved slowly into the Gulf of Davao. We had been at sea for two days and two nights on the 700-mile trip from Koror, retracing the path early Malaysians traveled over 4,000 years ago when they first sailed from the Philippines in ocean-going log rafts. The Palauans still consider the brightly colored ceramic fragments their ancestors carried from Mindanao as family wealth and dowry money.

By dawn our ship was surrounded by colorful double-outrigger canoes that clustered close around the hull darting back and forth between us and the nearby shorelike water-skating insects on the mirror smooth bay. Volcanic, cone-shaped Mt. Apo rose above Davao City shimmering in the morning haze, already bathed in the heavy humidity of a tropical day.

Money changers clambered up the gangways besieging us with bargain exchange rates for pesos as we made our way to the Philippine custom officials who obviously were not expecting us. Alien passengers from overseas seldom arrive in Davao since all scheduled air and ocean traffic was halted between Borneo and the Philippines following President Ferdinand Marcos's territorial claim for portions of Malaysian Sabah in North Borneo. Weary officials endorsed our passports with a barely readable rubber cachet from Cebu. No one in their memory had ever arrived from Palau.

Their warning to us was very serious. Davao City had sustained severe damage from recent street riots. We were advised not to travel beyond the city limits and under no circumstances to "drive across the island to Cotabato where Muslims were killing Christians." It was a "religious war," they said.

The warnings reminded me of similar cautionary instructions I had earlier received before driving from Manila south to Tagaytay. I took an armed bodyguard with me for that trip, traveling only during busy morning hours, remembering not to stop for cattle blocking the road, and being prepared to make a highspeed U-turn at any moment. I was told privately that Philippine constabulary stationed in guard houses were not always to be trusted, and that sometimes they actively collaborated with the bandits, as local communist cadres were known. The best defense was fast driving, a show of weapons, and plenty of pesos to buy protection from police in the next town.

As part of a long-range economic development program and in response to political pressures to carry out promised land reforms, President Marcos inaugurated a homesteading program to develop the wild unsettled interior of Mindanao. Qualified residents of Manila could apply for land permits granting them several acres of jungle which they would clear, plant, and—after erecting a house—eventually own as their own property. Manila Filipinos flocked to the government land office for homesteading rights, and soon hundreds of city dwellers were busy carving out their country home in the jungle. Government officials, backed by generous United States aid money, were pleased to help clear tropical hardwood trees covering homestead lands; and the rich soils, never before opened except by primitive slash-and-burn agriculturists, were turned by steel plows and planted with seeds developed by American specialists.

Peace Corps volunteers helping the homesteading program were proud of their contribution toward establishment of a prosperous new community where only primitive Muslim tribesmen had lived before. They were somewhat surprised when the Muslims objected. This had always been their land, they insisted: "Our ancestors have hunted and lived here for generations."

President Marcos, ensconced luxuriously in Malaccan Palace, scoffed at their protestations, saying it was time the Muslim country people became civilized instead of living in the jungle, and accelerated his homesteading program, encouraging remote villagers to leave the interior and move to the new towns that were springing up near sugar and pineapple plantations.

Muslim tribesmen retaliated by setting fire to homesteaders' huts and destroying their crops. When Marcos dispatched armed troops to protect settlers, Muslim hillsmen mounted attacks in strength. It was only a short time until Manilan Christians and Zamboangan Muslims were killing each other on the streets of Cotabato in vicious skirmishes that Marcos branded a "religious war."

He could not have been more wrong. His American advisors could easily have explained the problem. Pioneers clearing the land and settling the western United States encountered the very same difficulties when American Indians—then described by government officials as "primitive savages"—resisted the taking of their land. Two hundred years later, with the help of United States advisors and weapons, Marcos was dictating the same land ethic and enforcing its conditions upon a people who preferred to live without subdividing the landscape or logging the rain forest giants that had been growing undisturbed in the mountains of Mindanao as long as anyone could remember.

But Marcos had succeeded in selling millions of acres of timber concessions to foreign and domestic corporations, and professional timber cruisers from overseas were out scouting for more forested acreage, identifying every tree of commercial value and determining methods of dragging valuable logs out of the wet jungle for export to Japan and the United States. Prodded by loggers, landgrabbers looking for defaulted homesteads, and ore geologists, Marcos's Panamin agency, headed by Interior Secretary Manuel Elizalde, Jr., utilized every means to evict indigenous settlers from their land and throw it open to logging, mining, and commercial development directed from overseas. To crush the unexpected resistance, Philippine constabulary squads terrorized remote provinces in Cotabato, forcing thousands of refugees to flee across the Celebes Sea to Islands in the Sulu Archipelago. The fight for their land became a civil war when sixty-five Muslim men, women, and children were slaughtered inside the Barrio Manalili Mosque in Cotabato by twenty-three men wearing red-striped military uniforms from Ilocos Sur Province north of Manila.

In 1971, timber cruisers exploring the unmapped jungle of Cotabato del Sur came upon an unknown Malayo-Polynesian people living peacefully on the slopes of Tasaday Mountain. They quickly became celebrities when anthropologists described their "stone age" culture over American television.

The Tasaday hills have not yet turned brown and mangy from strip-and-run logging operations. Only the persistent smoky haze hanging loosely amid the dipterocarp forest canopy—the entrails of slash-and-burn agriculture—reminds rare visitors that someone is living here in the convoluted coral limestone caves and confused jungle of vines and spindly trees. It is a rugged country that has successfully resisted road builders and rubber planters over the years, but the whirring chop of helicopter blades has ended grand isolation of the Tasaday people—people who, according to Jesuit anthropologist Frank Lynch, are an "apparently healthy, happy people living in close and seemingly contented harmony with their natural environment."

"One of the most desirable things in life," the Tasaday say, "is to live together in our forest home, a counsel left us by our ancestors, so that we could take care of the trees and the rocks around us. . . ." Oligarchic administrator Elizalde assumes otherwise. Business financed Panamin, described in *Orientations* magazine as an organization dedicated to preservation of the culture and the uplift of ethnic minorities in the Philippines, has established research-and-development centers near traditional homes of tribal minorities and is destroying their cultural traditions in the process of converting subsistence living patterns into cheap labor for a money economy.

Apparent contradictions between the Tasadays' expressions of contentment with their life-style and outsiders' insistence that their standard of living must be "improved" by shifting from communal relationships to a competitive money economy—with all the traumatic cultural shock involved—seems unnoticed by even the most well-meaning spokesmen for conservation and cultural causes.

Colonel Charles Lindbergh spent eight days at a Panamin relocation camp for Ubos and T'boli tribesmen in Surala, Cotabato, and met later with Imelda Marcos and Elizalde to discuss "plans to improve the living conditions of the [Tagabili] tribe while preserving its cultural traditions." The contradiction in goals seemingly escaped Lindbergh, who at a later press conference also supported timber and mining operations in Mindanao. He said, "Conservation is in no way opposed to the exploitation of natural resources. . . . It is, in fact, in the interests of further exploitation of nature that conservation methods should be taken."

When I later asked Lindbergh if this observation might be misunderstood, he told me he was "tremendously interested in the work Secretary Elizalde and Panamin have been doing in their attempt to assist the national minorities, but I have not tried to interfere with political activities and local relationships." Lindbergh said, "I have constantly emphasized the importance of preserving the Philippine forests and establishing an overall plan of conservation."

Lindbergh forgets that most of Mindanao and Sulu are

traditional Muslim lands and are not subdividable by arbitrary dictum from Manila, granting homesteads to Luzon Filipinos or quarter-million-acre timber concessions to foreign corporations. Forests cover sixty percent of the Philippines and the Marcos government claims they own ninety-seven percent. This rationale would leave the Muslims with none.

It is a matter of fact to even the Philippine government, who in an official publication listing the "Factors that led to the present open conflict in Mindanao," state that, "Foremost among the measures perhaps which earned the bitter resentment of the Muslims against the government and its Christian neighbors is the granting of land titles to new settlers from the Visayas and Luzon, the granting of special lumber concessions to big firms, and the massive relocation program of the NARRA (National Resettlement and Rehabilitation Administration)."

Goodyear Tire abandoned its Basilan Island rubber plantation when it became evident that two-thirds of the island was under control of Muslim rebels. Other American corporations are increasingly apprehensive about their investments as fighting intensifies between Philippine army troops using United States-supplied weapons and Muslim revolutionary forces with captured munitions and new Russian and Belgian rifles smuggled in from Libya via friendly Malaysia.

Business continues as usual at four large American companies which are clear-cutting virgin forests at a rate reportedly nine times the expected reforestation rate. Weyerhaeuser, Boise-Cascade, Georgia-Pacific, and International Paper gained control of thirteen percent of Mindanao. Operating under long-term concession agreements, they have precipitated a logging boom marked by widespread political payoffs. A Georgia-Pacific corporate spokesman, responding to National Council of Churches objections, stated that, "because the U.S. would run out of certain domestic fibers in the near future, it was necessary that timber companies gain concessions as a 'bank deposit' for future needs." All their production is exported to Japan and the United States.

Typical Filipino families employed by United States timber companies are part of the eighty percent of Filipino families who divide forty-five percent of the low national income. Fifty-four percent of Philippine income enriches only twenty percent of the population, a disproportionate split equaled in few other countries.

Georgia-Pacific's 231,000-acre timber concession is across the island from Cotabato on Lianga Bay, well beyond the range of rebel guns. Georgia-Pacific considers itself a responsible investor, not waiting for government pressure to take action on good forestry procedures it considers important. The company was the first timber concessionaire to commit itself to a reforestation program and has annually carried out a replanting program utilizing Philippine mahogany seedlings from its own large nursery. Its forest research group is reportedly experimenting with even faster growing seedlings native to tropical soils to help regenerate logged forests. But mechanized logging equipment still churns up five-foot-deep topsoil that becomes a perpetual quagmire in the 300 inches of annual rainfall.

The company has helped its 800 employees build a church and a fifty-bed hospital; it has raised wooden sidewalks in the company town to clear the mud and erected pleasant employee housing. Yet, the nagging cries of "imperialists!" still ring in the ears of Georgia-Pacific international vice-president on his frequent visits to Mindanao. To him, it is a bewildering accusation.

Economic well-being is not necessarily a solution to political unrest. Evidence is accumulating that uncontrolled aggression in man, whether it be expressed in Chicago gang wars or indigenous revolutionaries, is not a feature of stable and integrated societies, but contrarywise, perhaps direct evidence that the particular community has disintegrated to the degree that one's social identity is constantly in doubt. When societies fail to provide opportunities for individuals to build a satisfying social identity, aggression will probably result. And the loss of identity is a frequent concomitance of rapid social and economic change set in motion by a weekly paycheck and the company town.

Bananas, pineapples, and sugar are harvested on Mindanao in addition to timber. Pineapples are exported to Japan, the United States, and Europe by two American multinational food corporations, Del Monte Corporation and Dole Philippines (Dolefil). Dolefil is a subsidiary of Hawaii's Castle & Cooke, the world's fifth largest food grower and processor. Dolefil cultivates over 13,400 planted acres on Mindanao, supplying their automated pineapple cannery with 275,000 tons of fruit annually. The fruit ripens in carefully planned increments, controlled by hormone spraying and chemical fertilizing to prevent the two-year crop from maturing all at once.

Organized with considerable fanfare by a pioneering group of Filipinos and Americans, Dolefil was a typical joint-venture enterprise with an original investment of 199,940 pesos by an American holding 79,994 shares and six Filipino nationals investing 60,000 pesos. The nationals own one share each. The president of Dolefil is Geronomo Velasco, a Filipino, who is also president of Republic Glass Corporation, sixty-one percent owned by Castle & Cooke. Dolefil's land-acquisition agreement with the Philippine National Development Company seemingly gives Dolefil the right to acquire almost the entire province of Cotabato del Sur for its operations.

Looking back over the ten years since Dolefil's beginnings on Mindanao, the early company pioneers that remain agree that Dolefil has conquered the frontier. "The contrast between 1963 and 1973 is almost unbelievable," says general manager Phil Schrader, one of the original five Americans who came from Hawaii to live at an old coffee plantation and help start it all.

Writing in *Castle & Cooke Report*, Penny Rogers tells of Elesio Duley, now sixty-five, who worked in those early days as a surveyor for Dole. "I'm still doing the same work today, and I enjoy it. I came to Cotabato with Gen. Paulino Santos in 1940 to do the first surveys for farm lots for the original Christian settlers, so it was not hard for me to continue with Dole. I do remember being chased many times with bolos when farmers here didn't agree with our boundary layouts, though," he chuckled with his foreman, Domingo Dimaclid. "It was barren land with no water, just cogon grass . . . and now there's electricity . . . so much progress."

"After the ceremonial planting," writes Rogers, "Dolefil swung immediately into action, planting a quarter acre the first day the planting material arrived by boat from Hawaii and four acres the next day. . . . In the early days, at least fifty percent of the male populace carried guns for protection." "This was a melting pot. I was really frightened," said Becky Tan who came with her husband in December 1963.

Violence and employee problems plagued the reign of Dolefil from the first year, but as these issues were resolved production of pineapple increased and local business grew. Polomolok district became a first-class municipality and Dadiangas village, originally a one-store-road intersection became General Santos City with all the appropriate urban amenities.

Five thousand people now work there and an early morning look at the local Kalsangi school yard tells it all. "Children of Dolefil families, dark and fair, towhead and brunette," according to Rogers, "stand together to sing the Philippine national anthem—a picture of cooperation and understanding, Filipinos and Americans working and learning together."

But the sound of gunfire is not far from the Kalsangi school yard. In the summer of 1974 more than 19,000 persons fled their homes following pitched fighting between local rebels and government troops from Luzon in the swampy valley west of Midsayap city, 65 miles north of Dole's pineapple fields. U.S. built F-86 jet fighters flown by Filipino pilots dive bombed rebel positions, their swooping clearly seen from the streets of Cotabato city.

For every new acre Dole plows in Mindanao an acre is abandoned in Hawaii. Ironically this process displaces contract laborers who were recruited from the Philippines in 1946 to inundate Hawaii's unionized labor market with low-paid competition for orientals then working the plantations. The move to grow and can Hawaiian pineapple in Mindanao has been a continuing economic success as consumer prices for pineapple on United States supermarket shelves rise sharply while total costs averaged between Hawaii and the Philippines decrease. Martial law imposed by Marcos helped preserve Dolefil's upward-spiraling profits when decrees were announced prohibiting strikes and requiring compulsory arbitration. Marcos created a labor board with exclusive jurisdiction over employer-employee relations including disputes and grievances leading to strikes, lockouts, and shutdowns. Dolefil has little to worry about from disgruntled employees, even though the last Dolefil strike resulted in a wage increase of only one cent an hour for most workers. In the unionized Hawaiian pineapple industry, Dole pays wage rates of $2.93 to $5.25 an hour. The same company growing the same pineapple on Mindanao pays a low of fifteen cents to a high of forty cents an hour.

Hawaii Representative Patsy Mink, in explaining why Hawaii's pineapple industry is closing canneries and abandoning once intensively-cultivated fields, agrees that "Most of the cutbacks in Hawaii's pineapple industry are due to the competition of low-cost foreign pineapple [these same companies] import into the United States." The cheaper Mindanao Cayenne pineapple is identical to the Hawaiian product and often sells at the same price. The Hawaii-based industry makes higher profits on pineapple because it pays Philippine workers less and puts Hawaiians out of their jobs. It is an unreal world that sees Representative Mink and Senator Daniel Inouye both introducing legislation to increase tariffs on foreign pineapple, tariffs that would allow the pineapple companies to compete with themselves! The major pineapple companies, true to their history, have refused to testify in support of higher U.S. tariffs. A century ago, when they first planted pineapple in Hawaii to benefit from cheap labor, they helped to overthrow the Hawaiian Kingdom in order to gain favorable reciprocity rights in American markets. Mink and Inouye fail to appreciate the fact that few American corporations have ever exhibited an understanding of social responsibility. Corporate bureaucracy is dedicated to maximizing profits—not saving an industry. Corporate morality is no better symbolized than in Castle & Cooke's decision to convert several hundred acres of Hawaiian pineapple land into a memorial cemetery to bury the dead.

President Marcos's popularity continues to gain increasing support from United States businessmen as he implements presidential decrees favorable to foreign capital and generally unfavorable to labor. At the same time strikes were made illegal, capital gains for individuals were made tax exempt. Stock transaction taxes were reduced from two to one-fourth of one percent; foreign tourists and travelers were exempted from hotel room taxes; and previous court decisions were rescinded which limited foreign land ownership and corporate control by expatriate corporate directors.

Almost thirty percent of Philippine government revenues go toward paying interest on their rapidly rising foreign debt. Over sixty-five percent of the debt is owed to Japanese and American creditors. Also, substantial sums are owed to the World Bank. Thus the Philippines is in an unusual situation: a sovereign country with worsening foreign exchange deficits exceeding $100 million, is beholden to private trading partners and two foreign governments to stave off impending bankruptcy.

The declaration of a national emergency by Marcos and the usurpation of dictatorial powers may be less of a response to communist insurgency, as Marcos claims, than reaction to a worsening economic situation. Under martial law, the government has been able to fend off economic disaster by encouraging unlimited foreign investment, exploitation of natural resources, and liberal profit taking.

United States businesses already dominate the Philippine economy. They account for over three-quarters of all foreign investments and assets estimated in excess of $2 billion. It appears they also control the destiny of a country.

While business flourishes in the environment of martial law, the anti-Marcos rebellion flares anew, threatening to involve all the Philippines. Marcos desperately attempts to quell continued fighting in Sulu while opposing raids by the Communist New People's Army in Luzon. Increased U.S. military involvement to protect huge American investments and secure debt payments becomes a possibility as Philippine armed forces utilize all its resources on two fronts. A Muslim minority wants only to recover ancestral lands. But a newly-aroused communist rebel movement is intent on completely overthrowing capitalism in the Philippines.

United States Special Forces civic teams—the Green Berets—are working side by side with Philippine forces, ostensibly only to "help with medical and veterinary programs." Their work is an on-the-job function of the Joint U.S. Military Advisory Group in the Philippines to create a favorable physical and psychological infrastructure for future military operations in support of the Manila government. It is the same role the Group served in Vietnam.

The U.S. Military Assistance Agreement is directed "to assist in creating an internal security capability in the Philippines," and "develop self-sustaining capabilities within the Philippine Armed Forces. . . ." But for some time there have been questions about the so-called advisory capacity of United States military advisory groups. According to Philippines Congressman Joaquin Roces, there have been occasions when the United States "issued orders directly to subordinate-level commanders" of the Philippines Air Force (PAF), forgetting that PAF is not a part of American forces.

In June of 1974, the U.S. Pacific commander in chief and co-chairman of the Philippine-U.S. Mutual Defense

Board, Admiral Noel Gayler, flew to Manila from his Hawaii headquarters at Pearl Harbor, where he personally received the Philippine Legion of Honor decoration from Marcos. Admiral Gayler was specifically honored for "Exceptionally meritorious and distinguished service rendered to the Republic of the Philippines . . . to enhance the development and modernization of the Armed Forces of the Philippines by accelerating the delivery of critical equipment and vital supplies needed to strengthen the defense of the Philippines and to support civic action projects of the armed forces. . . ." It was in the same month that the U.S. Mactan airbase was used by PAF jets in renewed bombing strikes against rebels on Mindanao, which may explain the critical need for vital supplies in "defense" of the Philippines.

It is not stipulated in any agreement or treaty between the two countries that American forces may intervene in Philippine internal affairs. But it is apparent that United States bases and personnel are directly involved in air support for Philippine army forces on Mindanao. It is reported that at least two squadrons of F-86 and F-5 fighter jets, piloted by Filipinos, operate out of the United States air base on Mactan Island, 120 miles north of Zamboanga del Norte in Mindanao.

Military aid to Philippine forces by the United States was widely discussed during 1969 hearings before the Senate Subcommittee on U.S. Security Agreements and Commitments Abroad. The exchanges between Senator Stuart Symington and Pentagon witnesses serve to reveal the extent of United States involvement in present Philippine fighting:

General Robert Warren, deputy assistant secretary of defense for military assistance (replying to Symington's questioning about the real purpose of Philippine military assistance and his assertion that assistance is really a means of keeping the Philippine government friendly to the United States): "In my opinion, to a

degree, yes, sir. But it is also to help Filipino forces to physically protect U.S. forces in the Philippines."
Senator Symington: "From whom?"
General Warren: "Internally, sir; to maintain internal security and stability and thereby make our own activities over there more secure."
Senator Symington: "In other words, we are paying the Philippines government to protect us from the Philippine people who do not agree with the policies of the government or do not like the Americans."
General Warren: "To a degree, yes, sir."

Later in the testimony, subcommittee counsel Roland Paul questioned Lt. General Francis Gideon, commander of the 13th Air Force in the Philippines. He asked about the apparent waste of money involved in assigning 600 U.S. Air Force support troops to the rural Mactan Air Base to service only about 160 U.S. military flights per month, compared with 20,000 per month at Clark Air Base:

Counsel Paul: "In light of this minimal function, could you tell us why Mactan, if I may ask a direct question, should continue to be an American facility?"
General Gideon: "Yes, we continue to reevaluate these questions, and that one is being reevaluated at this time, as are all the bases."
Senator Symington: "With respect, General, I do not think that answer is quite responsive. Why do you keep the base open?"
Gideon: "Well, from my own point of view we keep it open because I am instructed to carry out the mission."
Symington: "Let me approach it in another way. Six flights a day. Do you think it worthwhile on the basis of six flights a day?"
Gideon: "My own personal opinion is that if this were the only reason for the retention of the base, no; that would not justify the retention of the base."

When fighting waned in swampy Cotabato, Marcos mounted aggressive attacks in the Sulu Islands, bombing and strafing the capital city when Jolo Mayor Aminkadra Abubakar joined rebel forces. Six thousand Muslim refugees fled by boat to Zamboanga as Major General Fidel Ramos, commander of the Philippine constabulary, attacked rebel forces following the secessionists' capture of the headquarters of the Philippine 1st Army Brigade and after they overran the island's only airport.

Marcos later tried to make amends by what he called "an innovative experiment to return power to our people," by giving the lands of Jolo to its Muslim residents. He said, "All the lands within the territorial boundaries of the municipality of Jolo will be titled in the name of the entire community and turned over to the residents subject to their approval by referendum." An offer was also made to grant full amnesty to Muslim rebels who are willing to negotiate with the government and lay down their arms. "We will accept them as brothers," said Marcos, "and forget whatever they have done." There was little response.

It was a rebellion that wouldn't go away. And with spreading sympathy for the Muslims and growing opposition to Marcos's suspension of constitutional rights and liberties, the Mindanao rebellion remained a serious threat to Marcos's regime. Growing resistance from the ordinarily conservative Catholic Church, the dominant religion in the Philippines, further undermined Marcos's ability to govern effectively. According to *The New York Times*, militant priests and bishops have asserted "the right and duty of the Church to campaign for social justice, regardless whether such a campaign coincides with the government's program."

A letter over the signature of the Most Rev. Francisco Claver, Bishop of Bukidnon Province in north-central Mindanao said, "We probably should begin asking our people what the Christian's prophetic role of witness means in the concrete situation of martial law. If equality and participation are basic rights of modern man, how are our people to insure that these rights are not totally lost in the kind of government they now have to live under?" Increasing friction with political activists has led to new arrests in all parts of the Philippines as Marcos attempts to silence dissatisfaction with his rule.

United States businessmen seem elated over the turn of events; martial law makes the Philippines eminently attractive to foreign investors. The vice-president of Caltex Petroleum is quoted in *Pacific Basin Reports* as being favorably impressed with reforms carried out under martial law. He reportedly told Marcos in a personal meeting that he would encourage other business executives to "go and see for themselves" about conditions in the Philippines.

It is a strange, unreal replay of the Vietnam record, replete with evasive answers by United States military assistance groups, plans to "protect our forces," and pleas by American business to help Marcos protect the Philippines from a "Maoist-inspired" communist takeover. But this time around the rubber plantations are not French; they are American. And foreign investments are not European, but American. It is evident that, should Marcos suffer a serious military setback in his "Plain of Jars" on Mindanao, and should he request direct U.S. military assistance to save his tottering government, the U.S. government will be faced with difficult political decisions. These decisions could easily involve the United States in another Asian military quagmire—a war to save "our" $2 billion investment and Weyerhaeuser's trees and Dole's ripening pineapples.

"On the fate of South Vietnam depends the fate of all Asia," wrote Richard Nixon in the August 1964 *Reader's Digest*. "For South Vietnam is the dam in the river. A communist victory there would mean, inevitably and soon, that the flood would begin! Next would come the loss of Laos, Cambodia, Thailand, Malaysia, and Indonesia which is only forty-five miles from the Philippines and next door to Australia. Can anyone seriously suggest that in such a circumstance the United States would not have to engage in a major war to save the Philippines from the same fate as Vietnam?"

As President Nixon and his guests enjoy their evening meal in the White House, it is of interest to visualize Nixon's Filipino waiters and servants, recruited in the Philippines by the Navy under a 1947 military bases agreement, acting out the daily throwback to colonial times at 1600 Pennsylvania Avenue.

11

Land Beyond the Wind

OUR freighter departed the crowded wharf in Samal Channel and moved south on a very humid morning, dodging canoes and rusty coastal vessels heavily loaded in every available space with a variety of cargo for Davao City. Evenly distributed in the holds of our Norwegian-built freighter, now riding deeper in the water, was almost one million board feet of rough-milled Philippine mahogany planks cut from the virgin forests of Mindanao. The cargo would be unloaded at Vancouver, Washington, on the Columbia River.

Our Norwegian captain ordered a course due south into Davao Gulf. The *Hoi Kung* was not going directly to Washington, but would proceed on a tramp freighter's traditional orders of "sufficient inducement." Our next port of call would be Borneo where the cargo hatches would again be opened to load tropical mahogany—the sugar pine of the orient—this time for shipment to furniture manufacturers in Long Beach, California.

Along the west shore of Davao Gulf a perpetual haze covers the lower hillside where slash-and-burn tribesmen carry on traditional agriculture in a roadless, tropical wilderness. The green spine dividing east and west Mindanao enters the sea in sharp escarpments, to rise again as twin volcanic islands offshore bordering Sarangani Strait, a

139

dramatic entrance to the Celebes Sea—in another century the unchallenged preserve of Philippine and Borneo pirates. By 1845, most of the pirates had promised the British that they would never engage in piracy again, and except for an occasional foray into southern Mindanao villages, they have kept their word. But there is a nagging suspicion that what Marcos describes as pirate raids may actually be supporters of Mindanao rebels smuggling arms across the Celebes Sea from Borneo where Malaysian government officials barely disguise their dislike of the Philippine regime. A favorite route of rebel smugglers is along the chain of islands ranging southwest of Zamboanga to Jolo and beyond where Philippine territorial waters extend to within fifteen miles of North Borneo. It is also the old route of Filipino motorboat operators who buy tax-free cigarettes in North Borneo to run past bribable Philippines customs into the highly-taxed home market. In Davao I saw government posters advising smokers to buy "healthy" Philippine cigarettes without the American cancer warning on the package.

Heavily loaded double outrigger canoes carrying as many as four black Mercury outboards, two on a side, easily out-pace high-speed patrol boats supplied to Marcos under American military assistance programs. If pressed in rough seas, the shallow-draft canoes detour along barrier reefs and escape into shallow waters where they are protected by mangrove thickets where the larger boats cannot follow.

Three high-speed navy patrol boats, originally built for river duty in Vietnam, cruised the Celebes Sea on routine patrol in the summer of 1973, giving United States sailors some idea of logistical problems in the unfamiliar Sulu Islands. The U.S.S. Asheville, Gallup, and Canon, each carrying a crew of thirty-four and capable of speeds above forty knots with the highest firepower-to-weight ratio of any American naval vessel, may have met their match in the Merc-powered canoes darting back and forth along the Sulu Archipelago like angry bees dislodged from their island nests.

We passed the blinking harbor lights of Zamboanga at midnight, and before midmorning we were half way into the Sulu Sea. I lounged in a shady deck chair on the starboard side, dreamily watching the far horizon for a pirate sail or some other romantic reminder of colonial days a hundred years ago, knowing I was on the correct side for a westbound, posh passenger—"portside going out and starboard going home"—to escape the hot equatorial sun. It was hot, and I tried to imagine the plight of steerage passengers on the *Hoi Kung* when the freighter called at coastal Chinese ports before Mao Tse-tung changed the Chinese life-style.

The Hong Kong license posted amidship below the bridge revealed a fascinating measure of passenger capacity based on race. Twenty-four white passengers could be carried in air-conditioned cabins if a doctor was aboard. The ship was permitted to sleep 900 Chinese in the six-foot-high steerage below the main deck and above the cargo holds. Their ticket provided only space on the steel deck. Water and daily rations of rice were dished out of huge rice cookers in a steerage galley below the mainmast deck. On longer trips carrying Muslim pilgrims to Jeddah, the ship was allowed to carry 1,200, sleeping many on the main deck in addition to steerage deck allotments immediately below. No passenger list by name was required on pilgrim trips, only the total number aboard. When pilgrims died at sea, their bodies were dumped into the ocean with little or no ceremony. The purser generally could account for every passenger by the time the ship arrived in Arabia because new births balanced out the deaths. It is difficult to believe this detached attitude toward life still exists in our times— an attitude which considers it good business to crowd 1,200 people sleeping on straw mats into the filth that must have accumulated on the long, fetid voyages. Norwegian ship owners' only accountability was to end up in port with the same number they started out with.

Sulu people once paid tribute to the Chinese emperor and in Chinese eyes the lands of the Sulu Sea are properly Chinese. The islands of the South China Sea and adjacent southeast lands were also considered part of China until 1840 when Britain, Japan, and France began to annex the tributary states and proclaim them colonial protectorates. Malaya was occupied by Britain in 1895, Indochina was seized by France in 1885, and Taiwan ceded to Japan under the treaty of Shimonoseki in 1895. During the nineteenth century China was forced to abandon the elaborately ritualistic tribute system. And under duress, when faced by superior European military forces, China signed treaties demarcating specific boundaries on the Asiatic continent that severed almost two-thirds of nominal Chinese territory from control of the Manchu Emperor.

Perhaps in part because of the fiercely independent Sarawak and Brunei sultanate, Manchu influence never extended to Borneo Island, and even British influence was felt only lightly when white Rajahs ruled paternally by invitation of the Sultan.

The *Hoi Kung* sailed past Brunei fifty miles from shore, waiting until dawn in the brown, muddy waters of the South China Sea off Sarawak before venturing upstream twenty miles to a jungle anchorage in the Rajang River.

Shifting mud banks make permanent wharf facilities impracticable. No village or construction scar mars the surrounding jungle of nipa palm and swamp mahogany. In places only dimly seen in morning fog that clings to the river banks, dipterocarp giants spread umbrella canopys over the forest plain, projecting leafy cut-outs along the lower edge of a gray sky where a single bright spot covers the rising sun. Tropical birds skim low over the river in the wake of rough-skinned crocodiles sliding smoothly from muddy lairs into the murky waters.

Houseboat dormitories for longshoremen and bargeloads of saw timber are secured alongside. The loading of lumber destined for the United States, once begun, continues night and day until the cargo holds are filled. Even the unused pilgrim steerage is stacked with lumber until the *Hoi Kung* settles in the water to the safe load line painted on its rusty hull.

One of the first tropical lands to be affected by commercial forestry operations was Borneo. It sits astride the equator and is divided between three countries—Malaysia, Brunei, and Indonesia. Sarawak on the west drainage and Sabah on Borneo's north coast constitute the Malaysian portion. The tiny British protectorate of Brunei (apparently protected mostly because of its oil) lies on the coast between Sarawak and Sabah. The remaining two-thirds of Borneo is Kalimantan, part of Indonesia.

Borneo boasts one of the richest floras in the world—at least 11,000 species of flowering plants are known. Eighty percent of Borneo is still covered by tropical forest, despite age-old shifting cultivation by native peoples and increasing logging since the turn of the century. The interior is still mostly virgin forest, undisturbed by man.

This primary forest is evergreen and tall. Seen from the air it gives the impression of a woolly blanket. The crowns of the trees form a continuous canopy of leaves, broken only by an occasional lone tree forcing its way through the forest cover, sometimes reaching 150 or even 200 feet in height. Under the canopy grow shade-loving plants, short and sparse in the perpetual twilight that barely penetrates the cover overhead. The forest floor is open, and wildlife and humans find it easy to move about. Monkeys and birds monopolize the canopy.

Along rivers and footpaths where sunlight reaches the ground more easily, a dense ground vegetation is found. These are woody climbers, palms, and bamboos. Many of them appear to have more than their fair share of thorns, like the rattan cane. High in the forks of trees are ferns, epiphytes, and orchids, while the trees themselves are often parasitized by climbing vines, figs, and other plants. Insect-eating nepenthes cling to exposed root systems and dry underbrush.

The Borneo primary forest contains a bewildering variety of trees. Rarely do large numbers of the same type of tree grow together. Because of this, timber is more expensive and difficult to exploit compared to temperate countries where almost pure stands of trees like fir and pine occur. Though called evergreens, the trees do lose their leaves; but they are so rapidly replaced, the forest never has the seasonal bare look seen outside equatorial regions of the world.

When the primary forest is logged, vegetation slowly recovers, and gradually a complete secondary forest naturally regenerates. But it is quite unlike the primary forest. The first ground cover after cutting is stiff grasses such as lallang, ferns, bushy shrubs and palms. As tree seedlings grow and reduce the amount of sunlight, lallang and other vegetation die off, but the resulting forest never opens into broad avenues of straight, tall trees. It is often very difficult to traverse, frequently thorny and close-growing. Without extensive planting of trees and crops of commercial value, in a hundred years the secondary forest will become a wasteland of little value to man or wildlife.

Large areas of Borneo are being logged in a reckless manner, with noncommercial timber being bulldozed or poison-girdled to allow regrowth of only presently-recognized commercial timber in naturally regenerated forests. Future generations may never benefit from the vast forest riches of Borneo. Unknown to us, the waste trees of today could be the most useful trees tomorrow—if they are saved.

Malaysia is the world's largest exporter of tropical hardwood logs and lumber, surpassing the Philippines and Indonesia. Most of the wood exported is known as Philippine mahogany, called *lauan* in the Philippines and *meranti* in Borneo and Indonesia. Floated down interior rivers to seaports at Samarinda in Kalimantan and to the Sulu Sea port of Sandakan and the Celebes port of Tawau, the peeled logs are guided into storage basins and hoisted aboard specially designed timber vessels for shipment to Japan.

The first shipment of timber from Sabah was made in 1885 to Australia when an agricultural concessionaire found it more profitable to sell the timber from his cleared land than to grow crops. This speculative practice still plagues government administrators who promote land resettlement programs. A profitable market at the close of the century was Hong Kong. Belian, an extremely hard and insect-resistant timber, enjoyed ready sale for railroad ties on the rapidly expanding mainline Chinese railroads. Since 1958 timber has brought in more foreign currency than rubber. In 1968 it accounted for more than fifty-five percent of Sabah exports, and timber production (Hoppus measure) reached about 163 million cubic feet compared with one million in 1910. Of this total, 160 million cubic feet were logs of which over seventy-five percent was shipped to Japan. Most of the saw timber goes to Australia.

The cost of shipping timber outside south and east Asia is high. Coupled with inefficient, expensive logging operations, including the use of elephants in past years, shipping costs have prevented East Malaysian timber from going in great quantities to Europe or the United States. In most cases the freight costs to Europe are greater than the actual value of the logs—twice as much to Europe as to Japan—accounting for domination of the Borneo timber industry by Japanese buyers. Because the Japanese are interested only in logs, several large sawmills have been idled in recent years. The government has attempted to enforce certain percentages of exports in milled lumber, but this has proved unworkable in practice. Little milled lumber is exported other than veneer planks.

The Sabah government also has failed in its efforts to encourage people in crowded communities to move out and clear the jungles and populate the countryside. Continuing attempts to create new farming communities are no nearer fruition now than when they were first initiated a dozen years ago. The plan has served only to benefit incumbent politicians and to assure them long tenure in office.

Under the plan, special licenses for natives were awarded to leading Sabah politicians. Tracts of timberland varying from twenty to 100 square miles were to be logged over a ten-year period, then replanted in oil palms, coconuts, or rubber. Ideally the program would have perpetuated income from the land and promoted continued tax receipts and employment, a desirable goal in any developing economy. In practice, the economic development schemes revealed the practical motives of aggressive politicians. Ordinarily unsophisticated natives immediately sold the value of standing timber to local Chinese contractors and indulged themselves in a city house, a new car, and maybe a trip to Singapore for radios and tape-recorders. Leading politicians who received licenses were expected to divide the opportunity for development among politically aspiring associates and party supporters. But in practice majority ownership in the companies, organized to develop cleared forest land was most often held by the original licensee with little distribution of equity among the party faithful. Some licensees have found it more comfortable to live abroad on their rather too-conspicuous income.

The Sabah government granted title to 88,000 acres of land. The eighty licensees were expected to plow timber profits back into land development by creating ten- to fifteen-acre farms to be settled and worked by the owner. Only about two or three farms ever came into existence after timber was logged. Of 88,000 acres, less than 6,000 were planted in the three Borneo money crops—rubber, coconut, and oil palms. The scheme obviously did not work and recent grants have been restricted to corporate concessionaires, both domestically organized and foreign. But every concession involves political loyalty and preferential treatment of individuals and companies deemed sufficiently loyal to the regime in power to merit receiving valuable timber rights.

To involve the general public in their timber bonanza and generate political loyalty toward the government in power, Sabah has developed a scheme whereby every citizen is given free a one-unit share of certain forest reserves under concession agreements. Substantial acreages have been transferred by the Sabah legislative council to the autonomous Sabah Foundation. This foundation was created by the council and is administered for life by the foundation President Tun Datu Haji Mustapha. He is also the Sabah Chief Minister, and he appointed the members of the council. It is a convenient method of preserving influence and income in perpetuity.

To obtain his share, a citizen simply applies with his identity card to the local foundation office and his ownership is registered. It is estimated that at the present rate of timber logging, the share this year may pay off at about $8.40. But by the 1980s, when most foreign logging concessions will expire, what has been derisively called by the U.S. Embassy in Kuala Lumpur as the "Great Ali Baba Scheme," should appreciatively enhance foundation dividends, not only to citizen shareholders but especially to the trustees. Sabah authorities plan to accomplish this by turning over all foreign concessions to the Sabah Foundation, which would accept bids from existing concessionaires wishing to continue to cut under local Sabah management.

Sabah's timber exports, up 1,000 percent in the last decade and increasing, supply the major part of government revenue. Timber royalties and taxes on timber operations pay more than half of the government's budget. They primed a development program that has transformed the old chartered British colony from a backward economic dependency to a booming independent state fully recovered from the economic ruins of 1945. The capital city, completely destroyed in World War II, has changed its name from colonial Jesselton to the indigenous Kota Kinabalu. A modern city and a prosperous state have been built out of potentially divisive elements, perhaps the best example, excluding Singapore, in Southeast Asia of postwar economic recovery. It is a shining example for the Federation of Malaysia, yet Sabah is a hotbed of rebellion. Tun Mustapha is in fear of his life and there have been several attempts at his assassination. The state is held together by repression of the Chinese and non-Muslim indigenous people combined with forced conversion to Islam. Chinese merchants are regularly shaken down for contributions to

Tun Mustapha and the Chief Minister has turned a fairly straight-forward, honest administration into possibly the most corrupt of the three Malaysian states. There is no tolerance of cultural diversity in Sabah.

Writing in the *University of Redlands Foreign Policy Research Journal,* University of California professor Ibrohim Clark comments on the necessity for close cooperation between science and technology if the people of the world are to fully benefit from self-proclaimed technological solutions to problems generated by our contemporary dependency on manufactured products utilizing limited natural resources.

"Advanced planning for the use of science and technology can preclude some of the hazards of unbridled, unplanned growth we have experienced in the west," says Clark. "Science and technology need not lead the peoples of Southeast Asia down the road of environmental abuse and destruction, machine domination, and weapons brinksmanship. . . . If we look for a balance between social and spiritual development on the one side and economic, scientific and technological development on the other, then the infusion of science and technology may accrue lasting benefits."

Clark writes that, "the tropical areas of Southeast Asia have been, and are, most vulnerable to haphazardly planned projects and area development and to outright exploitation of natural resources. The almost fanatical surge of public interest in the 'quality of environment' now being expressed in the United States should serve as a flashing red light to the peoples of Southeast Asia—a warning for careful planning that will include preservation of the purity and beauty of land, water, and air for many decades hence!"

All the world's tropical rain forests, with the exception of a few acres preserved in parks, could be destroyed in the next three decades, a loss that would inevitably have important consequences for life on earth, although the nature and magnitude of these consequences cannot be foreseen.

Writing in *Scientific American* magazine, Paul Richards concludes, "One effect that is certain, and probably already irreversible, is that man's impact on the tropical forest will permanently alter the course of plant and animal evolution. Biologists are generally agreed that much of the existing flora and fauna of the world, perhaps including man himself, originated in the humid Tropics. The rain forest has for millions of years served as a factory and storehouse of evolutionary diversity from which plants and animals able to adapt to more regorious environments have migrated to populate the subtropical, temperate and colder regions. This role the tropical forest can play no longer; the destruction of forests and other ecosystems has already cut the lines of communication and made these migrations impossible. Even if the present, very reduced areas of rain forest were to be conserved, they could hardly play the same role as the much more extensive forest did earlier. Man has diverted the process of evolution permanently."

The tropical forest of Borneo is a unique and rich community of plants and animals, including many of the most beautiful and useful forms of life. If we believe that all living things should be a source of wonder, enjoyment and instruction to man, we should be very concerned, for a vast realm of potential human experience may soon disappear before there is even a bare record of its existence.

The impending ecological disaster in Borneo threatened by continued land clearing, agricultural and urban expansion, oil and mineral extraction, and timber exploitation, presents a clear challenge to humankind. Borneo is also an island—like a spacecraft with limited resources. Its natural resources, related to land area, are comparable to the United States', yet the ecological lessons we have learned in recent years are not taught or practiced in Borneo. The corporations that have almost exhausted the natural wealth of America to satisfy insatiable appetites for high living, have quietly retired from the scene of carnage, without apology, to further impose their advanced technological skills on an unsuspecting developing nation.

For its lifetime, the island of Borneo has been protected from natural disaster by its providential location which is east of deadly typhoons originating in the South China Sea. Borneo is located beyond the wind, but directly in the path of technological disaster.

12

Taking Up the Corporate Burden

AMERICAN multinational corporations seem totally insensitive to the complex problems involved in extraction and exportation of oil and timber from developing countries. Their corporate decisions reveal a strange lack of concern over what could be eventually serious adverse consequences, politically, economically, and culturally. The corporations involved simply do not know what the long-range effect will be of timber logging and oil drilling on indigenous peoples.

Little is known of the complex ecological impact of logging tropical forests. In some areas where selective cutting and removal of commercial species has exposed interior jungle plants to the sunlight, smaller trees remaining in the cut-over areas do not grow into a new forest but are often smothered by the accelerated growth of vines and undesirable grasses competing for sunlight. Mechanical equipment churns the earth, forcing nutrients to the surface where they stimulate still more undesirable flora in a new forest that may have no resemblance whatsoever to the old. The precise climate and ecological mix that created the giant dipterocarp forests being cut today cannot be duplicated. And the demise of this forest will force the extinction of unique wildlife and possibly many valuable plants and trees still undiscovered and unknown. Loss of

151

the forest by environmental die-back following clear-cutting eliminates the tropical food and fiber supplies. And this, in turn, will force the abandonment of interior jungle villages and longhouse communities that have been the communal home of Borneo tribesmen for generations.

One need not look far to find examples of corporations that willingly sacrifice the future for present commercial gain. With the last large available tracts of private timber in the Pacific Northwest already acquired by competitors and with their own acreage being intensively clear-cut beyond its capability to regenerate within commercially acceptable recycling periods, Weyerhaeuser went multinational in 1961. It has major investments in British Columbia, South Africa and France. By 1966, according to *Pacific Basin Reports*, Weyerhaeuser had investments in seventeen countries. One-third of its foreign sales were to Asia, mostly Japan.

In that year Weyerhaeuser reported, "International markets provided the company with the opportunity to balance and select what products to market and when, to realize highest returns, minimize the effect of demand cycles and dispose of surplus raw materials." By 1970 international markets accounted for twenty-two percent of total sales. Profits zoomed. The company was helped considerably by its Kennedy Bay Timber subsidiary on Borneo which reportedly returned a profit of more than thirty percent on timber sales. Even with extraordinary expenses in starting up logging operations and high shipping costs, Weyerhaeuser profits far exceeded the ratio of payoff to investment that the corporation realized on home grounds in the Pacific Northwest.

Weyerhaeuser's senior Vice-President C. W. Bingham said: "The tropics in general . . . provide the next major region for forest development, both in hardwood and in softwood plantations. They will be a major source of incremental world wood supply in a few decades, and we are positioning ourselves now to participate in that development."

Weyerhaeuser has exclusive cutting rights on over two million acres in Southeast Asia. When the firm acquired a majority interest in International Timber Corporation, holding 1.5 million acres of tropical hardwood forest lands in Kalimantan, Borneo, it became the world's largest timber concessionaire. It controls over eleven million acres in Canada, Malaysia, the Philippines, and the United States. Weyerhaeuser already owned the world's largest private fee simple timber acreage—5.7 million acres in the southeast United States and Pacific Northwest—yet its Borneo holdings alone exceed an estimated ten billion board feet, roughly fifteen percent of Weyerhaeuser's domestic timber inventory.

The company thinks of itself as working both ends of the investment street, and says, "When we talk about Europe and Japan, perhaps we are thinking about paper machines and the converting end of the business; and when we talk about the less developed countries, we are thinking about logging, saw mills, perhaps pulp mills. . . . In one case we go after the market and in the other we go after the raw materials. Since we are interested in being a worldwide company in the forest industry, we are going to go after both of them."

Weyerhaeuser signed a twenty-one-year agreement with the Indonesian Department of the Army for the Borneo concession. It squeezed out another American firm by means of a $3½ million advance payment to the Indonesian military which needed cash after overthrowing the leftist Sukarno regime. The concession agreement would eventually pay $65 million to the Indonesian Army. It could bring $300 million in gross revenues to Weyerhaeuser in return for capital investments of only about $30 million during a ten-year development period.

Weyerhaeuser Corporation sees no problem here, only benefits to everyone concerned. It plans to shift from its present selective cutting to clear-cutting the tropical jungle as soon as its request to the Indonesian Directorate General of Forestry is approved. Granting of this request will permit

the logging of everything in the forest. By current regula-
tion, Weyerhaeuser can cut no trees less than fifty centi-
meters (twenty inches) in diameter. By clear-cutting and
clearing the jungle completely of indigenous growth, Weyerhaeuser hopes to replace the slow-growing tropical hardwood trees with a fast-growing softwood forest of even-aged
trees to be grown and harvested like corn, plantation style.
Nurseries have already been established to grow pine and
fir seedlings that may not only replace the tropical jungles
of Borneo, but may also make unnecessary the maintenance of expensive, sustained-yield forests and mills in the
Pacific Northwest.

While Weyerhaeuser is establishing a nursery for new
trees and gathering extensive field-trial data to prove the
desirability of clear-cutting and expanded forest harvest
levels, the social impact on the people involved receives
little objective study. There is considerable research in the
"growth of desirable forest species, both long-fibered and
short-fibered," but no research at all has been made into
the consequences of destroying the homes of a semi-no-
madic forest people living a life-style unchallenged for
centuries who must now move their families to a downstream company town.

Weyerhaeuser is aware of the issues involved, but corporate officials have taken the position that American-style
economic development in Borneo can only be beneficial.

Weyerhaeuser Vice-President Bingham agrees that
"Any major investment brings major changes in the economic arena, and those changes tend to translate gradually
into social change . . . and to that same extent, I am sure we
do disrupt primitive societies. I do *not* think we cheapen
their cultural values, unless one believes that hunger and
early death are cultural values, or inherent human rights.
. . . Nor, do I think we corrupt cultural values. After all,
compared to many forms of consumer gadgetry, a two-by-
four has little corrupting potential. It is possible, however,
that by making visible alternative life-styles, major investments can plant the seed of political or social upheaval.

This is a risk the governments are obviously willing to take; the alternatives of starvation, further economic decline, expanding population and epidemic diseases and despair are considered even more dangerous."

But Bingham's view is backward. These obviously undesirable alternatives to foreign investment are not the result of maintaining the status quo. They are, on the contrary, the long-range adverse consequences of foreign economic exploitation. Bingham is not describing the self-sufficient life-style of natives living in the Borneo interior; he is describing the plight of millions of Indonesians on the verge of starvation in Java and Sumatra, the suffering humanity born of colonial exploitation in a past era. After years of postwar oil royalties and foreign aid cash, these people still are facing depleted resources and continued substandard living conditions in a country that has never developed a self-sufficient economy because of deliberate decisions by multinational foreign concessionaires.

Bingham says, "We are, in the process, (of) changing the local society to some extent, by providing technological skills, medical and educational services, permanent housing, and a cash economy." Weyerhaeuser is planning to build a sawmill and chip plant at their Samarinda concession, now shipping only logs. But this is only tokenism to satisfy concession agreements. What Indonesia needs, Weyerhaeuser cannot supply. The corporation intends to recover its $30 million investment and send home millions more in profits before the twenty-year concession agreement expires. Weyerhaeuser must deliver profits to its stockholders in the United States. It cannot create a timber industry that will return *all* the timber wealth to Indonesia.

Bingham's explanation sounds morally just. He says, "We *are* utilizing a renewable resource, owned and controlled by Indonesia, *on Indonesian terms* to bring about economic development in one of the remoter areas of the world, selling the products domestically and in neighboring economies." The emphasis is Bingham's, but he could be a Dutch colonial officer of fifty years ago explaining the "white man's burden" as he shipped away the islands' wealth in exchange for cheap foreign wages. Economic development and economic self-sufficiency are not the same. By any measure, Southeast Asian people should have first refusal on the overseas sale of their limited natural resources until they have developed the capability and technological skill to utilize these resources to enhance their own standard of living.

Cheap wages and royalty payments may provide the money to rent a small shack and build schools for a tiny minority, but any substantial beneficial effect on the overall economy by foreign concessionaires and corporations is illusory. The lesson of Central and South America is available for those who would question the fact. According to some informed estimates, Indonesia is the fifth richest country in the world in terms of its natural resources—minerals, oil, and timber. But its per capita income, averaged among its 110 million population, is only $82 a year. As a result of worldwide inflation, which also affects Indonesia, even that low income is decreasing.

Bingham expresses his belief that Weyerhaeuser's economic involvement in Indonesia, Malaysia and the Philippines is a positive, beneficial act. "I do not believe," he says, "that disease, poverty, and illiteracy are inalienable human rights, or that primitive societies should be *forced* to remain primitive, simply to provide museum pieces for their more affluent world neighbors' entertainment. I feel no apologies are necessary for offering the members of those societies a choice."

But the nagging question remains—are the people of Borneo really offered a choice? Or like the islanders of Micronesia, are they being sold a mixed bag of very costly merchandise with the true price tag carefully turned upside down? Americans are learning very belatedly, and somewhat sadly, that industrial progress, even if attainable, is extremely costly in terms of the quality of life. Two cars in every garage is a worthy achievement perhaps, but if the price includes subway muggings, racial ghettos, tenement slums, and breakdown of family relationships with juvenile delinquency and permanent unemployment, then the price may be judged a little expensive.

Almost 200 timber concessions have been granted in Kalimantan by the Indonesian government, but the nine granted to American companies probably account for seventy-five percent of the aggregate concessions. Numerous small concessions, some only a few hundred acres in size, have been signed over to Malaysian Chinese companies while larger acreages are logged on a small scale by Japanese, Filipino, French, and Korean companies. Most of the huge Japanese consortiums that once dominated the logging operations have bogged down in internal bickerings and sold off their concession rights. They seem content now to engage exclusively in the purchase of logs at the dock for overseas sale.

Exclusive concessions have been granted to Japanese rayon manufacturers to log the extensive mangrove forests along Sarawak's west coast. Mangrove wood fiber is of uniform quality, necessary for the manufacture of rayon, and recent investigations have proved the feasibility of mechanical harvesting of swamp mangrove as wood chips for bulk shipment to Japan.

The ecological ramifications of mangrove logging may be enormous. Yet concession agreements reportedly were granted without investigating the adverse effects of mechanized mangrove logging on bird and fish habitats, swamp wildlife breeding, or the physical protection that mangrove forests provide tidal lands in monsoon weather. The entire river delta system of western Borneo—established over many hundreds of years—may be radically altered by extensive mangrove logging. There are no studies underway to determine the ability of slow growing mangrove swamp forests to naturally regenerate after they have been clear-cut by a swamp mower.

Cultural and biological impact surveys have not been done to determine the eventual adverse or salutary effects of timber harvesting in tropical conditions. Little thought has been given to environmental consequences, not even to the extent of serious forestry studies to determine the number of years required to regenerate a tropical hardwood forest. The soils of Borneo, once cleared of timber, generally leach out and erode under the heavy equatorial rainfall. Unless the government initiates expensive operations promptly, planting food crops or reforesting with fast-growing conifers, the land may be lost forever. Most timber companies use heavy tracked vehicles in their operation. The thin top soil, once chewed up by these machines, washes away in the first spring rains, rendering the land useless for planting crops.

Concession agreements do not require reforestation. It has been assumed—without benefit of research and in the face of considerable contrary evidence—that the forest will naturally regenerate itself. Optimistic Sabah forestry officials had been saying 100 years would be sufficient for recovery; but political pressure for increased royalty and tax payments in recent years has resulted in a doubling of allowable cut with no announced change in biological studies to support the increased yield.

Sabah arbitrarily changed the cutting cycle from 100 years to forty years (one-fortieth of the forest to be cut every year instead of one one-hundredth). No one really knows how long it will take for a tropical hardwood forest to reach maturity under present climatic and soil conditions. The forest has never before been cut over thousands of acres. The previous residents, native slash-and-burn agriculturists, hardly left a scar. Trees harvested in the next generation may require many more years to mature than the giants being logged today. The current crop is about sixty years old, an age considered to be the absolute minimum for commercially valuable dipterocarp. It is clear that sustained-yield programs claimed by United States concessionaires are simply not being followed. It is apparent by any calculation that the timber wealth of Southeast Asia will be totally consumed overseas—probably within the lifetime of present concession agreements. Within twenty years the proverbial golden goose will have been plucked.

Even where underdeveloped countries have asked for professional advice in preparing concession contracts for exploitation of raw materials, the American consultants have considered only direct economic functions. They fail to question possible harmful effects to the ecosystems of the forest or the native peoples. The immediate benefits that might accrue from halting shifting agricultural practices and putting tribesmen to work in sawmills was greeted unquestioningly as a permanent benefit. No effort was made to measure long-range pernicious effects of racial and social disruptions that could ultimately effect the basic political stability of the government and require correction through costly social services and perhaps military action.

Where economic consultants did not possess anthropological and ecological expertise, the issues were ignored. Mitigating conditions were never considered by possibly more knowledgeable concessionaires who, after all, were negotiating for the lowest possible costs. The extensive experience gained in logging Pacific Northwest timber has never been put to work in the long-range best interests of the native peoples of Borneo.

Environmental impact statements would be most desirable. An "ecological consequence evaluation" should be mandatory. Sometimes even the most elementary economic evaluation has been missing. Mistakes that are a financial loss to the company lay waste to the tropical landscape with far longer lasting adverse consequences than the investors dollar loss.

Sarawak government agencies do not require a feasibility study of any kind before granting concession rights. The General Timber Company, a United States affiliate, began logging in Maputi Valley in northern Sarawak, but according to the Sarawak Forestry Department, "after bringing in vast quantities of equipment and beginning work on a long access road near Lawas, they gave up the license without even reaching the area . . . a severe lesson on the need for an elementary feasibility study before commitment."

The Sharikat Long Hegan Timber Company was licensed to log on the Batang Tinjar but, "soon surrendered the area because it was too poorly stocked and the terrain was too difficult." The Forestry Department report added, "Again an elementary study would have saved everyone a great deal of expense and time. Such considerations seem to carry no weight with applicants for timber licenses, who will cheerfully apply for the most difficult, inaccessible and poor areas. . . ."

Vast areas of tropical forest are now being cut. The results are unnecessary degradation of the ecosystem, irreplaceable loss of wildlife unique to the Borneo jungles, elimination of entire ethnic communities, and disruption of village cultures. An entire society and language, once isolated in the relatively unexplored jungle interior, could be lost without knowledge that it ever existed. It is too early to determine the eventual cost of such a loss, but it would seem that we must at some future date suffer from the consequences. The cost of our own unbridled development can be measured in terms of pollution, racism, urbanization, and steady depreciation of quality of life and values. The very least that a socially responsive corporation would do would be to raise the question of anthropological and ecological consequences that may result from the taking of timber, minerals, and oil. Is it clearly too much to ask that they consider the ethics of taking all this for the social enrichment and economic well-being of Americans at the expense of Southeast Asian peoples?

Today, the endangered orangutan can travel the entire length of Borneo—800 miles from Mount Kinabalu in the north to Indonesian Banjarmasin in the south. This unbroken forest canopy, which has thrived for a million years, is a necessity for the orangutans' survival. Yet American technology has the capability of breaching this forest canopy within the year and seems intent on doing so in order to satisfy corporate dividends and Japan's and their insatiable demands for timber to fuel its resource-consuming economy. When the orangutans' home is destroyed, the people's jungle heritage will also disappear. In the path of timber-logging crews, the native inhabitants are forced from shifting agriculture to the instant slums of shifting lumber camps.

Throughout Borneo it is official government policy to encourage native hill tribes, Iban and Punan, to settle down in permanent homes and cultivate crops. Most refuse and continue their nomadic ways, hunting in the forest and practicing slash-and-burn, shifting cultivation in the jungle interior. Local missionaries practicing religious salvation since before the days of British and Dutch colonial rule have never succeeded in converting interior headhunters to Christian life-styles. The Punan and Iban rigidly maintain their animist ways, passed down through unnumbered generations. Perhaps lumber barons will have more success than missionaries.

The orangutan traveling the length of Borneo swing through mostly primary forest jungle along the mountain ridges, but also across extensive secondary forest created by indigenous slash-and-burn agriculturalists in the valleys along river systems. In doing so, they cross village territories of many different ethnic groups, for perhaps 75 percent of all Borneo land is under native tenure. Most remote village territories are still occupied by descendants of the original inhabitants, although more and more secondary forest lands and these unique village territories are being abandoned as native people migrate to city slums and cash employment.

The Iban people have been offered exceeding favorable opportunities to leave their mountain homes and participate in elaborate land development schemes that will end their shifting agriculture life style and break up traditional longhouse dwellings common to the interior tribesmen. They are forced under various pressures into separate family dwellings and cash crop farms.

They are promised financial assistance to plant commercial crops such as rubber, wet rice, pepper, and oil palm, under the mistaken assumption that their old methods of slash-and-burn agriculture destroyed the jungle ecosystem. In fact, slash-and-burn farmers live in a fairly good relationship to their natural environment, and this is why, after many hundreds of years, the orangutan can still travel the length of Borneo until it runs into the clearcutting timber operations of Weyerhaeuser.

For some reason that escapes logical understanding, Indonesian, British, Dutch, and even Malaysian authorities consider the longhouse to be a den of iniquity—a communal living quarters of some kind. During my stay in an Iban longhouse on the Malaysian-Indonesia border, I was impressed by how similar the single village structure is to a modern townhouse, horizontal condominium. The longhouse is nothing more or less than an apartment building, but by bringing the various domestic families close together it provides a very convenient labor pool which is exchanged between the families, depending on the job to be done. With the breakup of the longhouse the degree of intravillage and family cooperation immediately disintegrates. It is obvious that any attempt to modernize a group of people must depend upon a certain degree of communal trust and communal economic exchange. In actual practice the shift from subsistence farming to cash labor results in total destruction of traditional cultural interchange, is acually detrimental to indigenous economic development, and results in a people who are poorer, both culturally and economically—no longer independent and self-sufficient.

Native hill tribes are endangered in still another way, and not just the Iban and Punan. There are various hunting and gathering groups in Borneo much like the Tasaday people on Mindanao, who in some ways could be described in the same generality as "Indians" are in America. They are without doubt a fragile people, and most susceptible to changes much less traumatic than those initiated by the timber companies.

To force the relocation of native people to company towns with all the delightful amenities that company towns have to offer, could be considered almost criminal in another context. Even for the Indonesian government to grant timber concessions to foreign corporations in village territory is open to question. To move the inhabitants, for no matter what reason, is tearing people away from their homeland. Home is where their ancestors are buried. It is the land they know as intimately as the back of their hand. Each individual stream, each individual grove of fruit trees, each individual hill, each depression in the valley, and each rock is named and brought into the native world view by ritual and legend.

Families dwelling in their village territories constantly plant valuable fruit trees and harvest from others whose ownership has been traced back for maybe seven generations. When an individual clears the jungle he establishes permanent ownership rights over that tract of jungle, rights that are inherited by all his descendants who then have the right to return to that area of jungle for generation after generation to slash-and-burn and recultivate.

Weyerhaeuser has announced its intention to remove all jungle tribesmen living in longhouse communities from their concession lands, and relocate them in new company towns, to make them accessible for hire to cut trees and saw timber. The company will build schools, churches, and hospitals. It will teach the people a new culture, preach a new religion, and save them from new diseases and nervous breakdowns resulting from their forced dislocation. A way of life, virtually unknown to the developed world, and possibly of great value if we should deign to consider its merits, will be destroyed by twisted intentions of Weyerhaeuser. No one knows how long it will take the forest to grow back to its present majesty—to regenerate into a second growth suitable for renewed logging by a future generation. Some have ventured to forecast—not before the wildlife and

birds and flora of Borneo are extinct, and not before a
native civilization is lost forever—will a second growth be
suitable for logging.

Timber operations on such a large scale now under
way in Kilimantan will obviously disturb the ecosystem,
further threaten endangered species in Borneo such as the
rhinoceros, the leafeating monkey, and orangutan, and
dislocate indigenous populations before anthropologists
have had the opportunity to record their cultures. Thus,
the potential loss to world knowledge is immense. This is
particularly the case with regard to the native herbs and
medicines of indigenous peoples. Anthropologist George
Appell, editor of the *Borneo Research Bulletin*, particularly
deplores loss of the local pharmacopoeia. He writes: "It
should be of major concern to both the research community and those involved in this timber development, as
much of the pharmacopoeia of modern medicine has had
its origin in the traditional medical knowledge of various
indigenous peoples around the world."

Appell further states that "the contamination and loss
of indigenous cultivars of the Kalimantan peoples also
poses a major concern to the research community. The
development of modern disease resistant, higher-yielding
crops depends on crossbreeding with just such indigenous
cultivars which are the result of thousands of years of
selection within the interior of Borneo. But there has not
yet been to my knowledge any major effect to preserve in
genetic banks the unique germ plasm of these indigenous
cultivars of Borneo. Thus the impending loss of indigenous
cultivars as the area shifts to a timber economy poses a
major threat to the development of tropical agriculture. It
can only be hoped that the research community in conjunction with those corporations that plan these timber
developments can rise to this challenge and initiate research and investigations of these endangered areas before
the loss is irretrievable."

With the introduction of commercial varieties of cultivated plants and palms through government agricultural

resettlement schemes scattered over Sarawak and Sabah, the genetic resources of native-grown crops are threatened with destruction. The indigenous plants cultivated by native peoples over many generations contain unique genetic material as the result of thousands of years of careful selection by native farmers searching for strains adapted to the humid, tropical climate and insect life of Borneo. These primitive plants contain valuable genetic materials for crossbreeding to develop higher yielding, more disease resistant varieties. The situation in Borneo has reached a crucial point where, if action is not taken in the near future, the loss to the agricultural sciences, plant breeders, and all of humanity will be inestimable.

The U.S. Department of Agriculture is currently screening gymnosperms from Borneo to determine whether they contain any anticancer constituents. To date the screening program for anticancer activity has included over 400 samples from all over the world. Sixty species in sixteen genera have shown sufficient anticancer activity to justify chemical fractionation to isolate and identify active constituents. Further screening of gymnosperms is urgent as the probability that other valuable compounds will be detected is high, and destruction of plant ecosystems in association with ancient forests is proceeding with possible loss of many important conifers and cycads in Borneo.

Indigenous living patterns are in danger of disappearing in the near future before an inventory identifying those cultures, languages and societies is obtained. It is discouraging to note that while we attempt to save the ocean whale from extinction, literally dozens of native cultures and languages may die out in Borneo without our knowing they existed.

The practice of government authorities to grant development concessions without adequate study of their economic practicality has resulted in abandoned strip mines, forest clearings, and deteriorating roads in many parts of the country. The General Timber Company, an American corporation, was granted an exclusive concession to log swamp hardwood. It expended several million dollars on access roads and other preparations before discovering that commercially suitable trees were so widely scattered in the swamp that economic logging was impossible. Their abandoned roads and bulldozer tracks through the forest testify to the folly of inadequate investigation by the company and to the apparent lack of concern about unnecessary forest damage by government agencies. After this experience the Sarawak Forest Department's only comment was that American companies seem to be fascinated by "blank places on the map," and habitually request concessions without accurately knowing what is on the ground. The government grants these concessions knowing full well that bulldozed tracks in the poor soil of Sarawak will not recover natural growth in the space of a human lifetime.

William Meijer, a former Sabah Forest official and botanist, put in writing his concern for current logging practices. In a report on the need for a study of Sabah forest botany before continued logging operations make this impossible, he said: "Pollen analysis . . . has taught us already that a great many elements of our lowland dipterocarp flora (the common tree in Borneo) have been here for at least thirty to sixty million years. Man himself has a history of less than a million years, but this clever and most destructive creature on the globe is now causing the disappearance of one of the richest floras in the world, at such a great speed that there is hardly time to save primary lowland forests for posterity.

"Modern man," Meijer continues, "is proud to conquer the planets around the sun, but in his greedy exploitation, his search for wealth, comfort and food, he is destroying earth-bound living communities of plants and animals which are unique. How many foresters and timber logging people, how very few agriculturalists and administrative officers, how very few simple kampong (village) people are aware of this? In the Smithsonian Institute in Washington (D.C.) I saw an exhibition of birds that have been exterminated by man during the last 1,000 years. This is the most sad part of all exhibits in this great museum. Shall we also have in our Herbarium (in Sandakan, Sabah) after 50-100 years, specimens of trees which by that time have been exterminated? If the present trends of exploitation continue, this will certainly be the case." Mr. Meijer is no longer with the Sabah Forest Department.

The consequences of severe damage to interior watersheds by unwise logging practices seems to be of little concern as governments clamor to collect timber royalties. Erosion scars and bare hills from traditional shifting agriculture practices are characteristic of mountains in both Sarawak and Sabah. Also characteristic are floods in sea coast towns along rivers that drain shifting agricultural lands. In tropical cloudbursts, the winding river that flows past Kota Belud has been known to rise seven feet overnight, with severe damage to rice paddies and village centers. It is only conjecture what will happen when the forests are devastated in the mountains above Sandakan where average rainfall probably exceeds 200 inches a year.

Wholesale killing of noncommercial trees with poison is routine forest silviculture in Sabah. After selective logging operations are completed, forestry department employees kill all useless trees still standing by cutting a frill in the bark completely around the trunk and inserting sodium arsenate into the channel. The tree dies within a year. The forest is then closed to allow natural regeneration of only useful trees, wasteful competition having been removed.

There is the beginning of awareness by Georgia-Pacific which, in apparent concern for its corporate image, has funded research on the ecological impact of Borneo logging. But the company still seems unaware of adverse cultural impact and the long-range economic consequences of extraction and export of natural resources overseas. Georgia-Pacific hopes its new payrolls in Kalimantan will "reduce the native need for hunting endangered species," and while agreed that "nature requires an ecological balance for good timber growing," are nevertheless proceeding ahead with logging operations before adequate information on local wildlife is accumulated.

Indeed, exactly the opposite of Georgia-Pacific's hopes may occur. As soon as improved channels of communication are established between the Borneo jungle interior and the outside world by logging operations, the low paid laborers will undoubtedly supplement their meager income through illegal trafficking in endangered animal species, thus increasing the threat of their extinction. The steady demand from overseas zoos and Chinese pharmacies will be more easily satisfied. It is a dilemma that will be difficult to reconcile for, understandably, the governments involved will be slow to inaugurate effective conservation practices that would inhibit royalties from their highest revenue producers.

Dr. L. S. B. Leakey of the Centre for Prehistory and Paleontology in Africa, said that American investigations have been "much too superficial" and advises that it will take a long-term effort like that of Jane Goodall with chimpanzees and Dian Fossey with gorillas to produce substantial findings. The president of Weyerhaeuser has written to Harold Coolidge of the International Union for the Conservation of Nature on the same subject, but it is not known just how far these American companies intend to go in seriously facing up to the major environmental problems they are creating in Borneo, other than to declare "we do not take our responsibilities lightly." Meanwhile logging continues.

Oil has been pumped from the rich fields of Borneo for sixty-two years since Shell discovered the black gold bubbling out of the beach sands of coastal Sarawak in 1911. Timber has been exported since the days of the ruling white rajahs and the British Chartered Countries of North Borneo. Only the names have changed in the intervening years, although Royal Dutch Shell seems to go on forever. Even with substantially increased oil and gas production, and timber exports—almost all to Japan—the plight of the common man in Southeast Asia remains little changed, even where he has succumbed to industrial blandishments and joined the cash economy.

Exportation of oil, rubber, timber, and spices, has done little more in the past hundred years than make the peoples of Borneo completely dependent on a money economy that barely provides a small minority a reasonable standard of living. It is quite evident that the exportation of unknown billions of dollars worth of oil and timber from Borneo has not returned an equivalent in value to the Borneo people. The few low-paying jobs that have resulted hardly compensate for the bare subsistence level of living suffered by many who abandon the farm for a city job. They eventually find themselves employed in a job-scarce economy manipulated by overseas multinational corporations under a government that forbids strikes.

Royalties and taxes on oil and timber represent only a fraction of their actual value. If Weyerhaeuser were truly concerned about the long-range best interests of native peoples, perhaps a wise decision would be to divert all timber production into the domestic economy at a rate that can be absorbed and utilized by the people themselves.

In this way, not only would tens of millions of native peoples enjoy modern housing for the first time, but they could also build their own self-sufficient industry, independent of foreign markets and unaffected by inflationary costs and artificial scarcities induced to maintain high prices in a profit-motivated economy. They would also save their forest and the great potential wealth it could eventually provide for all mankind when we learn how to properly manage a tropical jungle and the wealth it contains.

13

A Most Unsordid Act

IN MERLE MILLER'S intriguing biography of Harry S Truman, *Plain Speaking,* he tells how the Point 4 relief program for a war-torn world came about. "We always went ahead," Truman said, "and did what had to be done, and the Marshall Plan saved Europe, and that's something I'm glad I had some part in helping accomplish."

Winston Churchill praised Truman's Marshall Plan as "the most unsordid act in history." Historian Arnold Toynbee wrote, "This will be remembered as the signal achievement of our age."

Truman's Point 4 plan, which he insisted be called the Marshall Plan, was first described in a speech by General George Marshall at Harvard University in the summer of 1947. He spoke knowingly of Europe's plight following the successful conclusion of the war. "She must have substantial additional help," he said, "or face economic, social, and political deterioration of a very grave character. The remedy lies in breaking the vicious circle and restoring the confidence of the European people in the economic future of their own countries and of Europe as a whole. . . . It is logical that the United States should do whatever it is able to assist in the return of normal economic health in the world, without which there can be no political stability or secured peace. Our policy is directed not against any country or doctrine but against hunger, poverty, desperation, and chaos. Its purpose should be the revival of a working economy in the world so as to permit the emergence of political and social conditions in which free institutions can exist."

General Marshall's call was, indeed, a humanitarian act of great consequence, and the extravagant dole saved many lives, not only from malnutrition and disease, but also from riots and politically motivated revolt. Marshall's speech has been described by some historians as the first speech in the Cold War. Radical economists may identify the Marshall Plan as the expected concomitant of embryonic American economic imperialism. It would require only ITT and Exxon to eventually prove its success.

Wartime United States policy, as revealed by Daniel Ellsberg when he exposed the *Pentagon Papers*, confirms that, "At each key decisional point at which the President [Franklin Roosevelt] could have influenced the course of events toward trusteeship—in relations with the U.S., in casting the United Nations Charter; in instructions to allied commanders—he declined to do so; hence, despite his lip service to trusteeship and anticolonialism, FDR, in fact, assigned to Indochina a status correlative to Burma, Malaya, Singapore, and Indonesia: free territory to be reconquered and returned to its former owners. Nonintervention by the U.S. on behalf of the Vietnamese was tantamount to acceptance of the French return."

United States State and War Departments expected French troops to participate in the liberation of Indochina, but Roosevelt disagreed. The ambivalent American policy hardly supported Vietnamese independence under Ho Chi Minh's leadership, a fact that eventually led to the Vietminh being squeezed out by French authorities who forced a compromised Ho Chi Minh to agree on the return of French troops to Indochina.

This was no accident of international diplomatic one-upmanship. Rather it was the inevitable result of United States corporate leadership in determining the economic and foreign policy of America—a corporate policy presumed to be common with national interests—that formulated the United States' role in Southeast Asia. The foreign policy of corporate directors was translated by the State Department during the Roosevelt and Truman administrations into the Marshall Plan and military assistance agreements. The plan would never have been implemented by Henry Wallace; it was partly for this reason he was dumped as vice-president when it became evident that Roosevelt would not survive a fourth term and therefore would not oversee the postwar economic objectives of the free world. It was imperative in terms of a viable United States economy and a high standard of living for the American worker that industrial growth continue without pause. European and Asiatic markets had to be kept open to unlimited investment and trade, as well as friendly sources of oil and minerals for American manufacturers.

United States postwar policy called for restoration of the economic viability of war-torn countries and aid in regaining control of their colonial territories lost during the course of World War II. It was particularly important that ravaged economies be stabilized to prevent unrest, the possibility of a socialist revolution, and the establishment of independent nations unfriendly to United States corporate operations and free trade. It was in this context that we supported French colonialism in Vietnam without changing the plantation system, and then attempted to convince Chiang Kai-Shek and the Chinese Communists to work together without abolishing war lord feudalism.

United States aid to France, both in Europe and Indochina, was carried out to suppress revolutionary nationalistic Vietminh forces and to restore Indochina as a colony with proper respect for property rights of French businessmen. The loss of Indochina in itself would not have been serious in the context of all Asiatic investments. But the possible effect of forcing Japan into a business accommodation with a communist Vietnam or China would. In the

United States view, both threaten the stability and security of Europe and curtail American trade and investment in Asia. American aid for the French as they attempted to crush Vietnamese revolutionaries was only a small part of a much broader policy to retain all of Asia as a free world marketplace.

In corporate business philosophy, the loss of even one market is a serious loss, and the example set by successful indigenous nationalism in any one country might easily inspire its neighbor to proceed down the same jungle path of self-determination. The American revolution is still an example to follow in the jungles of Asia, but today America is the colonizer. The infamous "domino theory," which resulted in United States military intervention in Indochina followed by ruinous escalation of the war in 1964, is a U.S. State Department distortion. The native political movements that the "domino theory" was devised to explain were set up to overthrow oppressive colonial governments and to replace them with nationalist governments.

The United States directive for the procedure to follow in Southeast Asia was contained in a 1952 National Security Council memorandum: "The loss of any of the countries of Southeast Asia to communist control as a consequence of overt or covert Chinese Communist aggression would have critical psychological, political and economic consequences. In the absence of effective and timely counteraction, the loss of any single country would probably lead to relatively swift submission to or an alignment with communism by the remaining countries of this group." This policy and its effects are being felt throughout Southeast Asia today.

Two years ago I camped with a Malaysian Army patrol at the 12,000-foot level of Mt. Kinabulu, highest mountain in Southeast Asia. It was an unexpected pleasure, especially when I discovered most of the soldiers spoke English. They invited my companion and me to share a marvelous spiced chicken curry on rice dinner cooked by a Pakistani squad leader, cooled with the cold waters of a nearby mountain spring, and topped with a fifth of Scotch whiskey contributed by the Chinese commanding officer.

By enjoying their companionship I was violating a rule volunteered by anthropology researchers back in Kuching, warning me never to travel with Malaysian Army troops because they were prime targets of communist terrorists operating in the Borneo jungles. I was told that antigovernment guerrilla units never killed tourists (a comforting thought), but I should stay apart from soldiers in the field and avoid riding in official-looking vehicles. Their advice was valid. Just a week before I had passed a jungle search-and-destroy operation using British ferret armored cars near the Indonesian-Malaysian border at the southern extremity of Sarawak, only to be informed in the next village that the federal troops I met had been ambushed on the same road shortly after I passed by. According to newspapers the next day, six were killed and several injured.

Our Malaysian soldiers on Kinabulu were pleased to enjoy the comparative quiet of a mountain top, almost as if they were on a vacation from the strife below. Maybe they were, but their concern for Vietnam was real. They did not question the validity of the "domino theory" and did not like the idea of picking up the fighting chore when American troops left Vietnam. Members of an elite volunteer army, the highest paid soldiers in Asia, these men were loyal servants of the Federation of Malaysian States. They were convinced Vietnam would collapse without American military aid, and that with it would fall the carefully contrived federation created by the British to inherit the "white man's burden" in Southeast Asia.

On the other hand, socialist-oriented revolutionaries in the Philippines, who effectively fought Japanese forces throughout the occupation, now feel it was a serious mistake to accept American economic aid and allow American forces to reestablish colonial rule in the Philippines. It was a decision that allowed the United States to eventually proclaim independence under circumstances that perpetu-

ated feudal agricultural practices and resulted in abandonment of demands for land reform.

U.S. influence in the Philippines is pervasive. The
Quirino-Foster Agreement provided for the infiltration of
American Advisers throughout the Philippines governmental structure. The late Marv Gray, one-time CIA advisor to
President Raymond Magsaysay, explained to me personally
how he tricked revolutionaries into deadly ambushes and
how he advised the president and internal police of a sup-
posedly independent nation. It has never been possible for
any Philippine president, obstensibly elected by the Filipino people, to be nominated without the assent of Manila-
based American corporations.

In the 1969 Philippine presidential elections, Marcos
reportedly passed out 800 million pesos to bribe the voters.
Even food for disaster refugees was diverted for Marcos's
benefit. I remember waiting at a small military airport in
Batangas province to watch the unloading of needed relief
supplies shipped from Hawaii. When they finally arrived
a day late, accompanied by Marcos's beautiful wife Imelda,
all the boxes had been freshly stenciled with Marcos's
name.

Philip Shabecoff wrote a revealing article for *The New
York Times,* describing the political frustration and poverty that breed violence. He wrote, "There are many who
felt the same way as Mrs. Diagn Sena, the fried banana
seller of Barrio Magsaysay. 'I hate violence,' she said. A
revolution would be a terrible thing for the Philippines.
But I have ten children to feed. Prices keep going up but
not the money my husband brings home. If it takes a revolution to feed my children, then I say, let's have it!"

On my last visit to Manila I called on a businessman
living in the expatriate compound near Makati. His residence and the residences of his friends were situated on a
typical American tree-shaded street—except this street was
surrounded by barbwire-topped ten-foot-high concrete
walls with manned machine guns at each corner. At the
entrance I was searched and the armed guard called ahead

before I was permitted to enter. It was a strange kind of place to call home.

The consequences of free market economic policies followed in the United States- and Japanese-dominated countries of Southeast Asia is visible even in the most affluent cities. In Hong Kong, the very profitable trade and manufacturing economy fails to hide the sense of frustration and defeatism born of malnutrition and overcrowding. The floating slums of Aberdeen in Hong Kong harbor condemn thousands of Chinese to starvation levels of subsistence and economic stagnation within sight of wealthy tourists from Japan and America dining in opulent style aboard floating restaurants.

Singapore exists on the verge of racial violence and socialist revolt temporarily deferred by accelerating economic growth feeding new money into the city-state in the manner of a New Deal Works Progress Administration (WPA) project. So long as new capital is fed the workers of Singapore they will resist the supplications of socialism. While the people benefit from free trade and corporate enterprise, business rights are protected and applauded. But when capitalism fails to provide, it is given the blame for all evil, real or otherwise.

A study by the UN's Economic Commission on Asia and the Far East concludes that, "the conjunction of rapid population growth . . . with widespread unemployment and family poverty has led to a further precipitous decline in urban living conditions which in Asian cities have reached a stage of depression and disorder that practically defies description."

Between 1952 and 1968, almost twice as much capital went from the Philippines to the United States in the form of profits, interests, and dividends as went into the Philippines in aid or investment. One factor behind this is that eight of the top ten, and twenty-seven of the top fifty, non-financial corporations in the Philippines are American-owned. Important economic decisions concerning priorities and direction for the Philippine national economy are made by American corporations.

American investments in Philippine sugar plantations and mills—most of them constructed in Hawaii and shipped as prefabricated factories to an island nation deliberately deprived of its own industrial capacity—are enhanced by archaic share-cropping labor practices. The plantations maximize profits by requiring the cane cutter's family to live on one meal of rice a day while his small children work in the sugar fields so the family can survive. Sugar is a primary export commodity, most of it going to the high-paying United States market.

The much praised "green revolution" of miracle rice initiated by Rockefeller's fertilizer industry only intensified the sharecroppers' predicament because the landlords siphoned off all the benefits of the improved agricultural economy. Despite tremendous improvements in the production of rice, the staple of the agricultural sector, the farmers remain poor and rice-growing communities suffer from widespread poverty.

Farmers cannot afford to buy the rice they grow since Philippine rice is ordinarily exported to Singapore and Japan where higher prices prevail. Some 600,000 tons of rice are now imported despite the fact that the Philippines has some of the most fertile land in Asia. On my visits to rice-growing country near Legaspi in Southern Luzon, it was a rude shock to discover California rice identified as part of an American aid program for sale in small country stores completely surrounded by flourishing rice paddies in full cultivation. It is cheaper to buy U.S. rice.

Under such profitable arrangements for selling to the highest bidder while benefiting from favorable import tariffs and continuing foreign aid programs to permit depressed wages, it is easy to understand the reluctance of American business to tolerate any form of nationalism that would primarily benefit the farmer and the worker.

Malaya and Borneo were returned to their British

colonial administrators after the war to insure that independence did not mean economic freedom. Britain did not relinquish its rule until indigenous administrators were educated to carry on colonial traditions and economic philosophy and oppose any tinkering with the status quo. It was expected that there would not be any interruption of smoothly functioning bureaucratic machinery that directly benefited corrupt native ruling classes who obviously knew a good thing when they learned how to run it. It was only a different colored skin that carried the politicians' wealth to the bank.

The *Nation's Business* magazine stated precisely the nation's business philosophy in February 1968: "Certainly creation of trade and commerce has not been the motive of warfare, but laying down arms and the rebuilding and reappraisals that come with peace inevitably seed the fields for business opportunities. Now another such opportunity is near—a time when business will tap the rich expanses of Southeast Asia. The best thinkers on the subject in business and government agree that magnificent business opportunities await in Vietnam, Thailand, Laos, Indonesia, Malaysia and Singapore." The Marshall Plan had paid off. It was time to divide the loot.

Joined by their Japanese compatriots, now partners in foreign investment in Southeast Asia, the United States exploited the postwar economic benefits of victory at sea, from the advantageous position of a favored nation status assumed when Britain and France defaulted on their international obligations. The United States became the leader of the capitalistic world.

On the Malay peninsula across the China Sea, military requirements were mixed with economic development in the so-called Jengka Triangle scheme in a dense jungle area 120 miles northeast of Kuala Lumpur. It is close to where antigovernment guerrilla units operate in the jungle on both sides of the Thai-Malaysian border, much to the discomfort of government authorities. In order to deprive the antigovernment units of forest cover and a jungle shelter, the United States-controlled World Bank has financed an agriculture project to clear 93,000 acres of virgin jungle now occupied by elephants, tigers, wild oxen, and guerrillas. The program has been described as a "kind of peaceful defoliation campaign." Population control will also be facilitated by establishing twenty-three settlements and three towns as part of the 270 miles of main roads and more than 1,000 miles of graded service roads. It is expected the project will pay for itself from export of palm oil, rubber, and the timber harvested to clear the land. The guerrillas and wildlife are expected to find another jungle sanctuary.

In the words of the World Bank, the Jengka is an effort, "to provide new job opportunities for the countries' unemployed and underemployed." Malaysia's official unemployment rate is over twenty percent in the volatile fifteen to twenty-four age group, but many country people and nomadic tribesmen in a country that is mostly jungle are not counted at all. Malaysian officials and their foreign friends consider the task of finding work for the unemployed a matter of political survival. Most of the captured guerrillas from both Borneo and Malaysia seem to be less politically indoctrinated in leftist ideology than they are frustrated and angry at a creaking economy offering no future and few decent-paying jobs.

Each agricultural laborer resettled in the project will be immediately in $5,300 debt to the Malaysian Federal Land Development Authority to pay for the cost of his house, clearing the land, and planting oil palm and rubber trees. He is expected to repay his debt by selling his oil and rubber at open market prices. According to *Pacific Basin Reports*, while the Jengka Triangle Project has "been lauded for its bold approaches, it has come under criticism for taking advantage of the desperate job situation to promote slave labor farms on which settlers must labor for years at low wages to work off their debt." The Malaysian government says if things go wrong, the debt will be cancelled.

The World Bank financed the technical assistance

grant that paid the foreign consultants who prepared the master plan and loaned necessary money to clear, plant, and settle the first stage. The technical end of the project is masterminded by a New York engineering contractor. A San Francisco forestry consultant firm prepared feasibility studies. The Security Pacific National Bank of Los Angeles is lending part of the capital, and three Canadian firms in Vancouver have management contracts to set up and run the timber operation, to direct logging and land clearing and to process the lumber. All the palm oil, rubber, and forestry projects will be exported.

The World Bank and United States foreign aid programs have been designed by the State Department precisely to develop the underdevelopment of the country. Beginning with the Marshall Plan after World War II, the United States has given the Philippines over $1 billion in economic aid, almost all being spent on rural development projects. Yet according to then Senator Wayne Morse, in 1966, ". . . The economy of the Philippines is in worse shape than it has ever been since the end of the war. It is described as sagging, stagnant, and in the rural areas, as giving rise to discontent and providing a seedbed for a new resurgence of communism." It has also provided the excuse for Marcos to abolish constitutional government and still further impoverish the very people the good-intentioned President Truman intended to save.

Accepting the advice of the World Bank, considering its source and leadership, could prove to be very gratifying to Third World government officials looking for attractive retirement bonuses. But if long-term benefits for the country and its citizens are of interest, one must look to other alternatives than those urged by World Bank executives. The comparison might be made between the industrial progress of India and China, two countries of similar geography and natural resources, which for decades allowed their hydroelectric, indigenous crude oil, and refined product production to languish while international petroleum companies and the Soviet Union marketed imported products in their respective countries.

Since 1952 and after the Great Leap in 1958, the growth of energy production in China has increased spectacularly, until today China exports oil and coal to Japan. India, on the other hand, still struggles along with insufficient energy for her own industry and with minimal development and exploration of indigenous resources including coal and hydroelectric power. China's commercial energy production is now substantially greater than India's on a per capita basis, and over a comparable period the growth of energy production and consumption in China has been double that of India, which is totally dependent on overseas grants and aid.

While China has been aggressively mechanizing coal production in newly discovered fields, utilizing its own internal financing, steps to expand shale oil production, develop hydroelectric power, and build an oil industry have proceeded undiminished. By using her manpower and skills on a timetable related to satisfying petroleum needs only in proportion to available supply and capability, China built an industry independent of foreign imports. National planners promoted exploration of new oil fields and construction of expanded modern refinery facilities.

The World Bank, by discouraging government resource exploration in undeveloped countries, permits multinational corporations to limit development of resources. Thus the corporations can maintain scarcity and, by manipulating supply and demand, command higher prices and profits. The consequence of privately financed resource development is to limit native oil resource exploration and development to the detriment of the host country's industrial expansion. Where commercial demand is met by monopolistic refineries whose product is primarily intended for overseas export, growth of the local economy is stifled by high fuel cost. Island economy becomes dependent on the whim of foreign-based corporations whose social accountability is considerably subordinate to profits.

The Malaysian state of Sabah has long considered Royal Dutch Shell's lack of interest in exploring for new oil in the South China Sea to be an indication of a primary desire on Shell's part to restrict supply. Tun Mustaph, Prime Minister of Sabah, says he does not understand why there should be no oil north of Brunei in Sabah territorial waters, when wells along the Sarawak shore have been steadily producing since they were discovered by Shell in 1911. Brunei's young prime minister also became disgusted with Shell last year, breaking Shell's sixty-year exclusive monopoly on Borneo's west coast. Drilling rights were granted to the American Clark Brunei Oil Company, a subsidiary of Sunray Borneo Oil of Oklahoma. It is expected that with a little competition there will be fewer dry wells drilled. Whether by choice or agreement most companies with concessions in Southeast Asia have seemed content to drill spasmodically or not at all since 1960. Their geologists believe the South China Sea holds tremendous oil and natural gas reserves, but in the ten years after 1950, of the 250 onshore holes, the drilling companies reported them all dry or noncommercial.

It has been rumored that many of these wells did strike oil but were temporarily capped to keep the location of oil strikes confidential, reduce the payments for concessions, or to stabilize the market—an oil company euphemism to promote scarcity and maintain higher prices. There is evidence, albeit elusive and deductive, that overseas oil exploration companies in Southeast Asia have until recently not been overly enthusiastic about discovery of new oil and gas fields. It is not an easy assertion to prove. A low exploration and wildcatting budget decided upon at corporate headquarters in New York would have just the desired effect without any memos to shred. With rising oil prices brought on by artificially induced scarcity, the oil producing nations may well cooperate with oil concessionaires in praising the unpronounceable acronym OGMB—Oil in the Ground is worth more than Money in the Bank.

According to a Gulf Oil advertisement, "The fuel industry has been warning . . . for the past decade, that if government regulations continued to keep oil and natural gas prices at levels too low to generate capital needed to fund more oil and gas, our nation would eventually run short."

If rumors floating around the South China Seas are any indication, however, it is not a shortage that has worried oil concessionaires for the past ten years, but a surplus of oil that would seriously depress prices in world markets. In 1948, when I designed the water and sewerage systems for Standard Oil of California's employee housing near their Sumatra oil fields in Indonesia, there was a competitive race on to get the oil out in a postwar scramble for markets. Within fifteen years the oil industry had caught up with demand and in the early 1970s production surpluses decreased oil company profit margins as independents competed in a buyers' market.

In 1968 Standard Oil Company of California prepared a memorandum for executive planning within the company that warned of further problems. "The overhang of surplus crude avails is very large," noted C. T. Carlton, manager of Standard's economics department. He projected a "large potential surplus" through 1973 and predicted even more troublesome excesses in 1978 when Alaskan oil was expected to enter the international market. In addition new Indonesian and Australian production would be "extending and magnifying surplus supply problems."

The Standard Oil economists proposed slashing total 1969 output in Egypt, Nigeria, Libya, Latin America and Indonesia in addition to closing down low-producing oil fields in the United States and elsewhere, such as Shell's old Miri fields in Borneo. The economists assumed that all major international companies would act in concert in their own best interests to hold production down rather than allow prices to drop. As it turns out, the performance of the various independent companies was remarkable. The drop in production in 1969 was within one percent of production cutbacks recommended in Standard's 1968 memo. In later years the performance continued.

In the early 1960s excess capacity was roughly six million barrels a day, a reserve sufficient for oil concessionaires to negotiate in a hard-nosed way with demanding foreign governments. Exxon vice-president George Piercy said, "We had alternatives, and when you have alternatives you have strength." By 1969 the surplus was four million barrels a day. By 1973 it was zero as demand rose to equal production.

In Iraq, according to a secret United States government document quoted in the *Wall Street Journal,* a venture of five Western firms known as Iraq Petroleum Company actually drilled wells to the wrong depths and used bulldozers to cover up others, all in the hopes of hoodwinking the Baghdad government. Partners in this scheme were Exxon, Mobil, Shell, British Petroleum (BP), and Compagnie Francaise des Petroles. In Iran another consortium (Standard Oil of California, Exxon, Gulf, Texaco, Mobil, Shell, and BP) shifted its reporting year from the Christian to the Iranian Moslem calendar, to give the appearance of rising output while actually restricting production.

In the Far East region, covering an area from Pakistan to Japan to New Zealand, there were 160 wells drilled in 1969 resulting in only four reported discoveries. In 1970, 190 wells were drilled in the widespread concessions with only five reporting significant discoveries. It is a record that may not only indicate the risk involved in drilling for oil, but the skill of some companies in hiding their successes.

Refineries constructed with private overseas funds and operated to produce petroleum for export are not able to satisfy undeveloped countries' domestic needs at a price their citizens can afford. Refineries designed to generate maximum profits for the owners, turn out products for sale in developed countries where the demand—and therefore the price—is greatest. Under prevailing circumstances this generally means gasoline, a fuel used by only a minority of Southeast Asian citizens. The product they may need most to enhance their standard of living and industrial growth at a price they can afford may be diesel oil or kerosene. But these products constitute only a small portion of refinery production. (It is interesting to note that modern jet fuel—kerosene—a major product of developed country refineries for use by airlines flying out of major metropolitan cities, is also an important need of underdeveloped countries. They use it for home lighting and to encourage literacy in rural villages lacking electrification.) In some Southeast Asian countries it would be prudent to forego refining of gasoline and concentrate on residual oils and kerosene, but the appropriate refinery must be built originally to meet these requirements. It would be unrealistic to presume that American-built oil refineries would devote their productive capacity to meet the needs of underdeveloped countries, instead of selling highly profitable gasoline to Japan.

In light of pleas by American oil companies that increased prices at the gas pump and higher profits are necessary to finance expansion of overseas exploration and refining capacity, it is worthy to relate arguments of the Philippines subsidiary of Mobil Oil, holder of a petroleum marketing monopoly in United States-administered Micronesia. According to the *Philippines Herald,* Mobil admitted at government hearings that it had been raising its capital requirements principally from Manilan sources mostly through the facilities of Bancom Development Corporation, a local money market coordinating concern for Bankers Trust of New York.

In a detailed paper submitted to the Philippines Constitutional Convention by delegate Alejandro Lichauco, formerly president of the Philippine Petroleum Association (he was arrested and imprisoned on the night martial law was declared), Lichauco related that, "In 1968 Bancom announced that in view of the tight money and foreign exchange situation it was advising its clients to borrow as much as possible. Bancom also revealed that American overseas companies, such as those operating in the Philippines, had been instructed by the United States government to raise as much as possible of their capital from the host economies where they are operating."

Raising capital requirements from domestic savings and credit institutions unfairly competes with local businessmen for scarce credit resources and depresses available money for domestic construction and development of natural resources by indigenous investors. The general development of the host country is thereby inhibited while foreign corporations finance their profit taking—all of which is remitted to American coffers—by paying a little off the top in local interest. In a 1969 speech to the Manila Rotary, Marcos himself alluded critically to this practice, revealing that profit taking by foreign companies amounts to as much as $120-150 million a year. At one time when Ford Motor Company was capitalized at 100,000 pesos, its local bank borrowing exceeded thirty million pesos.

Bleeding the host economy is also accomplished by overpricing imports as well as by self-serving royalties, refinery service fees, and manufacturers' representative fees, all of which are paid out overseas to their parent countries. Philippine subsidiary oil refiners are on record as importing crude oil from their mother companies at costs consistently higher—sometimes twenty percent higher—than world market prices. Thus a substantial subsidy is being paid by unwitting Philippine consumers. The resulting higher local transportation and manufacturing costs deter establishment of local small businesses and, again, favor foreign consumer imports.

Hearings before the Philippine government oil industry commission revealed that the Exxon refinery actually paid interest to its mother company for temporary credits extended to the local refinery in connection with importing crude oil from oil fields owned by Standard Oil Company of New Jersey. Incredibly, the interest payments for selling to itself amounted to twelve percent if paid beyond an agreed forty-five-day credit period.

In testimony before the U.S. Senate Interior and Insular Affairs Committee in 1973, the counsel for the Federal Energy Office said its auditors found significant pricing violations by domestic oil refiners that may have occurred in transfer pricing—the price foreign affiliates of American oil companies charge parent companies.

Apparently, some foreign affiliates have been overcharging their parent companies, and these charges are being passed on to consumers in the form of higher gasoline prices. The U.S. Energy Office issued "remedial orders challenging approximately $40 million in cost passthroughs at the refinery level," according to counsel William Walker.

In comments made at a United Nations seminar, Emilio Collado, vice-president of Exxon, said, "Manipulation of transfer prices is usually neither feasible nor desirable," and, "in general, multinational corporations follow normal commercial practices in their interaffiliate transactions, and prices charged realistically reflect the market values of the goods or services transferred."

Collado's explanation sounds reasonable but it does not account for the fact that the Philippine Mobil Oil affiliate arbitrarily raised the price of its refined product in Guam, the Philippines, and Micronesia while their prices for crude oil in Indonesia remained unchanged. There was no attempt made to maintain low fuel prices in Southeast Asia, an area of the world where fuel requirements can be completely satisfied from Indonesian and Malaysian sources. After all, it is a closed circuit in Asia—the same companies own the wells, the tankers, the refineries, and the gas stations. The only change was a substantial price increase on the Japan market outside of Southeast Asia due to Arabian price increases on Japanese oil imports and steadily increasing Japanese demands for petroleum products.

It is difficult to understand how American oil concerns could entertain such a complete lack of social responsibility in their quest for overseas profits. It may be that an international "Code of Ethics" describing principles of acceptable behavior overseas would contribute to better behavior by multinational corporations. It would serve to discourage corporations from the kind of activities which generate ill will for multinational corporations as a group, and condemn certain undesirable forms of behavior—such as speculative foreign exchange operations, distortions in international transfer prices, and attempts to circumvent either host government policies or realistic royalty and tax payments.

Others have a different vision. Dow Chemical Company Chairman Carl Gerstacker wants his company to own an island in international waters where Dow can operate "beholden to no nation or society," as he puts it.

Gerstacker said this would allow Dow to operate in many different nations without being thought of as an American company, and would prevent the United States from forcing subsidiaries of multinational corporations to conform to American interests. They would apparently be outside the law.

It is not altogether clear whether socialism or capitalism would better enable the people of Southeast Asia to enjoy an improved standard of living, for a pragmatic test of socialism has never been allowed. It is quite obvious, however, that capitalism as practiced by independent Asian countries with considerable foreign investment continues the disgraceful system that subjects the majority population to a lifetime of poverty while elevating a small ruling class to absolute power and luxury. The benefits of abundant natural resources are not fully shared by the people who own the resources by right of national citizenship. The People's Republic of China is an all-too-obvious example of what can happen when an appropriately motivated leader points out the facts.

In the years after World War II, the United States could have safely supported reasonable nationalistic objectives, especially when they were motivated by unsophisticated peoples with little or no desire for Marxist goals, only an undisputable need for food, clothing, housing, and a few

acres to call their own. The Vietnamese peasants might
have been satisfied by simple agrarian reform, if United
States foreign policy had supported abolishment of archaic
feudal labor systems and confiscation of French rubber
plantations.

The modern history of China, beginning with the
establishment of the Republic of China in 1910 at a time
when most of Europe was still hobbled by the vestments of
royalty, might have had a distinctly different outcome if
European and American business interests had not insisted
on foreign concessions and investment opportunities—if
instead they had aided the Chinese people in creating a
workable democracy without the hated warlords and feudal land system. Almost as an afterthought, the old slogan,
"if you can't lick 'em, join 'em," was dusted off by Nixon
and Kissinger when it was realized that neither the French
nor the Americans would in the long run be able to guarantee a "free economy" in Indochina. The opportunistic
rush to bail themselves out of the Vietnam quagmire resulted in unseemly abandonment of old political friends in
Taiwan and Japan as the United States made up to Communist China with hardly an embarrassed blush. The
amicable liaison between Chinese Communist leaders and
American capitalists is reminiscent of the "friendship"
papers signed by Nazi Germany and Russia at the beginning of World War II, when it seemed prudent on the part
of both political and economic adversaries to postpone inevitable military conflict.

Former Undersecretary of State Eugene Rostow sees
no real détente in contemporary world politics, especially
the kind practiced by Nixon, asserting that China turned
to the United States for help because the Soviet Union has
fifty divisions in Siberia. "It takes two to détente," said
Rostow in a speech at an Anglo-American Press Association luncheon in Paris, "I see no sign we are doing much
more than rearranging deck chairs on the Titanic."

Meeting in Algiers, the Executive Commission of the
Nonaligned Countries recommended that "the interna-

tional community must urgently proceed to a radical transformation of the structure of economic relations which have been based up to now on inequality, domination and exploitation."

Calling for a complete overhaul of the world's economic system to benefit developing countries, the Commission said the developed nations ". . . must establish a new economic order founded on equality and the mutual interest of the partners, fully taking into account the existing disparity between the level of development of the industrialized countries and the Third World . . . with a view to bettering the terms of exchange which have never stopped deteriorating."

Industrial development in Southeast Asian countries does not return full benefits to the citizens involved, because emphasis and priority have been accorded export-oriented industries. The trend to manufacture for export is seen even in the case of industries which originally began manufacturing to satisfy domestic needs, but then shifted to more profitable overseas markets.

The Malaysian government in Kuala Lumpur speaks of a "somewhat limited domestic market of eleven million people," while to the concerned visitor it is obvious that the majority of working Malaysians do not enjoy the high standard of living their bountiful natural resources could supply. Instead of the people moving into better housing and sharing more technological amenities, they export increasing quantities of manufactured products, including textiles, wood, metal, and chemical products—all representing products that are needed domestically but are too expensive for the local market. The working people cannot afford to buy the products they manufacture. Instead, consumers in the United States and Japan buy inexpensive manufactured products made by the Southeast Asians toiling all too often at barely subsistence wages and under government regulations that forbid or inhibit unionization and strikes. Even where some tin, oil, and minerals are not exported but are converted locally into manufactured products, the Southeast Asian remains at the very bottom of the economic ladder and is cheated, sometimes by his own government, from receiving full benefit from the nation's natural wealth. It seems reasonable that a nation's own people should be the first to enjoy the standard of living their technology and natural resources can provide, and only then should surplus products and raw materials be shipped abroad, and those, perhaps, at a premium price.

A majority of Southeast Asians live in substandard housing, subsist on diets barely exceeding malnutrition levels, are ill-clothed, and utilize few technological advancements particularly in communications and transportation. At the same time their governments are encouraged by American and Japanese businessmen to establish detrimental export industries. Instead of making their countries self-sufficient in the minimum necessities for a quality lifestyle, their governments entice American businessmen with what the Malaysian Industrial Development Authority describes as an, "abundance of inexpensive and productive labor . . . and rich resources . . . that with the marketing expertise of foreign investors can result in mutually profitable arrangements." Labor that is "inexpensive and productive" is cheap and hardworking, and it is indeed unfortunate that these assets could not be directed exclusively toward their own well-being. Instead, Malay peninsula manufacturers reported a thirty percent increase in exports for 1972. This may explain in part why the strength of Malay guerrilla revolutionary forces also increased in the same year.

It might be reasonable to assume that if American foreign aid cash and Robert McNamara's World Bank loans had been used only for development of local industry for local consumption, the countries of Southeast Asia might be economically independent today, utilizing their vast oil, timber, and mineral resources to sustain a standard of living equivalent to ours—if that sort of future were their desire. By any measure, it would have been considerably less expensive to send industrial expertise and manufacturing facilities to Vietnam, rather than to send American troops to forceably prevent the expropriation of French assets and land by the Viet Cong.

Neither can Southeast Asians afford to buy their own oil. The marketing network created and controlled by American, Japanese, and European concessionaires, has allowed the highest prices paid in the world market to determine the price of oil in Southeast Asia. The people of the oil-producing countries are not even benefiting from a company discount. Some of the governments are sharing higher royalties, but these seldom filter down to benefit the man on the street.

The Bangkok suburbs boast of three American and Japanese owned refineries surrounded by eight oil concessions owned by a Who's Who of the American oil industry —Gulf, Conoco, Exxon, Amoco, Union, Marathon, and Tenneco. But the price of gasoline and residual oil in Bangkok is just as high as anywhere else. As a result, not only has local industry suffered, but prices of fresh fish in Bangkok soared far above regular levels because Thai fishermen operating in the Gulf of Siam went on strike, "until the Government helps us by reducing the price of oil."

Deputy president of the Fisheries Association, Damrong Phianpak, said he did not want to call the fishermen's action "a strike or a protest; but just a joint effort to produce positive help from the government." Almost 1,000 fishing boats were idle. Bangkok's municipal market, normally offering an abundance of fresh fish, was at one time almost bare of seafood. The small amount available sold at unprecedented prices, according to local accounts.

The cost of extracting and refining oil in Southeast Asia has not increased—only the selling price in Japanese export markets. No reasonable explanation can be offered to the average wage earner in Malaysia and Thailand who lives under the injustice of an economic system manipulated at the whim of foreign corporations whose only responsibility is to stockholders ten thousand miles away.

While the Thai fishermen in Bangkok were resisting

government entreaties to go back and fish, in far off Vienna petroleum ministers of the twelve-nation Organization of Petroleum Exporting Countries proposed a $3 billion fund to help poor nations buy fuel. The World Bank and International Monetary Fund, along with Iran, also announced plans to make $1 billion of Iranian oil revenues available as loans to developing countries to pay their energy bills.

To those Asians unacquainted with the complexities of capitalism and a free economy, the proposals were seen as only another method of keeping developing countries undeveloped and dependent. As the petroleum ministers met and as the Thai fishermen struck, the more militant Southeast Asians tuned by choice to Vientiane radio, which was reporting on Cambodian Prince Sihanouk's visit to the liberated zone in Laos. The Pathet Lao and the Cambodian Front for National Union (FUNK) reported they were for the first time "United in an expression of support for the struggle of the Thai people." Some day the initials "FUNK" may become just as familiar to Americans as "VC."

14

Dividing the China Seas

THE UNITED STATES is by far the largest oil consumer of any nation on earth, consuming more oil and gas than the Soviet Union, Japan, Great Britain and West Germany combined—six times as much per man, woman and child as the world average. Per capita consumption in the United States averages three gallons of oil and 300 cubic feet of natural gas every day.

Crude oil refined into petroleum products, along with natural gas, provides over three-quarters of all the United States energy. It is used to heat and cool homes and offices, to run trains, trucks, cars, and aircraft, to turn the wheels of industry, and to generate forty percent of the electricity. America's industrial civilization has flourished to a large extent on abundant, low-cost energy, most of it supplied from crude oil and natural gas wells within the continental United States. But domestic production is not enough, and American oil companies search the world for crude petroleum.

The historical lessons learned as a consequence of the original division of Asia and the insistence on foreign concessions in China 150 years ago, have been disregarded in the scramble for oil on the Asiatic continental shelf. The major powers are doing what is expected of them, again dividing up Asiatic resources for profit and higher living

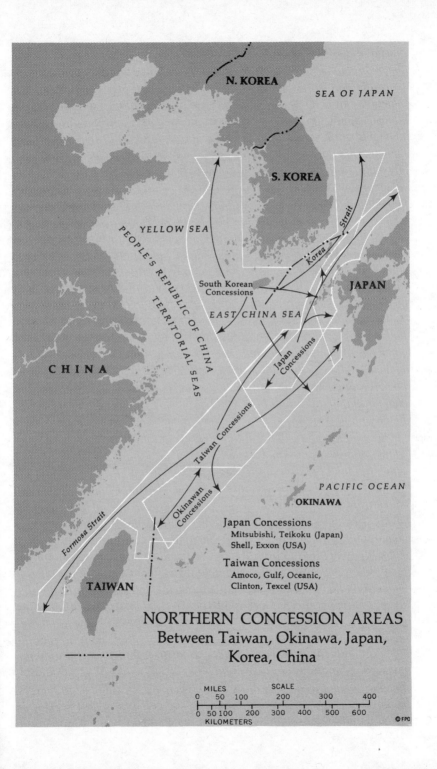

NORTHERN CONCESSION AREAS
Between Taiwan, Okinawa, Japan,
Korea, China

Japan Concessions
Mitsubishi, Teikoku (Japan)
Shell, Exxon (USA)

Taiwan Concessions
Amoco, Gulf, Oceanic,
Clinton, Texcel (USA)

back home. This time, instead of Great Britain, France, Holland, and Portugal, it is the United States—joined by Japan, out for a second try at exploitation—that is, dividing Asian resources.

The oil concession map of the Asiatic continental shelf and the South China Sea resembles the proposal of a speculative Arizona land developer dividing his desert acreage for sale to the highest bidder. This is exactly what the Asian nations have done with untapped undersea oil resources. Without benefit of international law, by tact agreement with each other and overseas buyers, the so-called international waters from Indonesia to Korea have been extensively subdivided by the United States and Japan. An occasional share is tossed to Italy, France, or Britain, almost as an afterthought. The rest of the world has been cut out of what has been described by some oil geologists as potentially the richest oil reserve on the earth, surpassing even the proven reserves in the Middle East and the extensive oil fields in China and Soviet Siberia. It is potentially so rich that in a very few years the vast fields could be competitive with Arabian wells, forcing a major world realignment of political forces.

American concessions, of course, have not gone without challenge. The Viet Cong have informed the United States they do not recognize the validity of oil concessions granted by South Vietnam to Mobil, Shell, Marathon, Sun Oil, Amerada Hess, Industrial Gas and Oil, and Conzinc Riotino Australia, which have already completed seismic exploration off the coast of South Vietnam. Even nominal occupation of islands located in the future undersea oil fields are being challenged by China. Last year China removed an American meteorologist and South Vietnamese troops from the Paracel Islands south of Hainan to reclaim the tiny islands as territory of the People's Republic of China.

This may well have been a warning to Japan which signed an agreement for joint development of oil in a large area lying between the tip of Korea and Japan's southern island of Kyushu. China has protested the agreement as an infringement on her sovereignty and warned that Japan and South Korea "must bear full responsibility for all the consequences" of their action.

China has restated its claim to all the Asiatic continental shelf, saying, "The Chinese government holds that, according to the principle that the continental shelf is the natural extension of the continent, it stands to reason that the question of how to divide the continental shelf in the East China Sea should be decided by China and the other countries concerned through consultations. But now the Japanese government and the South Korean authorities have marked off a so-called Japan-South Korea Joint Development Zone on the continental shelf in the East China Sea behind China's back.

"This act is an infringement on China's sovereignty," stated a spokesman for the China Ministry of Foreign Affairs, "which the Chinese government absolutely cannot accept. If the Japanese government and the South Korean authorities arbitrarily carry out development activities in this area, they must bear full responsibility for all the consequences arising therefrom."

China's claim is reinforced by historical acceptance of "tribute states" and territories that were under some form of Chinese control or influence prior to the British-instigated Opium War in 1840 when boundaries were forceably changed by European colonial powers and concession treaties were imposed upon a weak China.

South Vietnam has long claimed the South China Sea Islands, basing their claim on occupation by France in colonial days before World War II, and subsequently by Japan after the war, but the Hsisha Islands along with their neighbors in the South China Sea were officially taken back by the Chinese government during postwar territorial settlements. The Philippines government claims the Nansha Islands (which United States maps call the "Spratlys" and

which the Philippines have named, "Kalayaan" or Free-
domland), based upon their discovery and occupation by a
Filipino fisherman and adventurer in 1947.

But China claims these islands, too. On August 15,
1951, Foreign Minister Chou En-Lai pointed out in a statement on the United States-British peace treaty with Japan
that, "just like the entire Nansha Islands, Chungsha Islands
and Tungsha Islands, Hsisha Islands and Nanwei Island
have always been China's territory." Chou's comments
would seem to cover the Paracel Islands and all the other
islands in the South China Sea and is apparently the basis
for recent assertions by Chinese spokesmen "that the People's Republic of China has indisputable sovereignty over
these islands and the sea areas around them."

The more enforceable claims by China, and also those
most clearly defensible on the basis of recent historical
events, are the waters south of Hainan and the waters and
islands around Taiwan that were ceded to Japan under
duress by the Treaty of Shimonoseki in 1895 and in 1947
claimed by Chiang Kai-shek as a "province of China." The
Ryukyu Islands and Okinawa in the East China Sea were
occupied by Japan in 1910. But Chinese suzerainty over the
East China Sea and the many small islands extending
northward to the Japanese homeland has never been re-
laxed. Taiwan has staked out a concession area covering
the entire area and granting portions to Gulf Oil, Amoco
(Standard Oil of Indiana), Oceanic, Clinton Oil and Texfel,
an act that has not gone unnoticed by China. Japan has
granted concession rights to three Okinawan oil development companies in the Senkaku Islands immediately north
of Taiwan and completely within the area claimed by both
Taiwan and the People's Republic of China.

South Korea has designated concessions along its east
and west coasts extending southward to include the continental shelf northwest of Okinawa in the same area also
marked for concessions by Taiwan and Japan. Gulf Oil's
seismic research ship exploring in the Korean concession
area in the Yellow Sea has been asked to leave by the Peo-

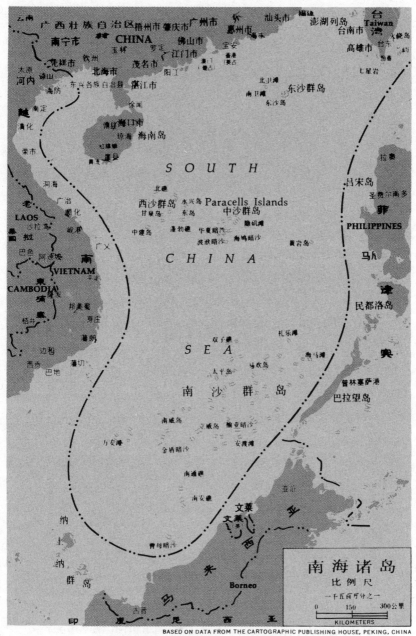

TERRITORIAL SEAS CLAIMED BY
THE PEOPLE'S REPUBLIC OF CHINA

ple's Republic of China, although their offshore operations on the west coast of Japan in the Sea of Japan have gone unchallenged. The U.S. State Department has informed operators of research ships in continental-shelf waters, "You are on your own."

Claims by every country to continental-shelf mineral and oil resources follow unilateral rights the United States has already assumed for itself regarding the continental shelf in the Gulf of Mexico and offshore Southern California. Congress now has under consideration legislation calling for designation of a 200-mile limit off New England to include rich fishing banks and oil reserves on the Atlantic continental shelf. Already the Maine lobster for 200 miles out is considered by law American property, not to be taken by foreign fishermen. It requires only an additional word to declare the oil within 200 miles also exclusive United States property. But the international implications would be quite different, for 200 miles is beyond the width of the continental shelf along the entire coast of China, and the United States apparently does not wish to restrict itself to recognition of everyone's 200 miles and 200 meters as defined by U.N. resolution. Their action in Micronesia supports this contradictory viewpoint.

In the Gulf of Siam, Standard Oil of Indiana (Amoco), Continental Oil (Conoco), Union Oil, and Gulf Oil operate on concessions granted by Thailand that overlap in a "no man's sea" of conflicting concession tracts also claimed by Cambodia and South Vietnam. These concessions, in turn, overlap into areas of the South China Sea claimed by Malaysia and Indonesia. Shell is pumping oil in an area claimed by China. Since Exxon has purchased concession rights from both South Vietnam and Malaysia, it is possible they may experience less problems in the future than other corporations that find themselves drilling in waters claimed by competitors and other countries. Conflicting territorial claims for these Southeast Asian waters, traditionally international since the innocent passage of British warships and the defeat of Borneo pirates a century ago, must soon be negotiated if serious jurisdictional rights are to be resolved, especially between Thailand, Cambodia, and South Vietnam.

Oil is already flowing from wells on both sides of the South China Sea with major investments committed. When important discoveries are made in disputed areas, the scramble by competing oil companies to claim territorial prerogatives in potentially rich-producing tracts could make the Oklahoma land rush look like a Sunday picnic. Most concession agreements in Southeast Asia, as far as is known, provide that the granting country "shall do everything necessary (to enable the oil company) to carry out its operations freely, efficiently and fully, and . . . they shall do everything necessary to prevent third parties from impeding the free exercise . . . of the rights granted."

It would appear, under these provisions, that the countries of Southeast Asia are obligated to take whatever action is necessary to protect the rights of their concessionaires. The situation is fraught with danger unless there is considerable restraint by all parties concerned, a degree of restraint that may be difficult to realize with billions of dollars in profits and royalties at stake. The political and economic ramifications of the American and Japanese subdivision of Asian waters could easily result in the return of United States military forces to protect American interests. It remains to be seen whether the oft-expressed goal of American self-sufficiency in energy requirements will include providing military protection for American-owned oil rigs pumping in self-proclaimed sovereign waters overseas.

The 1950 United Nations conference on the Law of the Sea adopted a definition of the continental shelf as "the seabed and subsoil of submarine areas adjacent to the coast (and islands) but outside the area of the territorial sea, to a depth of 200 meters or beyond that limit, to where the depth of the superjacent waters admits of the exploitation of the natural resources of the said areas." By this definition, signed by Cambodia, Malaysia, Thailand, Indonesia,

the Taiwan government, and the United States, the territorial claims of Southeast Asian states are supported, particularly within the Gulf of Siam and the South China Seas
between Vietnam and Borneo. A logical extension also supports the claims of the People's Republic of China to the
East China Sea area claimed by the Taiwan government.

The state of the art at present keeps oil drilling to
waters well within conventional continental shelf limits—
600 feet. But the swift advances in seabed mining capability should be sufficient warning that our ability to extend
drilling operations to much greater depths with attendant
political problems is only a matter of time. The U.S. Department of the Interior has issued oil leases under the
Outer Continental Shelf Land Act covering areas only forty
miles offshore in waters 4,000 feet deep. The Secretary has
also issued exploratory permits to conduct core drilling in
the Gulf of Mexico in waters 3,500 feet deep and on the
Atlantic seaboard for waters 5,000 feet deep and 250-300
miles offshore. All of these acts can be construed as an assertion of jurisdiction by the United States. They could be
duplicated by the People's Republic of China and the Soviet
Union to exploit resources in the Philippines Sea and beyond, also a geological extension of their continental shelf.
"The magnitude of the claims which have been made in offshore areas has been so great," according to the *Natural
Resources Journal*, "as to give concern both to the United
States and most nations in the world community that there
may be, in the words of President Johnson, 'a race to grab
and to hold the lands under the high seas.' "

In December 1969 the United Nations adopted a resolution pending the establishment of an international ocean
regime, saying, "States and persons, physical or juridical
are bound to refrain from all activities of exploitation of the
resources of the area of the seabed and ocean floor, and the
subsoil thereof, beyond the limits of national jurisdiction,"
and that "No claim to any part of that area or its resources
shall be recognized. . . ." It would seem proper for the United States to accept the principles of this moratorium; it

makes good common sense. Should American multinational oil interests seek to obtain rights to the seabed on a
first come, first served basis, we can expect the Soviet
Union and China to join in the ocean stake out for oil.

There may still be time for orderly development of the
sea to the benefit of all the nations involved as a common
heritage for all mankind.

It would be difficult to overstate the importance of
petroleum in Southeast Asia. The environmental advantage of crude oil from this region over other sources is the
low sulfur content, less than two-thirds of one percent. It is
a prime low pollution fuel, much in demand by American companies. Realizing the potential income, nations
controlling the natural resources of Southeast Asia have assumed an attitude of militant independence. They have
recognized how important it is to the United States and
Japan to have a politically stable source of oil. It is profitable
to American oil companies in particular to have cooperating governments which will not demand expensive safety
equipment and impose regulations on drilling operations,
oil pipelines, and pollution control devices. The spectre of
collision between an offshore oil platform and a super-
tanker in the South China Sea does not haunt Malaysian
government officials who granted extensive new concessions to Shell Oil with many paragraphs on tax relief and
royalties but nothing about environmental protection.

The impressive gathering of giant corporations drilling competitively for oil in Borneo waters, operating from
long stilt-legged platforms and ocean-going barge rigs in
the rush to bring in new wells and win concession bidding, will herald either a prosperous future for Southeast
Asia or ecological and economic disaster. The consequences of a major oil platform blowout or pipeline rup-
ture in the South China Sea are unknown, for in the
seventy years of Borneo oil production, no major oil spills
have been reported. It remains to be seen how the marine
life of the South China Sea will be affected by large-scale
oil pollution.

Thirteen oil firms and assorted consortiums cover Borneo's continental shelf waters with exclusive exploration concessions. Shell has been in Borneo since 1911 when the first oil was taken out of Sarawak fields. Today, Shell's pumping platforms and ocean-going drilling rigs are a familiar part of the Borneo horizon. The infamous Sea-Dyak pirates of yesterday quietly tap rubber in the Borneo interior while new pioneers noisily tap the earth with clanging drill pipes echoing new techniques in the search for oil.

The list of companies exploring for oil in Borneo waters reads a little like the who's-who of the petroleum industry: Esso, Aquitaine, Teiseki (of Japan), Union, Japex (Japan), Union Carbide (in collaboration with Kyushu of Japan), Gulf, Amoco, Frontier, Conoco-Getty, and Shell (essentially a Dutch corporation). Shell has a virtual monopoly on land concessions in Sarawak, Brunei, and Kalimantan.

Brunei Shell Company, a member of the Royal Dutch/ Shell Group headquartered in the Netherlands and operating in the British-protected Sultanate of Brunei, has finally gotten around to finding more oil after years of public statements that Brunei's and Sarawak's oil reserves would soon be pumped dry and that expenses of continued production would depend on tax rebates and relaxing of safety standards. They were all promptly granted. Shell now affirms that recently-proved offshore oil deposits will hold out until the year 2000 or so.

Sarawak Shell Company, another member of the Royal Dutch/Shell Group, continues drilling operations off the western shore of Sarawak, near where the first Borneo oil was discovered in 1911. In 1971, Sarawak Shell announced a joint venture with Mitsubushi Shoji Kaisha to develop natural gas fields discovered off the Malaysian Borneo State of Sarawak. An estimated $1 billion will be spent on the Sarawak project which calls for supplying about six million tons of liquefied natural gas (LNG) a year to Japan, a total of more than sixty-five million tons in the next twenty years.

Most of the financing will come from Japan and the Netherlands, but United States goods and services required in the construction of the huge liquefaction plant at Lumot, across the border in neighboring Brunei, will be covered by First National City Bank of New York credits. *Pacific Basin Reports* said the loan was guaranteed by the Export-Import Bank of the United States which also loaned additional sums for construction. Operating company for the Brunei facilities will be Brunei LNG, Ltd. The project will be forty-five percent owned by the Royal Dutch/Shell Group, forty-five percent by Mitsubishi Group firms, and ten percent by the Sultanate of Brunei.

The State of Sarawak is said to be not too pleased with arrangements for splitting royalties. *Far Eastern Economic Review* reports that, under Malaysian law, state's rights in the Federation of Malaysia end at the three-mile limit in the South China Sea, leaving Sarawak with royalties from onshore wells and very little else. In Sarawak and Brunei, offshore wells out-produce onshore wells by ten to one. Offshore concessions claimed by Malaysia, Indonesia, and South Vietnam meet somewhere in the center of the South China Sea.

The partial story of one American oil company's overseas operations may be somewhat illustrative of them all. The sign of the "76" has established its oil presence, from Seoul to Sumatra and Tokyo to Thailand, through a group of at least eleven subsidiary companies set up to find, refine, and market oil in Southeast Asia.

Union Oil Company of Thailand (with eighty percent ownership) operates collectively with three Japanese companies called Southeast Asian Petroleum Exploration Co. Union's first wildcat well in the Gulf of Siam uncovered commercial quantities of natural gas and petroleum condensate, the first announced offshore find in the area since drilling commenced in 1970 when Conoco began activity in an adjacent tract.

Union Oil Company of Indonesia is drilling offshore wells on a continental shelf concession along the southwest shore of Sumatra, exploring onshore sites in Borneo and Kalimantan. It is pumping a 100,000 barrel-a-day oil field in the Makasser Strait east of Borneo. All this is done as a contractor-concessionaire to the Indonesian government oil monopoly, Pertamina.

Unoco Limited in Hong Kong is the eyes and ears of Union Oil in the Far East, coordinating sales and crude oil tankers deliveries between the Persian Gulf, Indonesia, and Japan. It serves Union's refineries in Borneo, Taiwan, South Korea, and its Japanese affiliate, Maruzen Oil Company, the fourth largest refiner of petroleum products in Japan.

Union Oil shares with its friendly American oil associates—Amoco, Gulf, Conoco, and Tennoco—drilling concessions adjacent to the narrow Isthmus of Kra where the Thai government plans a 100-mile-long canal to allow passage of Japanese supertankers from the Middle East to Asian waters. Malaysia and Indonesia have refused to allow supertankers of more than 200,000 dead-weight tons through the narrow and shallow straits of Malacca west of Singapore. Present plans call for a route using Ban Don Bay and the Phum Duang River basin. This is the end of Union Oil's land concession where Muslim insurgent guerrilla separatist movements in the four southern Muslim provinces have objected strongly to oil company operations.

The idea of a Kra canal was first discussed in 1858 when the British annexed Burma. Ferdinand de Lesseps of Suez Canal fame actually surveyed the Kra area for the French in 1882, but the Thais objected. *Pacific Basin Reports* says the estimated $1 billion project is under study by a consortium of four American firms, including the Lawrence Livermore Laboratory in California where Edward Teller, who first assembled the hydrogen bomb, studied the possibility of using atomic devices to blast the canal out. It has been estimated that necessary nuclear explosions to excavate the canal would contaminate over 4,600 square miles of land and force evacuation of about one million people.

Another unique aspect of the canal's planning is the

hiring of Hudson Institute's futurologist, Herman Kahn, to forecast economic, political, and social implications of the project. This would be possibly the first time that the social and cultural impact of a major development in Southeast Asia has been considered in planning, though the depth and concern of the consultant for the aspirations of Thai people may be questioned in light of Kahn's words in the *Far Eastern Economic Review*. Regarding the drastically increasing gap between rich and poor countries, he wrote, ". . . this should not be disastrous either morally or politically since, as I have suggested, there are very few peasants, workers, or even businessmen in Latin America, or in Africa or in Asia who care much about gaps. . . . "

Malaysian Prime Minister Tun Abdul Razak probably reflected a more accurate view of local feelings when he said that developing countries "could not continue to serve passively as suppliers of raw materials and as markets for manufactured goods." The Kra guerrillas would applaud that comment even as they were shot by Tun Abdul's troops.

Oil exploration in the interior of northeast Thailand by Union Oil has encountered continued harassment by guerrillas firing at riggers. The guerrillas distribute leaflets to villagers asking them not to cooperate with government authorities and to deny Union Oil permission to drill on their property. Thai government authorities dispatched troops to the drilling site at Kuchinarai to protect Union Oil workers. They are operating not far from the United States airbase at Nam Pong.

Union Oil controls the 12.6 million acre onshore concession with eighty percent ownership. Other participants are three Japanese firms, including Maruzen Oil Co. Adjacent to the inland Union Oil tract is a 2.3 million acre concession held jointly by Meridian Oil Co. of San Antonio, Texas, and Prudential Funds of New York, all with agreements requiring the Thai government to protect them from Thai people who object to oil exploration by Americans.

American oil technology acquired through years of innovative exploration and drilling in domestic fields was long ago exported overseas by United States multinational corporations investigating new oil sources and new markets in all parts of the world. While advocating responsibility toward providing energy fuels for the American market first, actual corporate decisions have been made to maximize profits by producing, refining, and selling on the international market primarily in Europe and Japan. While giving lip-service to home consumption, major oil companies have invested in extensive production facilities abroad for distribution to more profitable foreign markets.

At the same time Gulf President B. R. Dorsey was speaking at Gulf's 1972 annual meeting, saying, ". . . it is our economic obligation to provide the energy which our nation depends upon for survival," his own company had almost ceased building domestic refineries while expanding production overseas for foreign markets at a greatly accelerated rate. Gulf's refineries in Korea, Okinawa, Singapore, and Taiwan market all their products for Asian consumption. Gulf's 65,000 barrel-a-day Singapore refinery, completed in 1973, has contracted sixty-five percent of its capacity to Japan, and Gulf "expects to market the remainder in Singapore and surrounding markets." Nothing from Southeast Asia will appear very soon at the corner Gulf gas station.

Much of the cost of Gulf's Singapore refinery was paid by local investors, including the Development Bank of Singapore and Oceanic Petroleum, a subsidiary of Summit Industrial Corporation which operates a major oil refinery and distribution network in Thailand. The use of foreign investment capital and World Bank funds is a traditional manner of financing for American companies in the Far East. Their advertising pleas defending high profits in the United States to finance expanded overseas operations to "discover and import more fuel for Americans" does not agree with actual overseas performance. It would appear the companies concerned are spending considerably more dollars on domestic advertising than on overseas oil exploration for American consumption. The complaints of certain companies that only in recent years have profit levels been satisfactory compared with previous years' low profits, seem difficult to understand. Gulf Oil's "advance royalty payment" to the Portuguese regime's Angola Government of $15,051,183 in 1970 would appear to make annual financial reports meaningless, if it were repeated often on any appreciable scale.

Exxon's national advertisements produce a strange mixture of information that we have little need to know and not much of anything important. My letters to fifteen major oil companies in the United States requesting information on their overseas operations elicited in most cases no answers at all or vague evasions. In overseas newspaper reports on foreign operations, localized company names effectively hide interlocking corporate action and financing behind a corporate maze of subsidiary companies and banking interests. It appears that corporate secrecy as a way of life keeps more than just competition uninformed. It hides full disclosure of profits from host countries and wards off disparaging comments by socially-minded expatriates and newly independent nationalists who have questions concerning actual benefits of oil development in an undeveloped country.

Obtaining information on foreign oil operations in the South China Sea has emphasized the role of Singapore, rapidly becoming the financial Switzerland of the Orient. Singapore is a stable market for hard currencies and gold and has considerable respect for secrecy. The able Prime Minister Lee Kuan Yew cooperates unstintingly with any company willing to spend or keep money in his booming city-state. He offers free hard currency exchange—unlike Tokyo with its burdensome regulations—and levies no tax on dollar deposits, compared to Hong Kong's withholding of fifteen percent. And to the researcher looking for information, Minister Lee prefers that business transactions remain a secret even to the extent of turning down a request from the United States government to examine a bank account and initiating passage of a law allowing Swiss-style numbered accounts.

Does an overseas concession operation benefit the people of any foreign country? Gulf Oil Corporation asks the question rhetorically, then answers it in the affirmative: "We believe we very definitely do."

In the economists' words, it is a shift from a communal society to capitalism with all its implications. Gulf says, "In Okinawa the Gulf refinery was the first major industrial installation and provided jobs and income for a number of people who up to that time were farmers." The postscript may be added: and who probably never will be farmers again, and will be forever dependent on the largess of overseas employers whether they like it or not.

The impact of foreign corporations is in some respects quite remarkable, particularly for native politicians who have inherited the colonial mantle and now share in royal prerogatives, skimming the top of every royalty payment and accepting opportunities for remunerative contracts. In some countries of Southeast Asia, specifically Indonesia and Borneo, the oil has been flowing outside the country for sixty years in great quantity, first for the Dutch, then the Japanese, and now a mixture of buyers including American. (Most of the crude oil for Hawaii's Standard Oil of California refinery comes from Sumatra.) And while the Indonesian government oil monopoly, Pertamina, today extracts a considerably larger share of the oil profits, the demands of Indonesia are so great that few benefits dribble down to the Indonesian farmer and fishermen. The question is always asked, "What if all the profits were retained by Indonesia?" But even more pertinent is the alternative of simply leaving the oil in the ground and permitting its use only at the rate Indonesia can use it.

At one time the people of Southeast Asia accepted with few complaints the malingering effects caused by warping and retardation of economic and social development under European colonial rule. The impact of colonialism destroyed their own developed and sophisticated societies and deliberately prevented normal growth patterns, pushing them further and further backward into an undeveloped status. Continued extraction of oil and minerals without full application of these resources within Southeast Asia—at a rate the raw materials can be fully utilized within the indigenous economy—can only perpetuate the existing underdeveloped countries. The taking of oil, even at a price agreeable to the seller, to feed the wasteful and extravagant economies of Japan and the United States can only spread further the gap between the rich and poor, the unhealthy gap between the developed and undeveloped nations, and between the major powers and the Third World nations.

To selfishly consume the limited oil resources of Southeast Asia, a resource of unknown quantity, while we expedite design and construction of nuclear energy facilities to use when our oil and theirs run out, is a moral affront to the Third World and a fact that cannot escape notice by indigenous nationalists in Southeast Asia who are asking, as does Gulf Oil, Does foreign oil development "directly benefit the people?" They are saying that China is possibly right in reserving their oil for use in the future, selling only small, limited amounts on the foreign market and even in these sales retaining all the income and controlling all production facilities itself.

At one time, in the distant past, the undeveloped nations—poor by our standards—accepted the occasional handouts of the rich without complaints. Today, the poor nations are demanding more. And restless segments of the population, having read the thoughts of Mao, are demanding everything.

French economist Paul Alpert, who worked twenty-five years in the United Nations, wrote recently, "As long as the poor countries get poorer and the rich remain stingy, the world is risking a confrontation that could far exceed the worst days of the East-West struggle."

An Asian diplomat is quoted in an Associated Press story, saying, "In America each family is thinking in

terms of a third car and of television in every room. We are
still worrying about how to get enough busses."

Underdeveloped countries the world over are bur-
dened with external debts totaling over $800 billion. More
than a third of the new foreign aid grants and bank loans
they receive each year goes immediately back to the "giving" country to pay on the principal and interest of earlier
loans. The Philippines are so deeply indebted to the United
States that some have referred to the island nation as an
American company store.

The looting of natural resources is the quickest way
of creating the superprofits needed to protect the growing
pyramid of investment paper. It is also the quickest way to
disaster and ruin for countries which continue to view the
Third World as nothing more than a place of cheap labor
and cheap oil to maintain the wealth of Japan and the
United States.

15

That's All There Is

It is a well-known environmental axiom that applies equally to cultural and social aspects of a society: Every act of development of necessity involves an act of destruction.

The destruction, whether measured in social, ecological, economic, or political terms, is seldom accounted for by planners and consultants, the experts who advise the decision-makers. Yet the destruction of a culture and the pollution of a fragile environment may in the long run—if not sooner than expected—generate costs that far outweigh benefits arising from development, even neglecting reckless profiteering by socially irresponsible governments and multinational corporations.

Failure to fully account for the costs of development, whether it be timber harvesting or oil drilling, forest clearing or land reclamation, arises sometimes from failure to realize the adverse consequences of development. But more often than not this failure is a calculated risk undertaken with full knowledge of possible losses by political opportunists and business executives whose goal is self-enrichment and corporate profit. Many times the well-intended developer attempting to solve complex needs of Southeast Asian undeveloped countries is simply not provided with the proper conceptual tools needed to uncover the total social and ecological costs. Unexpected harmful social effects and irreversible ecological damage frequently occur long after it is impossible to halt a project, or after political graft and managerial profits reach levels that make it more practical to hide future side-effects in the file. It is obvious that many land development schemes would be abandoned in early stages when they still are paper plans and discussions if true social and ecological costs were included in an honest cost-benefit analysis.

Expert advice and consultive services can be most misleading, depending on the source and the ultimate intentions. It is obvious why the United States has never provided foreign-aid funds for oil exploration in underdeveloped countries. Assistance of this kind to overseas governments would run counter to developed countries' philosophy of fostering private enterprise and keeping Third World countries dependent on American cash and technology. Even the Soviet Union in this regard has a tendency to export the manufactured products rather than the factory and the technical know-how, although Soviet offers of assistance for governmental oil exploration are continuing. Attempts of developed countries to insure colonial dependence on their technology can be traced back to the reluctance of Great Britain to allow export of cotton-spinning machinery to New England to maintain Britain's overseas markets and competitive advantage. Not until Samuel Slater went to work in the English mills to study British textile mill operations, memorized machinery details, and sailed to Providence, Rhode Island, with his head full of everything needed to start textile mills spinning in America did the revolutionary colonies develop their own thriving textile industry that would eventually make them completely independent of their overseas mother country.

Advice is often woefully inadequate or downright misleading, and unsuspecting government officials may be misled by apparent objective expertise. Take the World Bank (which has also refused to lend money for government oil development) and their study for Third World countries on the "Implications for State and Private Enterprise" in the search for oil. Prepared by a prominent New York oil consulting firm, the report, obviously intended to influence drafting of oil exploration policy in a quite prejudicial manner, stresses everything negative about state development and everything positive about private investment—using overseas corporate experience, of course. The report labels Brazil's government effort as "disappointing" because little oil was found. It criticizes the government-owned oil operation in Mexico, a country self-sufficient in crude oil, as not earning an adequate return on capital invested. It failed to measure the social benefits of self-sufficiency and low consumer prices which benefit the public and industry in general.

Where the consultant sincerely desires detailed information that measures not only favorable returns on the dollar but also the widespread benefits obtained when refined oil products are distributed at cost and products produced are geared to national needs rather than overseas markets, he is frustrated by the sudden ignorance of developed countries. The ecological consequences of extensive timber harvesting in Borneo, jungle clearing in Malaysia, or seabed mining in Micronesia are unknown. What are the economic effects of clear-cutting tropical wood on Savai'i in Western Samoa when the trees are all gone and inshore fisheries have been disrupted by fresh water runoff from a denuded landscape—when there are no longer jobs in logging and the fish are gone? What are the social consequences of wiping out complete ethnic communities in the Borneo interior or the political consequences of homesteading in Mindanao? What is the future of rim countries around the China Sea when the tin, oil, and timber are gone? How long will the natural resources of Southeast Asia last at the present rate of foreign consumption? What would be the consequences if Third World countries in Southeast Asia were to reserve their oil and timber for their own exclusive use?

These questions are valid and relevant, yet neither the

social scientist, the planner, the overseas investor, nor the Third World leader presents the answer. Irrevocable decisions are being made today (and have been made for several years) on the basis of totally inadequate information: decisions that may condemn an entire nation to servitude or revolution, poverty or prosperity; decisions made in ignorance, self-serving political aggrandizement, or straight profiteering; decisions that in many ways will determine the future of the world, as Vietnam inevitably produced a conscience for America.

The developers of foreign countries behave not unlike an American speculator. They ignore at the very beginning the total ecosystem in which the development will take place, as if nothing they did would affect anything else. Developers fail to consider the fact that human society lives in a complex ecosystem and is linked with that ecosystem in a complex relationship. A fragile relationship threatened by each action in turn, whether it takes place in the economy, or is the result of a new variety of rice—even if the action is only a simple idea implanted in the mind of a school child by a Peace Corps volunteer, an idea that destroys cultural village relationships and traditional communal life-styles.

A well-known aspect of ecosystem degradation is pollution, belatedly recognized in America as a harmful by-product of industrial growth, but yet to be fully measured in terms of cost. It may be that a city cannot measure the cost of pollution until they can count the dead and dying. But it may already be a truism that the question of whether we can afford to pay for pollution abatement is fully answered by the rhetorical plea, "can we afford not to?"

There is also what may be called the "ecological boomerang" to development—another area where no cost analysis is available. When a development throws an ecosystem out of balance, a counteraction by natural forces within the ecosystem frequently cancels out all the anticipated gains. It has often been pointed out that construction of the Aswan High Dam on the Upper Nile has in some respects proved to be more of a liability than an asset because of the increased spread of schistosomiasis in newly cultivated areas and the changes in river flow that have seriously affected fisheries at its mouth on the Mediterranean Sea. Similar proposals for dams on the Mekong River in South Vietnam may have disastrous consequences on food production in the lower delta country.

In neither project has any data been presented on costs for disease control nor for losses of productivity for farmers and fisheries. The actual cost of the Aswan Dam has never been calculated because the losses are not known. The eventual cost of the Mekong River project is likewise unknown; the social cost may exceed the total value of hydroelectric power and irrigation waters. Only unsettled political conditions delay the start of construction.

Another crucial aspect of ecological degradation stemming from unwise development is the extinction of various species of wild plant and animal life occurring in Southeast Asian land-clearing and timber-harvesting operations. At present it is difficult to determine the full loss to humanity of any plant or animal, for we have gathered no information on these values and many species and varieties undoubtedly disappeared before we even knew they existed. It may be possible only to pose the problem in terms of potential values.

Dr. George Appell of Brandeis University points out that "each ecosystem contains a unique inventory of wild flora and fauna. Looking at the world as a single ecosystem —it has also been cogently viewed as a space ship with limited resources—the inventory of flora and fauna that has evolved over aeons is in serious danger of depletion. Within the past 2,000 years 110 species of mammals alone have ceased to exist, and in the past 200 years, 600 species have declined to the point of extinction."

Appell says, "It is rational to conclude that survival of the human race is threatened when any development project contributes to the extinction of any one species of plant or animal, because the disappearance of any species diminishes man's ability to adapt to future conditions on the earth. The degradation of man's ecosystem already proceeds apace.

"Musk ox are being domesticated in Alaska to serve as an economic basis for developing herding communities on the underpopulated tundra areas. It has also been recently pointed out that the African game animals are more productive of animal protein than the cattle replacing them and that these wild ungulates could better serve as a valuable source of protein food. The manatee, which is on the list of endangered species of the International Union for the Conservation of Nature, has just been discovered to be a more efficient controller of the water hyacinth, which is clogging fresh water inland waterways, than chemical or mechanical methods are. Unfortunately, they have been hunted almost to extinction.

"Wild species of animals have another utility that highlights even more starkly their potential contribution towards the adaptation of the human race to the earth. This is for medical research. Without monkeys our control over poliomyelitis would not have been developed as rapidly; and cancer in hamsters has produced rewarding results for the understanding and control of human cancer. There is a continuing search to find animals in which human diseases can be induced experimentally, and there is the need to study abnormalities in animals which do not contract the human diseases but which display those impairments that closely duplicate human illnesses. This field of comparative medicine is as yet little developed, so to deplete our resources before they have been adequately studied is indeed foolish.

"Man's capacity to adapt is lessened by the loss of any of the world's fauna. This also applies to the extinction of any species of flora. For we do not know to what uses a species may yet be put. One example of the unexpected value of flora for man's survival is the recent discovery that certain gymnosperms have compounds that display anticancer activity. And this discovery has led to a world-wide search for other species of gymnosperms that may have similar compounds.

"But there is perhaps a more immediate threat to man's ability to adapt through the loss of indigenous cultivars. These indigenous cultivars have provided and can continue to provide a genetic pool from which new crossbred and hybrid varieties of crops are designed for resistance to new plant disease and for greater productivity. But few of these are being collected and studied to determine what contributions they might make to the development of higher yielding, more disease resistant varieties. Few indeed are being preserved in genetic banks against the day when a new challenge appears from new disease agents. Yet these indigenous cultivars are being displaced and permanently lost in all parts of the world by agricultural experts who introduce the more developed, genetically refined varieties of cultivars from the more advanced countries."

In conclusion, Appell emphasizes the point, "that flora and fauna of the less developed regions of the world are being destroyed by development projects before they have been analyzed for the contributions that they can make to man's welfare. Yet they are the mechanisms on which man may have to depend at some future point in order to adapt to a changing world environment. The benefits of a full use of the genetic resources of the indigenous cultivars of Southeast Asia might conservatively be put in terms of billions of dollars per year in increased agricultural production. With regard to rice alone, recent crossbreeding experiment with indigenous varieties has raised the yield per hectare from 1 to 1.5 tons to six or eight tons. Yet these indigenous varieties are being rapidly lost as people from the interior regions move to development projects and give up their indigenous agricultural system."

For a competent cost-benefit analysis of the society being developed, to actually determine if it is worthwhile to be developed—or be left alone—it is necessary to possess an inventory of knowledge of the ecosystem that will be developed. It would also be worth considering the local ecosystem as a valuable asset owned by the ethnic community, and not for sale to the highest corporate bidder or for debasement by ill-informed teachers imported to inform the natives of a better way of life.

Considering development only as a corporate act to turn a profit could be very misleading. Development or improvement is generally considered the province of developed nations overseeing the care and welfare of underdeveloped nations. Colonialists called it "the white man's burden," assuming the "primitive savages" had no civilization or religion and therefore needed to be civilized and converted.

The early European colonists were developers in every sense of the word. But equally so are the Peace Corps school teachers and the local doctor, as well as the United States civic action team bridge builders, and the economic agricultural and education experts who work in government centers as advisers and who are ultimately responsible for the behavior of the lowest-rated native civil servant. Even the prying anthropologist researching the village life-style of a Borneo longhouse community can leave an alien imprint on ancient cultures that may never be erased.

Ordinarily innocent acts of helpfulness and enlightenment can eradicate age-old cultural traditions and destroy individual self-esteem and pride held by members of the ethnic group, an unwitting act that can produce pernicious stresses within the native society. The visiting forestry botanist, economic adviser, or teacher of ordinary reading, writing, and arithmetic, can all destroy within short periods of time the accumulated human experience acquired over thousands of years of experimentation with a tropical ecosystem.

Any reasonable evaluation of education would presume that the pupils are in need of education and that there can be a worthy improvement in their status by imparting worthwhile knowledge. However, the expatriate teacher in Micronesia imparting ideas to island children that have absolutely no relevance to an island environment and have little or no value in learning to live on an island is hardly educating, unless the insidious purpose of Peace Corps instructors is to develop an indissoluble dependence on American moral values and administration.

Perhaps their object is not so much to intellectually enslave unsuspecting islanders as it is to inculcate an exploitative attitude toward nature and wildlife more in keeping with western "civilized" values. It is a way of suggesting that it is better to live "on" the land than "with" the land and its accommodating ecosystem. It is the philosophy of advanced, progressive ways that prove a self-made outrigger canoe to be old-fashioned and primitive, while to be "with it" is to go out and work and buy a fiberglass Boston Whaler.

Anthropologist Appell, reflecting on the considerable time he spent in Southeast Asia, tells of his experiences among the native people in Borneo, when "a new school was built within walking distance of our field station. The young pupils were told by the new teacher and the Chinese shopowners in the shop area where the school was located that they could not wear their native dress or carry their belongings to school in their native baskets. Instead they were told to buy shirts, shorts, and school bags from the local stores. Thus began the slow process of disarticulation of the people from their ecosystem. Their native dress, tailored both from cloth purchased at the shops and from the cloth they weave themselves from their own cotton, will give way to manufactured clothing which requires a great cash outlay. And to obtain this cash, these people must become more closely integrated to the national cash economy through taking up wage labor rather than maintaining their tradition of being small, independent farmers. As a result, their agricultural products used in clothing manufacture will no longer be raised, and the forest products formerly used to make a variety of basketry materials will be forgotten as well as the skills and knowledge needed to produce these.

"Furthermore, other important skills linked with the ecosystem in which they live will also be replaced with nonfunctional, but modern skills. For example, the school teachers for a local district fair taught the school children to do calisthenics rather than encouraging them to put on a demonstration of athletic skills that they themselves must learn either to survive in their environment or which they engage in for pleasure, such as climbing bee trees, spear throwing, felling trees, and leg wrestling.

"Another example of the destruction of valuable local knowledge and its replacement with doubtful knowledge from overseas was provided by the actions of the head of the local agricultural school, operated by a group of missionaries. On taking up his post, he told me that he was going to teach the local people, among whom we were living, to plant fruit trees as these would provide a valuable supplement to their diet. I had to point out to him the great variety of fruit trees already owned and inherited. In some cases I was able to trace the inheritance of these valuable fruit groves through seven generations. Furthermore, anyone who knows how to read the jungle could look across the hillsides and pick out these groves of fruit trees from the surrounding jungle. However, because of his high status as head of the agricultural school and teacher, his vastly inferior agricultural knowledge would be transmitted to the young school children to replace that which arose from thousands of years of accumulated agricultural experience. In this manner the people will become separated from their local environment to the detriment of themselves and mankind as a whole. For with their accumulated experience displaced by an inferior knowledge, they are less able to adapt to the challenges of their ecosystem. And with the loss of their knowledge of their ecosystem, with the replacement of their crops and fruit trees by those from outside, mankind loses another part of his inventory of knowledge and tools that was won by trial and error over many generations.

"A further striking example of the way in which the people will become parted from the ecosystem in which they must live is provided by the missionaries who operate the agricultural school. The natives believe that groves of trees along river banks, in ravines, and around springs are the home of spirits who will become angered if this forest is cut in the preparation of swiddens. Thus these spirits will vent their anger on those involved in such forest cuttings and cause them to become ill. The missionaries told the people that if they became Christians, they would be protected from such spirits. Furthermore, they argued that then the people could cultivate these virgin areas with impunity and, by taking advantage of the rich soil, make a lot of money from the higher agricultural yields that would be produced.

"However, the people believe that in addition to angering the spirits, if they cut these groves, their land will become hot and dry up. Thus the natives demonstrate that they have a greater knowledge of cause and effect in their agricultural system comparable with modern concepts of agriculture, than did the missionaries who staffed the agricultural school."

The society living in a specific ecosystem, particularly in fragile tropical climates, must know how to deal with that system. Those who would erase indigenous knowledge of the ecosystem destroy the ability of the native inhabitants to adapt to it, and preclude any successor society of ever learning secrets.

D. J. Prentice, writing in his dissertation for the Australian National University, describes the Timugon Murut of Borneo who have taken up rubber planting and, on the urging of government economists, abandoned their old nomadic life-style. He says, "The change to a cash-economy has, as usual, proved a mixed blessing. While it enables people to survive a bad rice harvest without too much difficulty, and while it has brought such commodities as penicillin and zinc-roofing within their reach, it has also caused the disappearance of such arts as weaving of hats, mats and baskets, since all these articles are readily obtainable in the shops. . . . Moreover, the availability of cheap tinned foods from the same source has led to the large-scale abandonment, not only of the traditional hunting and fishing activities, but also of the traditional methods of preserving emergency stocks of food . . . by fermenting meat or fish with rice, or by roasting and smoking pork, venison, and game. The resulting unbalanced diet has produced a greater incidence of diet-deficiency diseases than formerly. More importantly, these households which are now dependent on shop-foods are often placed in considerable distress when the cash-income fails through illness or a fall in the price of rubber."

When any society loses its skills and knowledge in adapting to an alien system of living, no matter how convenient and profitable it may seem, it becomes a losing society, along with the human race of which it is a part. How can we be certain that the methods of environmental adaptation discovered and invented as a result of thousands of years of experimentation will be rediscovered and re-invented at some future point when they may have crucial importance for human ability to adapt to a much crueler world when our natural resources are also diminished to a level of extinction?

This point is vividly illustrated in another scientific analysis by Appell, whose conceptual knowledge of the interrelation of anthropology, botany, and zoology in the ecosystem gives considerable understanding to a complex subject. He points out that jungle inventories of native herbs and medically useful plants are based on ancient beliefs and broad experience, "a knowledge that is quickly destroyed in the missionaries' zeal to replace native superstition with modern beliefs," not realizing in their arrogance that "the germ theory of disease to which they subscribe, is really only modern folk belief that is now under considerable revision.

"The introduction of Western medicine," asserts Appell, "is also one of the major destroyers of the indigenous chemotherapeutic knowledge. The success of cures by antibiotics but particularly the attitude of physicians to the indigenous medical belief systems puts the native pharmacopoeia into disrepute, and it slowly erodes away. Yet at one point before the development of synthetic products to duplicate the properties of natural drugs there were over 200 drugs in the *United States Pharmacopoeia* that were derived from the American Indians. The number of native-discovered drugs incorporated into Western medicine is astounding, yet today we systematically destroy at each cultural frontier such indigenous knowledge. For example, I know of no ethnobotanical expedition to Borneo for the purpose of inventorying the local pharmacopoeias, and yet these are rapidly disappearing."

A striking example of the value of traditional knowledge from indigenous peoples about their ecosystem and its uses in medical treatment is reported by Tabrah, Kashiwagi, and Norton in *Science Magazine*. On the suggestion of "an elderly woman of Hawaiian race who had experienced many of the native Hawaiian medical practices," a tropical sea worm was tested for antitumor activity and found to inhibit growth in treated mice. According to their informant, indigenous "cancer patients had shown clinical improvement after drinking an infusion of cooked sea worm tentacles daily for several weeks." Another native Hawaiian anticancer method involved sucking the body fluid of live sea worms through a fine bamboo tube.

The oil and timber consultant, hired to determine the economic feasibility of a project, is primarily interested only in how much it will cost in labor and equipment to mine the ore, drill the oil, and log the timber. And how much profit will be made after totaling up the expenses. But the expenses never include the cost to the indigenous people, the loss to them of a traditional life-style, perhaps even political and economic independence. The changes can have injurious effects on their physical and mental health with few benefits even temporarily accrued and then generally only to an opportunistic minority. Apparent improvements in housing, health standards, and food availability that accompany a change from subsistence farming to a cash economy are often illusory and temporary—in some cases they may disappear entirely when the oil wells dry up or the forest is denuded.

There is the widespread example of Iban people in Borneo, who moved to a village, ceased traditional slash-and-burn agriculture, and cleared the forest to plant rubber trees, only to have the price of rubber drop below starvation levels when overseas rubber buyers decided synthetic rubber was cheaper. Micronesians on Ponape and Chinese on Sarawak were both advised to clear the jungle to plant pepper until the world market became glutted and the price fell to a level below the farmers' ability to buy food they no longer grew themselves. The Marshallese who long ago were required by German colonists to clear the jungle and plant coconut trees, buy canned fish instead of taking the time to build a canoe and fish themselves. They now have found the depreciated price of copra below the price at which they can buy canned fish from Japan. Their fate is compounded when it is discovered that the canoe lying unused on the beach has been destroyed by dry-rot and their age-old knowledge of the sea is no longer a valued asset to their children.

When Boston missionaries decided the "naked savages" of Hawaii had to be clothed, respirational diseases and flu became fatal illnesses. Along with the white man's syphilis and smallpox, these diseases almost wiped out the small island population. Modern hospitals and doctors in no way cancelled out the insidious, pernicious effect of the missionaries' presence. The net cost of religious conversion and a cash economy to the Hawaiian people was racial genocide.

The people of Yap in the Micronesian Caroline Islands have been noted by visiting anthropologists for their small families. Apparently the young Yapese man desired a sexually experienced wife, and general sexual relations were common until the desired experience was acquired, but the man did not want his future mate to have given birth. Yapese women developed years ago a method for producing abortion that is not dissimilar to the modern plastic coil. When her period was missed, the single girl rolled a handful of fresh hibiscus leaves into a cigar shaped tube and inserted it temporarily into the cervix. It worked, and older Yapese with whom I have talked claim that adverse side effects were far less common than death from childbirth. The age-old traditional practice apparently continues in some areas, for United States administrators have characteristically expressed concern over the low birth rate in Yap.

Who is to say that Yapese sexual relations and the community living of Borneo longhouses are not the best life-style for their environment? Some Americans have suggested that we adopt life-styles that are in many ways inspired by native civilizations a thousand years old. Women's liberation in America has a long way to go in emulating Palauan society where the woman's name is used in family relationships and where family property rights are passed on from woman to woman.

Ill-considered changes in native life-styles for "improvement of the general welfare," without full understanding of local traditions and the ecosystem that is obviously an integral part of the local culture, results in destruction of community relations that cannot be replaced in a generation by contemporary morality. To destroy valuable cultural assets and assertively replace them with alien society modes claimed to be more developed, more modern, and more productive, may in fact cause mankind to become, on the whole, poorer rather than richer. When we deplete our inventory of adaptive techniques simultaneously with the depletion of our natural resources we are headed toward an eventuality where our place in the world ecosystem is in serious jeopardy. It may well be mankind's greatest challenge.

As applied to local societies in underdeveloped Southeast Asian countries, the extinction of traditional culture without replacement by anything that is a worthy improvement may indeed be the very situation worthy of exploitation by indigenous radical leaders with knowledge of more culturally compatible economic and political systems. What may be ideally suitable for a dairy farmer living in Wisconsin, may not at all be best for rice growers in the paddies of Vietnam. Have the economic consultants figured the cost of revolution into their cost-benefit analysis?

What kind of emotional stress arises when a society is moved from its traditional home?—when the village is moved downstream to work in the lumber mill?—when the forest is cleared and hunters are forced to be employees?—when the rubber tapper is convinced that literacy and a bartender's job in Singapore is progress? Who will determine the social costs when his teen-age child becomes a juvenile delinquent in the city? Will the lowest paying industry (tourism) in any society fully pay for the greatly increased governmental costs when he becomes a city dweller? The evidence of Hawaii's possible bankruptcy indicates that tourism and the people who labor for its expatriate owners do not pay their own way. There is also a growing body of evidence in Hawaii and the South Pacific that the rural subsistence farmer may live many years longer than his fellow city dwellers, not taking into consideration the greater possibility of violent death on city streets.

As the United States and Japan piously preach the better life to so-called underdeveloped nations while we rip off the last of their natural resources for our own use in an incredibly wasteful society, it would behoove us to pause and reconsider our actions. As we recklessly deplete the last of our oil, minerals, and even growing plants, it must become evident that the end is near. At some point there will be no more, with ecological consequences at which we can only guess.

Our remaining hope—and that is all the scientists will give us—is for technological advancements that will enable us to survive on a dead world in an ecosystem that can hardly be imagined, much less tolerated. The first Apollo astronauts were plucked from Micronesian waters after their visit to a dead moon. It would indeed be ironic that we suffer the same fate as the moon in our children's lifetime. Or is the ultimate technological solution the evacuation of earth by space ship to a distant planet where we can start all over again?

What we are discussing here is a moral and political problem. For the selfish and exploitative methods we use in wheeling and dealing with the Third World peoples (and to some extent our own people), may actually be based on a highly distorted image of ourselves as civilized people.

James Neel in his *Lessons from a Primitive People,* writes of the "intellectual arrogance created by our small scientific successes" which must be replaced by a "profound humility based on the new knowledge of how complex is the system of which we are a part. To some of us," adds Neel, "this realization carries with it the need for a philosophical readjustment which has the impact of a religious conversion."

The inferior status that we confer on primitive people and citizens of underdeveloped societies may in fact be of our own making. Teachers from more sophisticated countries trained on a highly developed model whether derived from Japanese or American technology and history, drive out local knowledge and skills with so-called machine intensive skills, totally inappropriate for Southeast Asia. We expropriate their only natural resources—the last resources on earth—leaving in exchange the devastated earth and a crippled people unable to cope with their shattered world.

I remember the evening I visited a Polynesian Kapingamarangi Island village, the day before a United Nations inspection team was due. Both men and women proudly wore their colorful wrap-around skirts, bare from the waist up. The full breasts of the women were exciting and youthful, while the brown skin of everyone revealed a healthful and happy people very appropriately dressed for the humid tropical environment. The next day they "dressed up" for their important visitors. They pulled old wrinkled shirts, pants, blouses many times too large, and second-hand skirts from the bottom of damp storage places. It was a terrible sight. The once beautiful community was transformed overnight into the image of abject poverty, a humiliated and sad people. To the accompanying missionaries it was a tangible and visible symbol of the inferiority of the native. To me it was the product of a distorted Christian ethic created out of its own historical lack of tolerance for other customs. The inferiority that many American and Japanese businessmen look for in every race—black or brown—is used to justify their own racist world view. The result of this is that civilized interlopers from Japan and the United States turn out to be arrogant, pompous bores in the Pacific and the rest of the world as well.

The man with a car and an airplane assumes that people from cultures with simpler technologies than his more complex and garbage strewn society, have nothing to offer. It is the basis of education and the payment for exploitative privileges in underdeveloped areas. It is the philosophy of the Peace Corps. It is the philosophy behind every corporation, well-intentioned development programs, and foreign aid grants. And it is the insidious philosophy that every indigenous recruit to modern ways who advances one notch up the western scale of values shall apply to those below him. At a deeper level this attitude of civilized man toward simpler societies and life-styles implies a basic disrespect of people and the failure to respect fellow man's creations as an equal both in spirituality and endowed potentialities.

Any development project in which there is no exchange of ideas, knowledge, and skills from cooperating cultures, or any educational program in which exchanges fail to take place is hollow. The gains, if any, to the host country are ephemeral. The corporate exploiter takes all and spawns the cancerous growth of hate, which at some point will be consummated in violence.

The plea is not just another romantic overture for preservation of the native or a self-serving plea to save them from themselves. The plea is a cry to save ourselves from eventual loss of everything we hold dear. As we strip our fellow humans of their pride and their gold, if we are not to consider the moral consequences we must measure the eventual cost to ourselves and our children—the cost to humankind. We must assume the conscience of multinational corporations without a soul. Otherwise the future of our world is in doubt, and if we continue to strip and degrade the lands of simpler societies, we must face up to the fact that, no matter how covertly or subtly, we are racists.

Bibliography

BOOKS

Barnet, Richard. *Intervention and Revolution.* New York: Institute for Policy Studies, 1972.

Buchanan, Keith. *The Southeast Asian World.* New York: Doubleday & Company, Inc., 1968.

Buss, Claude. *Southeast Asia and the World Today.* New York: Van Nostrand Reinhold Company, 1970.

————. *Contemporary Southeast Asia.* New York: Van Nostrand Reinhold Company, 1970.

Carano, Paul, and Sanchez, Pedro. *A Complete History of Guam.* Rutland, Vt.: Charles E. Tuttle Co., Inc., 1964.

Crocombe, Ronald. *The New South Pacific.* Wellington, New Zealand: Reed Education, 1974.

Dashman, Raymond, et al. *Ecological Principles for Economic Development.* New York: John Wiley & Sons, Inc., 1973.

Fields, Jack and Dorothy. *South Pacific.* New York: Kodansha International, 1972.

Friis, Herman. *The Pacific Basin.* New York: American Geographical Society, 1967.

Katz, Robert. *A Giant in the Earth.* New York: Stein & Day Publishers, 1973.

Lifton, Robert, ed. *America and the Asian Revolutions.* New Jersey: Transaction Books, Rutgers University, 1970.

Magdoff, Harry. *The Age of Imperialism.* New York: Modern Reader Paperbacks, 1969.

Miller, Merle. *Plain Speaking.* New York: G. P. Putnam's Sons, 1974.

Myrdal, Gunnar. *An International Economy.* New York: Harper & Row Publishers, 1956.

Nader, Ralph, and Green, Mark, eds. *Corporate Power in America.* New York: Grossman Publishers, 1973.

Ridgeway, James. *The Last Play.* New York: E. P. Dutton & Co., Inc., 1973.

Tanzer, Michael. *The Political Economy of International Oil and the Underdeveloped Countries.* Boston: Beacon Press, 1969.

Wenkam, Robert. *Hawaii.* Chicago: Rand McNally & Company, 1972.

―――. *Maui: The Last Hawaiian Place.* San Francisco: Friends of the Earth, 1970.

―――. *Kauai and the Park Country of Hawaii.* San Francisco: Sierra Club Books, 1967.

Wenkam, Robert, and Baker, Byron. *Micronesia: The Breadfruit Revolution.* Honolulu: The University Press of Hawaii, 1972.

Wenkam, Robert, and Brower, Ken. *Micronesia: Island Wilderness.* San Francisco: Friends of the Earth, 1974.

ADDITIONAL SOURCES

Appell, G. N. "A Survey of the Social and Medical Anthropology of Sabah: Retrospect and Prospect." *Behavior Science Notes,* 1968.

―――. "Genetic Erosion in the Indigenous Cultivars of Borneo." *Plant Introduction Newsletter,* 1970.

―――. "Kalimantan Timber Concessions Pose Challenge to Urgent Research." *Borneo Research Bulletin,* 1970.

―――. "Overview of Research in Sarawak." *Studies in Third World Societies Journal,* 1974.

Bingham, O. W. "Multinational Issues: Some Observations and an Example." Unpublished paper by senior vice-president, Weyerhaeuser Corporation, 1973.

Clark, Ibrohim. "Patterns for Effective Use of Science and Technology in Southeast Asia." *Journal of the Foreign Policy Research Assn.* University of Redlands, 1973.

Hanna, Willard. "Three New States of Borneo." American Universities Field Staff, 1968.

Prentice, D. J. "The Murut Language of Sabah." Ph.D. dissertation, Australian National University, 1969.

Shapley, Deborah. "Ocean Technology: Race to Seabed Wealth Disturbs More Than Fish." *Science Magazine*, 1973.

Slansky, Cyril. "The Management of Radioactive Waste in the Nuclear Fuel Cycle." Report to the Federation of Western Outdoor Clubs. 1972.

Tabrah, Frank, Kashiwagi, Midori, and Norton, Ted. "Antitumor Activity in Mice of Tentacles of Two Tropical Sea Annelids." *Science Magazine*, 1973.

Verdad, Juan Razon. "The Philippine Crisis." *The Far East Reporter*, 1972.

"Petition." Translated by Micronesian Legal Services for the people of Maap Island, Yap, 1972.

Richards, Paul W. "The Tropical Rain Forest." Scientific American Magazine, 1973.

"Resolution of the Full Assembly of the Chiefs in Council." Translated by Micronesian Legal Services and signed by thirty-four chiefs. Maap Island, Yap, 1973.

"Manganese Nodule Deposits in the Pacific." Symposium/Workshop Proceedings. Honolulu: State of Hawaii, 1972.

"The Philippines." Chicago: Committee of Returned Volunteers, 1970.

"The Republic of the Philippines." CIC Brief Corporate Examiner, Corporate Information Center, New York: National Council of Churches, 1973.

"Indochina." Chicago: Committee of Returned Volunteers, 1971.

"The Pentagon Papers." Gravel Edition, New York: Beacon Press, 1972.

"Undersea Drilling." American Petroleum Institute, 1973.

"The Great South Asian War." New York: North American Congress on Latin America, 1971.

"Lessons from a 'Primitive' People." *Science Magazine*, 1970.

"The Lichauco Paper, Imperialism in the Philippines." New York: *Monthly Review*, 1973.

"People's Republic of China Atlas." Central Intelligence Agency. Washington, D.C., 1971.

"Oversight on Outer Continental Shelf Lands." Hearings before the Committee on Interior and Insular Affairs, U.S. Senate, 1972.

"Deep Seabed Hard Mineral Resources." Hearings before the Committee on Merchant Marine and Fisheries, Subcommittee on Oceanography, U.S. House of Representatives, 1972.

"Micronesian Minerals." Trust Territory of the Pacific Islands, 1971.

"Material Needs and the Environment Today and Tomorrow." Final report of the National Commission on Materials Policy, 1973.

"An Oceanic Quest: The International Decade of Ocean Exploration." *National Academy of Sciences Publication*, no. 1709, 1969.

"Petroleum Resources under the Ocean Floor." National Petroleum Council, 1969.

"Economic Effects of Deep Ocean Minerals Exploration." National Technical Information Service. Washington, D.C.: Department of Commerce, 1971.

"Possible Impact of Seabed Mineral Production in the Area beyond National Jurisdiction on World Markets with Special Reference to the Problems of Developing Countries." Report of the U.N. Secretary General, 1971.

"The National Territory: A Brief on Archipelagos." *New Philippines*, 1974.

"Dolefil Pioneers Look Back on Ten Years on Frontier." Honolulu: *Castle & Cooke Report*, 1973.

"Mindanao Report." Manila: Republic of the Philippines, 1970.

"The Facts about Sabah." Public Information Service. Manila: Republic of the Philippines, 1968.

"Annual Report." The Forest Department, Sarawak, Federation of Malaysia, various years.

"Introduction to Offshore Oil Exploration." Esso Exploration Malaysia. Kuala Lumpur, 1972.

"Statement of Emilio G. Collado, executive vice-president Exxon Corporation." Meeting of group of eminent persons to study the impact of multinational corporations on development and on international relations. United Nations, 1973.

"Statement by spokesman of the Foreign Ministry." People's Republic of China. Peking: *Peking Review*, 1974.

World Petroleum Reports. Mona Palmer Publishing Co., 1973.

International Petroleum Encyclopedia. Tulsa, Oklahoma: Petroleum Publishing Co., 1973.

"Tin State Industrializes." Singapore: *The Straits Times Annual*, 1971.